SLAVERY IN ANCIENT GREECE

SLAVERY IN ANCIENT GREECE

REVISED AND EXPANDED EDITION

YVON GARLAN

Translated from the French by Janet Lloyd

Cornell University Press

ITHACA AND LONDON

Originally published 1982 as *Les esclaves en Grèce ancienne* by
Librairie François Maspéro.

Translation and revisions copyright © 1988 by Cornell University

First published 1988 by Cornell University Press.

International Standard Book Number (cloth) 0-8014-1841-0
International Standard Book Number (paper) 0-8014-9504-0
Library of Congress Catalog Card Number 87-47963
Printed in the United States of America
*Librarians: Library of Congress cataloging information
appears on the last page of the book.*

*The paper in this book is acid-free and meets the guidelines for
permanence and durability of the Committee on Production Guidelines
for Book Longevity of the Council on Library Resources.*

To the memory of Moses and Mary

Contents

Preface

This book makes no claim to compete in its own field with M. I. Finley's *Ancient Slavery and Modern Ideology* (1980). Its purpose is at once more restricted and wider, for my aim is to consider the phenomenon of slavery, in all its aspects, within the limited framework of the ancient world. This thus constitutes a kind of "handbook" (in the better sense of the term, I hope) aimed not only at students but at all those who, working within a multidisciplinary framework of research, can tackle this subject only at second hand. In it, I have attempted to provide a synthesis of the rich international secondary literature that has appeared over the last decades, paying attention to the important questions of interpretation raised and, of course, taking the opportunity to suggest a few solutions of my own.

However careful, the author who approaches a topic as full of pitfalls as this one runs considerable risks: one will be considered naive by some and presumptuous by others; one will be taxed for theorizing too much or too little, for electicism or dogmatism, and so on. For me, the hazards would have been even greater without the comments on the manuscript provided, before publication of the work in French in 1982, by my friends M. I. Finley, Pierre Lévêque, Pierre Vidal-Naquet, Claude Mossé, and Edouard Will—as well as, later, Domenico Musti and many of his Italian colleagues who in 1985 organized a day of discussion on the book, under the auspices of the Gramsci Institute (*Studi Storici* 26 [1985]: 841–915). I am indebted to the Centre d'Histoire Ancienne de Besançon for helping to compensate for my physical remoteness from good libraries by making its documentary resources available to me, and to my wife for her information on numerous studies in the Russian language. Finally, I thank Paul Cartledge for his help in making possible the publication of this translation, which is based on a revised and slightly expanded version of the French edition.

I certainly cannot claim to have read everything on the subject, not for example the 5,162 works in the new edition of the *Bibliographie zur antiken Sklaverei* published in 1983 by E. Herrmann under the patronage of J. Vogt and H. Bellen. My reading has been wider than it may appear, however, for I decided to refer in my notes only to a selection of works: the most notable, the most recent, those that are less well known, or, on the contrary, those that are more accessible for linguistic reasons. Moreover, I have not indicated all my more or less conscious borrowings from M. I. Finley's book. To complement my bibliography the reader should consult the judicious choice of works suggested in that book or the bibliography that appears at the end of his collection *Slavery in Classical Antiquity* (2d ed., 1968, pp. 229–36). I have tried to limit the scope of my references so as not to confuse the reader. For convenience' sake, however, let me list the works to which I refer using abbreviated titles:

AJPhil: American Journal of Philology.

Analisi marxista: Istituto Gramsci, *Analisi marxista e società antiche* (1978).

Ancient World: Problems of socioeconomic history in the ancient world. A. I. Tjamenev Collection (in Russian, 1963).

ASNP: Annali della Scuola Normale Superiore de Pisa.

Colloque Besançon 1970: Actes du colloque d'histoire sociale 1970 (1972).

Colloque Besançon 1971: Actes du colloque 1971 sur l'esclavage (1973).

Colloque Besançon 1972: Actes du colloque 1972 sur l'esclavage (1974).

Colloque Besançon 1973: Actes du colloque 1973 sur l'esclavage (1976).

Colloque Besançon 1974: Terre et paysans dépendants dans les sociétés antiques (1979).

Colloque Bressanone 1976: Atti del colloquio internazionale di Bressanone 25–27/11/1976. Schiavitù, manomissione e classi dipendenti nel mondo antico (1979).

Colloque Camerino, 1978: Ceti dipendenti e schiavitù nel mondo antico, Index, 8 (1978/1979).

Colloque Gargnano 1975: Centro ricerche e documentazione sull'antichità classica. Atti, 8 (1976–1977).

Colloque Iéna 1981: Antike Abhängigkeitsformen in den griechischen Gebieten ohne Polisstruktur und den römischen Provinzen, ed. H. Kreissig and F. Kühnert, 1985.

Colloque Nieborow 1975: Actes du colloque sur l'esclavage, Nieborow 2–6 XII 1975 (1979).

DHA: Diologues d'Histoire Ancienne.

Escl. périph.: D. P. Kallistov, A. A. Nejchardt, I. Š. Šifman, and I. A. Šišova, Slavery on the periphery of the ancient world (in Russian, 1968).

Hell. Poleis: Hellenische Poleis, ed. E. C. Welskopf (1973).

JHS: Journal of Hellenistic Studies.

PP: La Parola del Passato.

Rech. int. 1957: Etat et classes dans l'Antiquité esclavagiste. Recherches internationales à la lumière du marxisme 2 (1957).

Rech. int. 1967: Premières sociétés de classes et mode de production asiatique. Recherches internationales à la lumière du marxisme 57–58 (1967).

Rech int. 1975: Formes d'exploitation du travail et rapports sociaux dans l'Antiquité classique. Recherches internationales à la lumière du marxisme 84 (1975).

REG: Revue des Etudes Grecques.

Slavery: Slavery in Classical Antiquity, ed. M. I. Finley (1960; 2d ed., 1968, with a supplementary bibliography).

Soziale Typenbegriffe: Soziale Typenbegriffe im alten Griechenland und ihre Fortleben in den Sprachen der Welt, I–VII, ed. E. C. Welskopf, 1981.

TAPA: Transactions of the American Philological Association.

ZPE: Zeitschrift für Papyrologie und Epigraphik.

Y.G.

Rennes, France

SLAVERY IN ANCIENT GREECE

Introduction

Henri Wallon published the first edition of his *Histoire de l'esclavage dans l'Antiquité* in 1847—virtually at the end of the campaign to abolish slavery in the French colonies, a campaign in which he was one of the prime movers. The abolition bill, introduced by Victor Schoelcher, was eventually passed during the period leading up to the 1848 revolution. The book's starting point had been a memorandum composed as a prize essay for a competition organized by the Académie des Inscriptions et Belles-lettres in 1837. The questions posed for the competition ran as follows: "What were the causes for the abolition of slavery in the ancient world? At what stage did slavery disappear altogether in western Europe, leaving agricultural servitude as its sole surviving form?"

In his foreword, the author concealed none of the sentiments that had prompted his research: "Partisans of the status quo appeal to Antiquity in support of their cause: it is worth investigating whether its evidence, taken as a whole, supports their claims. Even as we delve into the past, we shall thus be keeping the modern problem in our sights" (2d ed., p. iv). That aim is reaffirmed in his contemporary pamphlet on slavery in the colonies, which he appended to his book when it was reprinted in 1879. Denouncing his adversaries' favorite arguments (the main substance of which is echoed in the historiography of today), he here shows that to reduce slavery to an internal family conflict between generations, between a "race of fathers" and a "race of sons," is to postulate that it is an eternal phenomenon and that, by unilaterally underlining "slavery's claims to the gratitude of

[1]

mankind," its proponents have even been able to pass it off as a
liberal institution: those who perpetuate servitude being presented
as the only ones to "establish liberty" . . . *a contrario* (p. v). As for
slavery's influence upon society, he concludes that it is totally negative: "Just as slavery has not so much preserved as decimated races,
not so much refined as corrupted mores, not so much served as
ruined both the family and the State everywhere, equally it has not so
much promoted as hindered the progress of work and the development of intelligence. There was both good and evil in Antiquity: the
evil, as we have shown, unquestionably stemmed from slavery, the
good from liberty" (2:438).

As Moses Finley powerfully emphasized in the first of his lectures
at the Collège de France, published in 1980 under the title *Ancient
Slavery and Modern Ideology*,[1] Henri Wallon thus takes his place in the
tradition of all those, theologians and philosophers alike, who, especially from the Renaissance onward, had approached slavery from
a moral point of view, either to extol its happy consequences or, on
the contrary, to denounce its iniquities or at the very least its ex-
cesses.[2] It was an approach that subsequently fell out of fashion,
progressively disappearing in the modern world and, by the late
nineteenth century, was no longer to be found except among Catho-
lics such as Paul Allard who, following Henri Wallon, ascribed the
end of ancient slavery to Christianity,[3] and also to some extent
among historians who studied Antiquity in the light of the modern
workers' movement for which, in general, they felt scant sympathy.
One such historian was Robert von Pöhlmann, who, in 1893 and
1901, on the occasion of the electoral successes of the German
socialists, published a work with the highly significant title *A History of
Ancient Communism and Socialism*.

What, even today, confers scholarly value of a kind upon Henri
Wallon's work is the fact that it also drew upon an entire tradition
(which, for its part, was to enjoy considerable future success!), the
tradition of the "antiquarians" and "philologists" who devoted themselves to collecting exhaustive documentation on certain well-defined subjects. *An Inquiry into the State of Slavery amongst the Romans
from Its Origins to the Establishment of the Lombards in Italy*, published by

---

1. Cf. "Slavery and the Historians," *Social History* 17 (1979): 246–61.
2. L. Hanke, *Aristotle and the American Indians* (1959); D. B. Davis, *The Problem of
Slavery in Western Culture* (1966); G. L. Huxley, "Aristotle, Las Casas and the American
Indians," *Proceedings of the Royal Irish Academy* 80 (1980): 57–68.
3. See his *Les esclaves chrétiens, depuis les premiers temps de l'Eglise jusqu'à la fin de la
domination romaine en Occident* (1876); *Esclaves, serfs et main-mortables* (1884).

the Scot William Blair in 1833, is a fine example of this type of study, which, it is worth noting, is concerned less with Greece than with Rome.

But this method of approach, a combination of erudition and moral judgment, was subsequently overtaken, then progressively supplanted by two others, one political, the other economic. The former found favor mainly at the time of the first bourgeois revolutions, during the quest for a new type of formal and representative democracy, quite distinct from the Graeco-Roman model. In contrast to the Jacobin idolatry of the "ancient republics," what was now emphasized were their links with slavery.[4] The second approach, which was to be more enduring, originated with Franklin and Hume, in the context of a controversy over ancient demography,[5] and among contemporary economists who were trying to distinguish a number of stages in the development of humanity, on the basis of modes of subsistence and modes of organizing economic life. It was in accordance with criteria such as these that they began to debate the question of slavery in the ancient world. They appear to have concentrated, initially at least, on the reasons for its disappearance: for it is noticeable that Adam Smith, for example, continued to account for its appearance by considerations of a psychological nature.[6] A short work on slavery in Greece by J. F. Reitemeier,[7] which appeared in 1798 and whose originality Moses Finley was the first to point out, brings to bear this new perspective.[8]

But it was obviously above all through the work of Marx and Engels that this latter tradition influenced the historiography of ancient slavery. It is an influence that so far exceeds their personal views on the subject that before assessing the impact of the latter we must try to place them in context. First, we should bear in mind that both men (but especially Marx), like all the educated bourgeois of their age, had acquired a direct and very solid familiarity with Graeco-Latin literature and kept themselves abreast of the best historical scholarship of their times (although more in connection with Rome than with Greece). We should also remember, however, that they never undertook any systematic and detailed study of

4. See L. Canfora, *Ideologie del classicismo* (1980), 11–19; G. Cambiano, "Dalla polis senza schiavi agli schiavi senza polis," *Opus* 1 (1982): 11–32.

5. See G. Cambiano, "La Grecia antica era molto popolata? Un dibattito nel XVIII secolo," *Quaderni di Storia* 20 (1984): 3–41.

6. *An Inquiry into the Nature and Causes of the Wealth of Nations* (1776), 3:2.

7. *Geschichte und Zustand der Sklaverei und Leibeigenschaft in Griechenland.*

8. *Ancient Slavery*, 35–39.

ancient societies, which interested them only to the extent that they fueled reflection on the origins of capitalism; Marx and Engels used ancient societies to take retrospective historical "soundings" at a very general level. It would consequently appear to be just as unjustifiable to denigrate their personal skills in analyzing Graeco-Roman society (claiming for example that they thought through the ancient phenomenon only on the basis of the North American model[9]) as to limit oneself to a reverential exegesis of their texts (taking no account of either the subsequent advances made in this field of knowledge or the evolution in their own reflections on the place of slavery in the early history of humanity.[10]

As early as *The German Ideology* (1844–1845), Marx and Engels had broken away from the ethnocentricity of the prevailing trend in political economics, which applied modern categories to all the systems of the past, thereby masking the unique features of capitalism itself. Instead, they envisaged a history of the successive stages in the division of labor and of the corresponding forms of property (rather than a history of modes of production, a concept that was as yet not clearly defined): tribal property, then ancient property, characterized by a combination of communal property and private property, followed by feudal property. Slavery appeared as early as the first stage, as the earliest form of exploitation. "Latent in the family," where it simply extended the natural division of labor, it gradually developed within the framework of the tribe, "with the increase of population, the growth of wants and with the extension of external relations: both of war and barter" (*The German Ideology*, London, 1965, p. 33). But it is only with the second form of property, in which "the division of labor is already more developed," that "the class relation between citizens and slaves is . . . completely developed" (p. 33): for example, in Rome, where "slavery remained the basis of all production" (p. 78). In the *Communist Manifesto*, published in 1848, slavery was still being used to illustrate the famous proposition that "the history of all hitherto existing society is the history of the class struggle": "Free man and slave, patrician and plebeian, lord and serf, guild-master and journeyman, in a word, oppressor and oppressed stood in constant opposition to one another; they were

---

9. See W. Backhaus, *Marx, Engels und die Sklaverei: Zur ökonomischen Problematik der Unfreiheit* (1974), and his "John Elliott Cairnes und die Erforschung der antiken Sklaverei," *Historische Zeitschrift* 220 (1975): 543–67.

10. There are many articles on this subject in *Analisi marxista* and also in a special issue of the journal *Arethusa* 8 (1975). See also M. Vegetti's introduction to *Marxismo e società antica* (1977), 11–65.

engaged in a continuous struggle, now covert, now open, a struggle which each time ended in either a revolutionary transformation of the whole of society or common ruin for the classes involved in the struggle." In this statement, which is more subtle than has often been recognized, the slaves of Antiquity constitute but one of the "orders" or "classes" involved in a complex interplay of contradictions that were expressed and resolved in a variety of ways.

From 1853 onward, in particular, Marx was to begin to develop a keen interest in "eastern" problems. This interest was initially prompted by the debate on different types of land ownership in India which arose on the occasion of the renewal of legislation favoring the British East India Company. By 1857–1858, in a pre-paratory manuscript for his *Capital* known as the *Grundrisse*,[11] in particular in the chapter titled "Pre-capitalist Economic Forma-tions" (*Formen*), he was inquiring more deeply into the various types of precapitalist development.

One fact that emerges clearly here is the unique character of the Asian mode of production (AMP), in which surplus production is collected through the intermediary of an administration in the ser-vice of a "despot" to the detriment of village communities. Village development is thereby virtually arrested since the access of individ-uals to the means of production (the land, essentially) is controlled and any process of social differentiation is thus limited. In the *Grundrisse*, the AMP certainly represents one individual path that leads to the dissolution of the "primitive community," just as do the "Germanic" and the "ancient" modes of production. It is not seen simply as a form of transition leading to that process.

As for slavery,[12] what also emerges from the *Formen* is that it developed together with serfdom, as a result of operations of war and conquest imposed by the natural process of reproduction in communities whose members at a stroke thereby affirmed them-selves to be both members of a community and also the possessors or owners of the land which constituted their "inorganic body." These two modes of personal exploitation thus exist, potentially at least, wherever community life is essentially based on a relationship to the land. But they do not develop everywhere in equal fashion:

This they are least able to do in the Asiatic form. In the *self-sustaining* unity of manufacture and agriculture on which this form is based,

11. Karl Marx, *Pre-Capitalistic Economic Formations*, ed. E. J. Hobsbawm (1965).
12. See Y. Garlan, *Colloque Besançon 1973*, 58–65.

conquest is not so essential a condition as where *landed property, agriculture,* predominate exclusively. On the other hand, since the individual in this form never becomes an owner but only a possessor, he is *at bottom* himself the property, the slave of that which embodies the unity of the community. Here, slavery neither puts an end to the conditions of labour nor does it modify the essential relationship. [Pp. 91–92]

In these conditions one can speak only of a "general slavery" which, as Marx makes clear, is not slavery except "from a European point of view," since the worker does not "himself appear among the natural conditions of production for a third individual or community" (p. 95).

In the ancient community composed of small private properties, in contrast, slavery prospers to the point where it becomes its very "base" for three reasons. First, such a community could not manage without conquest. Second, "where the members of the community have already acquired separate existence as private proprietors from their collective existence as an urban community and owners of the urban land, conditions already arise which allow the individual to *lose* his property, i.e. the double relationship which makes him both a citizen with equal status, a member of the community, and a *proprietor*" (pp. 93–94). Third, in the towns a body of artisans and, above all, commerce developed, on the periphery of agriculture and dependent chiefly on foreigners. If it is the case that slavery, and serfdom, are to be found as a secondary mode of production in all the early class societies, ancient slavery, inasmuch as it is a dominant mode of production, thus results from the decomposition of a certain type of community, at well-defined periods and in well-defined sectors, when its growth is facilitated by a massive importation of servile livestock of "barbarian" origins.

That is the explanation for the well-known laconic statement which appears in the 1859 preface to *A Contribution to the Critique of Political Economy:* "In broad outlines, the Asiatic, ancient, feudal and modern bourgeois modes of production may be designated as epochs marking progress in the economic development of society" (London, 1971, p. 21)—"marking progress" essentially in their relation to the point finally reached, not "successive," as has often been understood.

The Asiatic mode of production was not explicitly abandoned in *Capital,* the first book of which appeared in 1867, but neither was it developed systematically either there or in Engels' *Anti-Dühring* in 1877. Furthermore, Engels made no mention of it in 1888, in his book *The Origin of the Family, Private Property and the State* in which, in the wake of Lewis Morgan's *Ancient Society*, he was content to study the "ancient" path, characterized by the appearance of private property and the rise of slavery as the principal form of exploitation. And it is this book, destined, because of its popularizing nature, to enjoy a wide readership, which tends to promote the notion that Engels, and even Marx himself, in the last analysis renounced the concept of AMP and came to recognize the dissolution of the primitive community and the formation of the first class societies in one form only— that of slavery. In reality, their correspondence from 1868 onward proves that, on the contrary, they continued to enrich and diversify their thinking on this point in the light of their studies of Russian and Germanic "communities."

At any rate, Marxism—reduced to the works published during the lifetimes of their authors—in the immediate event exercised scant influence upon the historians of Antiquity.[13] Such influence as it had was in part direct, through the intermediary of two Italian works,[14] which presented illustrations of Marxism that were brilliant yet at the same time marked by the reductionist economics of the Second International (*The Decline of Slavery in the Ancient World* by Ettore Ciccotti, 1899[15] and *Capitalism in the Ancient World* by Giuseppe Salvioli, 1906). Meanwhile, a measure of indirect influence was exerted through the use to which Marxism was put by sociologists such as Karl Bücher and, in particular, Max Weber, but here the originality of its substance was diluted by strong eclectic tendencies. Furthermore, the influence of Marxism was effectively blocked by the academic prestige of the German historian Eduard Meyer, who in 1898 wrote a synthesizing essay entitled "Slavery in Antiquity" (reprinted in 1910 and 1924 in the first volume of his *Kleine Schriften*). Reacting against those (Karl Bücher even more than Karl Marx) who saw history as a succession of "stages," he regarded Antiquity as an entity in itself, beginning and ending with serfdom and including an interlude of slavery the importance of which he minimized, providing it with a strictly political explanation. Slavery was simply

13. On the influence of Marxism on ancient history in the West, see A. Momigliano, "Marxising in Antiquity," *Times Literary Supplement*, 31 October 1975; D. Lanza and M. Vegetti, "Tra Marx e gli antichi," *Quaderni di Storia* 5 (1977): 75–87; L. Canfora, "Antiquisants et marxisme," *DHA* 7 (1981): 429–36.

14. On the Italian "ideological position" at the beginning of this century, see M. Mazza, "Marxismo e storia antica: Note sulla storiografia marxista in Italia," *Studi Storici* 17 (1976): 95–124.

15. Reprinted in 1977 with an introduction by M. Mazza which later appeared in *Klio* 61 (1979): 57–83.

the corollary, the obverse of liberty, that is, the product of a democracy that was itself born from the development of commerce and artisan trades. Now this thesis, which—standing as it did for fidelity to the facts and a rejection of all modernist ideology—naturally enough claimed that democracy derived from the capitalist "spirit" and depicted slavery as a juridico-political phenomenon with no directly economic basis, was greeted enthusiastically by positivist and anti-socialist historians opposed to any evolutionary view of society. In the wake of this work, the West witnessed a whole spate of monographs, many remarkable for the quality of their information but all conspicuously lacking any overall perspective. The article by the American William L. Westermann, which appeared in the *Real-Encyclopaedie* in 1935[16] and again in 1955 in the posthumous work *The Slave Systems of Greek and Roman Antiquity*, to some extent represents a synthesis of these partial and fragmentary studies. Ideological considerations aside, it must be admitted that, as Joseph Vogt remarked, the author "put together a mosaic made up of innumerable tiny pieces but was unable to achieve the broad vision required for a historical canvas."[17] Elsewhere, slavery was generally reduced to a position of minimal importance by specialists in economics and in the principal treatises on ancient history.

In a number of respects then, Soviet historians were obliged to assume the difficult role of pioneers in this area.[18] Few of them combined a solid Marxist education with a real understanding of the ancient world. But in the context of ideological struggle created, in their eyes, by the need to consolidate a socialist State threatened from all sides, it was their duty to endeavor to "construct" a firm and coherent representation of human evolution and, to that end, emphasize the most notable features of their own particular field of

16. "Sklaverei," *RE* suppl. 6 (1935): 894–1068.
17. *Ancient Slavery and the Ideal of Man* (1974), 182.
18. See M. Raskolnikoff, *La recherche soviétique et l'histoire économique et sociale du monde hellénistique et romain* (1975); Raskolnikoff, "Les recherches soviétiques sur l'esclavage antique depuis 1965," *Ktema* 1 (1976): 195–206; P. Petit, "L'esclavage antique dans l'historiographie soviétique," *Colloque Besançon 1970*, 9–27; S. P. Dunn, *The Fall and Rise of the Asiatic Mode of Production* (1982). See also H. Heinen's article on the latest Soviet works in *Historia* 24 (1975): 378–84; 25 (1976): 501–5; and 28 (1979): 125–28, and his collection *Die Geschichte des Altertums im Spiegel der sowjetischen Forschung* (1980), in particular the articles on 98–102, by E. D. Frolov, and 153–62, by I. S. Svencickaja. Of the Soviet works that have appeared since the 1960s, more than it is generally believed have been summarized in or translated into one or another Western language. However, they are mostly to be found in collections (such as those produced by *Recherches internationales*) and journals that have a relatively limited readership, such as the *Biblioteca Classica Orientalis, Soviet Studies in History, Soviet Anthropology and Archaeology*, and *Soviet Sociology*.

research. On top of these practical necessities, they were faced, on a more general level, with the theoretical deviation of so-called Stalinism, the deep causes of which lie outside the scope of the present book. The result, in ancient history as in other sectors of the social sciences, was the emergence of a dogmatic tendency which was liable to generate errors but which nevertheless prompted some passionate debates and the expression of a number of more or less acknowledged reservations—reservations that many Western critics, out of either ignorance or anti-Marxist dogmatism, prefer to ignore.[19]

In the years following the October Revolution, Antiquity aroused little interest and was not a subject of any official "doctrine." Some scholars even became contaminated by the cyclical theories of Eduard Meyer. It was not until about 1928–1929 that the problem of precapitalist societies began to be considered relevant to the debate provoked by the tendencies of the revolutionary movement in China. At that point the Asiatic mode of production was frequently condemned for its static and colonialist character, on account of the reactionary use to which it could be put by those determined to apply it to the contemporary Chinese situation. It was consequently agreed that the whole of humanity had followed—was bound to follow—a process of unilateral evolution passing through five stages (primitive communism, slaveholding, feudalism, capitalism, and socialism), each of which might, however, be traversed at varying rates of speed, depending on the historical circumstances. In support of this theory, in 1929 *Pravda* printed *On the State,* the lecture Lenin had delivered in 1919 to a gathering of cadres, years before Stalin in his turn was to speak, in his *Dialectical Materialism and Historical Materialism,* of "five fundamental types of relations of production" (without, however, specifying what should be understood by "fundamental").

Historians of Antiquity were directly interested in this problem and discussed it under the aegis of the recently created State Academy for the History of Material Civilization (GAIMK). In the course of the conferences on the subject of the AMP which took place in Tiflis and Leningrad in 1930–1931, the general view adopted was that it had never existed in contemporary China; but where Antiquity was concerned there were some disagreements. Some considered the AMP to be no more than a form of feudalism, while others regarded it as a stage in the transition from the primitive community to slavery—although that did not prevent Godes, in his closing speech, from radically condemning it.

19. A. I. Pavlovskaja, "Les recherches des historiens soviétiques sur l'esclavage en Grèce et dans le monde hellénistique," *Colloque Nieborow 1975,* 23–33.

At all events, during the 1930s the officially favored view was that the whole of Antiquity (Eastern and Far Eastern as well as Classical) could be explained in terms of slavery and that its class struggles could be assimilated more or less to those of the modern world. S. I. Kovalev and Vassili Struve eventually became the best known of these "pan-slavery" advocates. Each devised different ways of surmounting the difficulties raised by his own particular interpretations of the facts. Kovalev was of the opinion that, in certain ancient societies, slavery had been supplanted by feudalism, while Struve believed that strong traces of the primitive community survived in them and, accordingly, that they had produced no more than a "patriarchal" form of the slaveholding mode of production. It was the latter view that dominated the historiography of the socialist world right down to the 1950s. The Western reader may find an echo of this trend in the second issue of *Recherches internationales,* which in 1957 was devoted to slavery in antiquity, and also in the history of antiquity by V. N. D'jakov and S. I. Kovalev.

Unanimous agreement on this matter was never reached, however. Thus, as early as 1935, A. I. Tiumenev was emphasizing that in the ancient East production rested to a large degree upon a free, although economically dependent, population of village communities, and he concluded that, compared with Graeco-Roman slavery, Eastern slavery presented fundamental qualitative differences, not just difference of quantity and degree. In the East it was a matter of "generalized slavery," which implied a de facto rather than a de jure subjection of the mass of producers. Other historians such as V. S. Sergeev, A. V. Misûlin and A. B. Ranovič did not go so far along this line but did insist on the incomplete and original nature of the slaveholding system in certain ancient societies.

These criticisms, which were quite limited during the 1930s became developed from the 1960s onward, when use was made of the many detailed studies that had appeared in the intervening years and also of a whole series of works that, in a variety of ways, qualified (I. M. Diakonov) or contradicted (K. K. Zelin, G. A. Melikišvili) the pan-slavery view of the ancient world. Above all, a new theoretical situation had now arisen, following the denunciation of Stalinism by the Twentieth Congress and the readoption of the concept of the AMP as a result of the publication in Moscow, in 1939, of the *Grundrisse,* although this work became widely known only when it was reissued in Berlin in 1953.[20] The immediate effect of this "re-

20. See G. Sofri, *Il modo di produzione asiatico: Storia di una controversia marxista,* 2d ed. (1974).

habilitation" of the AMP, which owed much to Marxists of the Third World and the West (in particular the French CERM),[21] was to free the ancient world from the narrow shareholding label it had earlier been assigned in the linear schema of the evolution of humanity. It would, however, have been a limited rehabilitation had it resulted only in presenting a new set of rigidly defined alternatives and had this critical view of the weakest point in the Marxist "dogma" not been accompanied by two developments: (1) a general debate on the unity/diversity of precapitalist modes of production[22] and (2) a reassessment of the concept of the "economic formation of society," which provided new theoretical bases for the problem of the articulation of different modes of production and the interaction of infrastructures and superstructures.[23] So far as classical Antiquity went, all this led to a rejection of any monolithic view of slavery or slaveholding societies attained by a simplistic reduction of their historical characteristics. This critical revision, provoked essentially by factors internal to Marxist practice and reflection, gave rise to many projects of varying scope and ramifications. One was the program, set up in 1960, by the Soviet Academy's ancient history section, to produce a new series of works intended to cover the whole field of ancient slavery. Others were the establishment, by CERM (which has recently become the Institute of Marxist Research) and the Gramsci Institute, of specialized work groups[24] and the initiatives taken by Marxist historians to hold a number of international congresses on the subject.[25]

One work of a very personal nature, which lies outside this current, has attracted much attention. It is G. E. M. de Ste. Croix, *The Class Struggle in the Ancient Greek World from the Archaic Age to the Arab Conquests* (1981). The mass of evidence that it brings together makes it a valuable work, and its intentions are particularly commendable. I would nevertheless criticize it on a number of essential counts: for its underestimation of all non-British European works, its overly reverential approach to Marx's texts, and its propagandistic reduction of

21. *Rech. int. 1967*; *Sur le mode de production asiatique* (Ed. soc., 1969); *Sur les sociétés précapitalistes: Textes choisis de Marx, Engels, Lénine* (Ed. soc., 1970), with an important preface by M. Godelier.
22. This may be followed, in particular, in the German journal *Ethnographisch-archäologische Zeitschrift*.
23. A seminal article is that by E. Sereni, "De Marx à Lénine: La catégorie de formation économique et sociale," *La Pensée* 159 (1971): 3–49. On Antiquity, see for example V. I. Kuziscin, "The concept of socioeconomic formation and the periodization of ancient slave society" (in Russian), *Vestnik Drevnei Istorii* (1974), no. 3:69–87.
24. Which culminated in Italy with the publication of *Analisi marxista*.
25. Cited in the Preface.

all social conflict to class struggle. Furthermore, Ste. Croix under-
estimates the politico-legal dimension which the exercise of extra-
economic constraints invariably confers on relations of production
and which affects the corresponding theoretical positions adopted;
so we find him still using the "linear" and "continuous" concept of
ancient history. Marx was well aware of that crucial dimension of
Antiquity, but in Ste. Croix it is superimposed from outside upon the
class struggle. He thus speaks of "an astonishing development of real
democracy" in classical Athens, which, according to him, constitutes
"a good example of exceptional political factors operating for a time
in such a way as to counterbalance economic forces" (p. 97). It is
significant, in this respect, that to further his cause the eminent
Oxford professor, who is sometimes more Marxist than Marx himself, feels no compunction about emending (p. 66 and p. 91) a
number of passages in *The Communist Manifesto* and *The German
Ideology* on the subject of the opposition between slaves and free men
or slaves and citizens. He tells us that in these passages the opposition ought to be between slaves and slaveowners. But is it really
feasible to decree, without more ado, that this is "certainly a mere
slip" (several times repeated)?

In the reopening of the Marxist debate, a wholly positive role was,
on the other hand, soon being played by a few Western historians
whose relations with Marxism are as complex as are their contributions to it. Their views, which in some cases have evolved with the
passage of years, have produced a range of varied reactions. Such is
the case, above all, of M. I. Finley. His studies of ancient slavery,
which he often compares with slavery in the nineteenth century in
the American South,[26] form two chronologically separate groups
that share a common inspiration even if the emphasis shifts as his
theoretical position changes. Around 1960, it was essentially a matter of stressing the difference between chattel slavery, on the one
hand, and Helotry and other forms of personal dependency based
on extra-economic constraints, on the other.[27] This was in opposition to the postulate of an eternal category of slavery, upon which
Marxist doctrine of the 1930s to 1950s had based its notion of the

26. "Slavery," *International Encyclopedia of the Social Sciences* (1968), 307–13; "A
Peculiar Institution?" *Times Literary Supplement*, 2 July 1976.
27. "Was Greek Civilization Based on Slave Labour?" *Historia* 8 (1959): 145–64;
"The Servile Statuses of Ancient Greece," *Revue Internationale des Droits de l'Antiquité*,
3d ser., 7 (1960): 165–89; "Between Slavery and Freedom," *Comparative Studies in
Society and History* 6 (1964): 233–49. These articles are collected in his *Economy and
Society in Ancient Greece* (1981), 97–195.

"five stages." Finley's critical appraisal was based on an observation of how dependency in all its aspects functioned in several historically well defined contexts. Such an approach implied a diversification of the criteria of social classification in which he rejected the concept of "class" (reduced to its economic interpretation) and had recourse to the notion of "status," defined as a complex of rights and duties of various kinds. That is the theme which, in 1973, still characterized the chapter entitled "Masters and Slaves" in his *Ancient Economy*. The general evolution of forms of dependency, which only occasionally led to chattel slavery, is here presented as the result of a "structural transformation within the society as a whole."[28] This theme—the heuristic value of which has been demonstrated in France by the parallel studies of Claude Mossé and Pierre Vidal-Naquet—was certainly greatly developed in the lectures Finley delivered at the Collège de France in 1978, which I have already mentioned. However, this whole series of lectures seems to me to be principally inspired by a new preoccupation: namely, the idea of undertaking a radical critical appraisal of the "humanist" approach to the phenomenon of slavery, an approach that had earlier been resuscitated in West Germany as an antidote to Marxism.

As Marxist research relating to slavery in the ancient world developed in the years following the Second World War both inside and outside the socialist camp, it became increasingly clear to Western anti-Marxist historians that they could no longer content themselves with what scholars had done in the wake of Eduard Meyer, simply minimizing the importance of the subject. They decided that it was now necessary to engage in a hard-hitting dialogue on their own side and retaliate with an ideological counterattack nurtured by the "eternal" values of Western humanism. Hence the success of the program of systematic studies begun by Joseph Vogt in Mainz in 1951, right in the middle of the cold war period, and the vigor of the attack launched against the Soviet historians at the 1966 Stockholm Historical Congress, an attack that seems to have constituted "an international political act," as M. I. Finley puts it.[29] The major idea that emerges from the synthesizing articles of Joseph Vogt[30] and various,

28. *Ancient Economy*, p. 86.

29. *Ancient Slavery*, 62; and, in briefer form, "The Necessary Evil," *Times Literary Supplement*, 14 November 1975; "Progress in Historiography," *Daedalus* (Summer 1977), 133–39. Cf. the polemical, indeed almost defamatory, articles published by, for example, F. Vittinghoff in *Saeculum* 11 (1960): 89–131, and in *Gymnasium* 69 (1962): 279–86.

30. These articles were collected in 1965 as *Sklaverei und Humanität: Studien zur antiken Sklaverei und ihrer Erforschung*. The second, enlarged edition appeared in 1972

generally well documented studies published under his patronage[31] is that ancient slavery should be regarded as a life-giving and spirit-enhancing necessity, a precondition for the progress of the elite, who responded by improving the lot of the slaves. Emphasis is consequently laid upon assimilation and integration of slaves and free men—in line with a paternalistic tradition that was particularly strong during the nineteenth century, in slaveholding America, in *The Ancient City* by Fustel de Coulanges, and among his admirers in Maurras's group. For Vogt, the gratitude to be felt for the price the exploited paid for the cultural development of their exploiters ceases to apply with the modern world: for in modern times, it seems to him, humanist values must automatically impose themselves, regardless of all historical conditioning, in a society committed to "general equality and universal liberty" and totally oriented toward God. The same approach to the phenomenon of slavery is to be found among other German historians such as Hermann Strasburger (*Zum antiken Gesellschaftsbild,* 1976) and, as can well be imagined, in South African studies.[32]

Apart from these ideological problems, the history of slavery in ancient Greece, to which we shall henceforth limit ourselves, raises other questions, of a methodological and epistemological nature, which also call for a preliminary examination since, like the ideological problems, they will determine the course of our inquiry.

Some belong to Greek history in general and need only a brief mention here. One is the extremely fragmentary and uneven nature of our documentation, which immediately sets certain limits, if not to our questions, at least to our answers and makes it essential, within those limits, to conduct our inquiry in a particularly rigorous fashion, combining a minute analysis of individual cases (which it is often difficult to know whether to regard as norms or as exceptions) with an attempt to sketch in a coherent general picture.[33]

This endeavor is, as it happens, all the more risky because the Greeks left us no systematic study of the institution of slavery. the

---

and was translated into English in 1974 as *Ancient Slavery and the Ideal of Man.* Among Vogt's most recent articles, note particularly "Die Sklaverei im antiken Griechenland," *Antike Welt* 9 (1978): 49–56.

31. These will be referred to below as *Abh. Ak. Wiss. Mainz* and *Forsch. ant. Skl.* The main data, together with a full bibliography, are to be found in the recent synthesis by N. Brockmeyer, *Antike Sklaverei* (1979). See the collection of texts assembled in the same spirit by T. Wiedemann, *Greek and Roman Slavery* (1981).

32. *Ancient Slavery,* p. 25.

33. Cf. L. Canfora, "Immagini moderne della schiavitù di età classica," *Colloque Camerino 1978,* 104–20, in particular 114.

only treatise on the subject, of which no more than a mention has come down to us, is *On Liberty and Slavery,* written in the fourth century by the philosopher Antisthenes. It must have approached the problem primarily from a moral point of view, to judge by the only sentence that has survived ("The man who fears others is a slave without knowing it"). But if the Greek philosophers concerned themselves only indirectly with slavery, they did so not because they underestimated its importance, even less because they wished to conceal it. The reason was that it lay outside the field of their preoccupations, either too limited for it (as at the time of the pre-Socratics' cosmological speculations) or situated beyond it (as at the time of the post-Socratics, for whom happiness depended upon individual virtues). For similar reasons, it hardly rates as a major theme for strictly political reflection, concerned as this was with the organization of the city, the *polis.* Even less was slavery a topic for, for example, the official funeral speeches in which a city, celebrating its dead warriors, presented an image of itself as a military power, united, indivisible, and quite separate from all the "foreigners within it"—not out of any desire to erase the reality, but because there was nothing to be said about it at this level of abstraction and sublimation.[34] The fact is that, in the eyes of the Greeks, slavery was relevant only to the economic sphere, that is, to the art of managing a family unit, an *oikos.* But even the literary genre devoted to *oeconomica,* which began to develop in the mid-fifth century, is concerned only secondarily with the exploitation of slaves (in the degree that they contribute toward the leisure of their master) and to a large extent assimilates their situation as dependants to that of other members of the family. Such discourse is not centered on slavery, indeed sometimes ignores it altogether. But we should beware of automatically concluding its authors to be misinformed or even deliberately misleading on the subject. Rather, we should ask ourselves why the situation could not have been otherwise.

The same applies to all the ancient texts relating to slaves. We should be in danger of fundamentally misunderstanding them if we sought to interpret them outside the context of the literary genres to which they belong and, even more important, without reference to the place that they occupy within one or another system of representation.

We must thus recognize that the Attic speeches of the fourth

---

34. N. Loraux, *L'invention d'Athènes* (1981), 336–39 (translated, 1986, as *The Invention of Athens*).

century, which provide us with the best image of contemporary society,[35] can present no more than a partial and distorted view of the slaves' world. The number of slaves, in particular, is frequently underestimated to the extent that, for example, an orator may take account only of those who constitute a source of income, ignoring all the domestic slaves. In this type of documentation we must also expect to find more information about slaves' legal position than about their mentality, living conditions, or role in production.[36]

Attic comedy also found direct inspiration in daily life. Aristophanes, at the end of the fifth century, portrays it from a social and political angle; Menander, a century later, in terms of individual psychology. In both, consequently, slaves play an important role, as servants. But such depictions cannot be treated as hard currency,[37] for these are comedy slaves modeled according to the traditional rules of a clearly determined literary genre. It is true that Aristophanes claims to have distinguished himself from his predecessors in this respect. In the *Peace* (ll. 743–749), he claims he has "done away with the slaves who were constantly being ejected from the house, lamenting, to the sole end that a companion, having mocked them for the blows rained upon them, should be in a position to ask: 'Wretch, what has happened to your skin? Could it be that the spiked whip has invaded your sides and ravaged your back?' " Setting aside such inept sallies, such vulgarity and base buffoonery, he has created a great art for us. In the prologue to the *Frogs*, Xanthias reproaches his master Dionysus for having prevented him from delivering "any of those old jokes at which the audience never fail to laugh" (ll. 1–2) and so to have denied him the chance to crack "one of the jokes Ameipsias, and Lycis and Phrynichus, in every play that they write, put in the mouths of all their burden-bearers" (ll. 13–15). In the *Wasps* (ll. 58–59) and *Plutus* (ll. 797–799), the author congratulates himself on having avoided introducing on stage a "brace of servants

35. Cf. C. Mossé, *La fin de la démocratie athénienne* (1962), in particular the chapter on slaves, 179–215.

36. What is involved here, however, is a collection of homogeneous texts which the ancient history group of Besançon draws on, using the most sophisticated methods of semantic analysis; see the articles by F. Dunand, M.-P. Carrière-Hervagault, and above all M.-M. Mactoux in *Colloque Besançon 1970, 1971, 1972, Colloque Nieborow 1975,* and *Colloque Bressanone 1976.* The inquiry was extended to take in Aristophanes in the *Colloque Camerino 1978,* 7–47. The last three articles are also to be found, together with an introduction, a conclusion, and a chapter on Aristotle, in Mactoux's *Douleia, esclavage et pratiques discursives dans l'Athènes classique* (1980). See also "Langage et esclavage: Remarques méthodologiques," *Index* 11 (1982): 57–68.

37. E. Lévy, "Les esclaves chez Aristophane," *Colloque Besançon 1972,* 29–46; V. Ehrenberg, *The People of Aristophanes,* 2d ed. (1951), 165–91.

here, to scatter nuts from their basket out among the audience." Yet in his own comedies, Aristophanes himself is not averse to such procedures: his slaves shower the public with barley and water (*Peace*, ll. 960–972), never pass up an opportunity to crack dirty jokes, complain of possessing tanned hides as a result of all the beatings they have received, and wish that they had carapaces like tortoises. Like the slaves portrayed by his rivals, they too have empty stomachs, itching palms, coarse expressions, and calculatedly slow gaits. They are faithful to their stock image. And if one does by chance step out of this conventional role to serve as a foil for his master, that simply underlines the grotesqueness of the situation. In Aristophanes' last works, the *Clouds* and *Plutus*, for example, the distance between master and slave certainly seems to have shrunk; but the fact that they seem closer is explained more by the degradation of the master, who has lost his sense of civic values, than by any elevation of the slave.[38] Menander's typology of slaves, which is more complex, was immediately revealed to the public by the slaves' names and caricatural masks.[39] For example, there was a basic difference between the personalities of the Daos on the one hand and the Parmenons on the other, all of whom played leading roles: the former, who may have worn the mask of "the principal servant whose red hair was gathered into a bun" (no. 22 in the nomenclature established by Pollux), specialized in intrigue whereas the latter, sporting a crest of red hair (no. 27), were simple confidants, there to listen to the moralizing speeches of their masters. In both cases, their ruddy complexions betokened a harder, less protected life that that of their masters. However, they now certainly took a more active part in the unfolding of the action than they had in old comedy a century earlier. From being no more than agents employed to execute the plans of their masters, they had become plot organizers, proud of their intelligence and artfulness. They also played a more positive role in sexual matters: love affairs are far more important in Menander than in Aristophanes, for slaves as well as for free cou-

38. As is believed by F. Bourriot, whose views clearly coincide with Vogt's; see Bourriot, "L'évolution de l'esclave dans les comédies d'Aristophane et l'essor des affranchisements au IVᵉ siècle," *Mélanges d'histoire ancienne offerts à William Seston* (1974), 35–47.
39. See W. T. MacCary, "Menander's Slaves: Their Names, Roles and Masks," *TAPA* 100 (1969), 277–94; S. Charitonidis, L. Kahil, and R. Ginouvès, *Les mosaïques de la maison de Ménandre à Mytilène* (1970), esp. 277–94; A. Aloni, "Il ruolo de lo schiavo come personaggio nella comedia di Menandro," *Colloque Gargnano 1975*, 25–41; L. Bernabo Brea, *Menandro e il teatro greco nelle terracotte liparesi* (1981), 78–93 and 196–207.

ples.[40] Was the same true of real life? Obviously not, as M. I. Finley rightly observes.[41] The slave is a mirror image who on stage has simply assumed the psychological nuances his master has acquired. The fact is that slaves do not think (any more than Greek women do): they are useful to the free man, helping him to see himself in all his perfection but also with all his limitations and illusions.

There are also many slaves in the tragedies of the fifth century,[42] rather fewer in Aeschylus and Sophocles than in Euripides, who adapts the traditional mythological themes more freely to the mores of his own day. Occasionally he even places them at the center of the action, but not just any slaves, only those—usually women, such as Hecuba and Andromache (the mother and the wife of Hector, captured by the Greeks when Troy was taken)—who retain their princely souls in the midst of their tribulations. Ordinary slaves are usually present as mere foils for their masters and they play only minor roles (of confidants, janitors, pedagogues, nurses, and so on), indispensable yet insignificant on stage just as in real life. It is also the case that in Euripides slaves of all types are prone to echo the philosophers' contemporary thinking about slavery, but it is never clear whether such views coincide with those of the author or of his public—let alone with what slaves themselves may have thought! So, like the slaves of comedy, the slaves of tragedy should not be introduced without due precaution into any picture of real life.

There is hardly any documentation, written or archaeological, which can be claimed to provide an authentic or original image of slavery to set alongside these portraits of slaves constructed by the literate elite of free men and accordingly quite literally "mastered" by them. It is hard to gauge the personal views of writers of slave origin such as Aesop, the fabulist, in the first half of the sixth century and a number of philosophers of the fourth century and the Hellenistic period, given how little we know of their works.[43] Nor can we learn much even from archaeology.[44] Had greater interest

40. C. Leduc, "Le discours d'Aristophane et de Ménandre sur la sexualité des maîtres et des esclaves," *Index* 10 (1981), 271–87.

41. *Ancient Slavery*, 119–20.

42. See H. Brandt, *Die Sklaven in den Rollen von Dienern und Vertrauten bei Euripides* (1973); C. Synodinou, *On the Concept of Slavery in Euripides* (1977); H. Kuch, *Kriegs-gefangenschaft und Sklaverei bei Euripides. Unters. z. "Andromache," z. "Hekube" und den "Troerinnen,"* 2d ed. (1978).

43. The theme of the philosopher-slave became firmly established at the time of Epictetus, around the mid-second century A.D. It is worth noting that this is the period when Hermippus of Berytus composed a treatise entitled *On Slaves Famous in the Cultural Domain*; see S. Mazzarino, *Il pensiero storico classico*, II 2 (1966), 131–99.

44. See N. Himmelmann, *Archäologisches zum Problem der griechischen Sklaverei*, Abh. Ak. Wiss. Mainz, *1971*, no. 13; J. Kolendo, "Eléments pour une enquête sur l'ico-

been shown in the matter, many more roughly built dwellings would certainly have been discovered, but we should still not know for certain whether the framework of the lives of slaves differed significantly from that of the poorest free men. As for the iconography of slavery as conceived in the popular and largely servile milieus of the ceramic industry, this too seems very ambiguous. To begin with, the heroic context of figurative representations generally demanded that servants should be depicted as free, young companions. But shortly before the end of the sixth century slaves began to become distinguishable from their masters (for the first time, on a black-figure clay tablet painted by Exekias around 530. It shows a bearded groom of noticeably smaller stature than the free men around him). The tendency became more marked in the fifth century, a period when the figure of the "barbarian" was acquiring more definite characteristics. A slave could now be recognized from one or more of the following details: a rough woolen tunic belted at the waist and reaching no further than the knee, sometimes topped with a goat-skin or a short jacket; a dog-skin cap; laced boots or sandals; a short "soup-bowl" haircut; a pointed beard; a face with coarse (sometimes negroid) features; above all, a sitting or squatting position and a small stature. Many of the characteristics, however, also appear in the representations of artisans[45] or free men of humble condition, so it is difficult to be certain.

From a theoretical point of view, I will conclude by saying that all our documentation relating to slaves is "overdetermined" in one way or another and, as such, demands a "diagnostic" or "symptomatic" reading. What is at work here, just as in Herodotus' writings on the barbarians, is a "rhetoric of otherness" founded upon certain textual constraints and a certain shared knowledge,[46] which as a general rule turns the slave into the reverse of a free man—that is, a subversive incarnation of incompleteness and disorder.

Without prejudging the limits assigned to the concept of slavery, we should also recognize that its basic terminology in ancient Greece

nographie des esclaves dans l'art hellénistique et romain," *Colloque Bressanone 1976,* 61–174; Kolendo, "Les esclaves dans l'art antique: La stèle funéraire d'un marchand d'esclaves thraces découverte à Amphipolis," *Archeologia* 29 (1978): 24–34; A. Waso-wicz, "Les serviteurs sur les monuments funéraires du Pont Euxin: Eléments pour une enquête," *Colloque Camerino 1978,* 232–40; W. Raeck, *Zum Barbarenbild in der Kunst Athens im 6. und 5. Jahrhundert v. Chr.* (1981); H. P. Laubscher, *Fischer und Landleute* (1982).

45. See J. Ziomecki, *Les représentations d'artisans sur les vases attiques* (1975).

46. See F. Hartog, *Le miroir d'Hérodote: Essai sur la représentation de l'autre* (1980), translated, 1988, as *The Mirror of Herodotus.*

was extremely complex and generally ambiguous—even in the classical and Hellenistic periods, by which time it had already acquired a fixed juridical definition.[47]

As well as the names used locally to refer to such or such a local people reduced to servitude (Laconian Helots, Thessalian Penestes, and so on), there existed a large number of generic terms which could refer to slaves but most of which were not reserved for them alone. Here it is not always possible to establish distinctions with any certainty on the basis of the context or customary usage alone.

The only term that never leads to confusion is *andrapodon*. Etymologically related to *tetrapodon* (being with four feet), denoting livestock,[48] a "being with human feet" in a military context denotes a prisoner, not in the technical sense of "captive," but regarded as an object acquired as booty, subject to the will of the victor and destined to be sold as a slave, and thus a slave as a thing, an object owned, and a resource to be exploited.

In the classical period, the word *doulos* (fem., *doule*) is even more common. Its etymology remains uncertain,[49] but a study of its semantic field reveals it to stand in opposition, either explicitly or implicitly, to the free man (*eleutheros*) and even more so to the complete man as represented by the citizen (*polites*) to whom the *doulos* is automatically assumed to be linked in a relationship of domination and possession. The word may consequently be found in juridical contexts, in theoretical discussions, and also in gnomic formulations relating to model types of behavior: wherever it is important to underline statutory differences and tensions. That explains how it is that, in the narrowest sense, it can denote the "perfect" slave, one deprived of all liberty, while in a wider sense, from either a juridical or a nonjuridical point of view, it can mean any type of submission to an alien force, be it submission in fact or simply of a psychological nature.[50] For Plato, for example, *douleia* denotes not only slavery in the strict sense, that is, of the Athenian or Spartan type, but equally political subjection, moral servitude, or simply subordination (of one part of the body in relation to another,

47. See F. Gschnitzer, *Studien zur griechischen Terminologie der Sklaverei*. I: *Grundzüge des vorhellenistischen Sprachgebrauchs*, Abh. Ak. Wiss. Mainz, *1963*, no. 13; II: *Unters. zur älteren, insbesondere homerischen Sklaventerminologie*, Forsch. ant. Skl. 7 (1976); U. Kästner, "Bezeichnungen für Sklaven," *Soziale Typenbegriffe*, ed. E. C. Welskopf, 3 (1981): 282–318.

48. R. Lazzeroni, "Etimologia e semantica del greco *andrapodon*," *Studi e Saggi Linguistici* 10 (1970), 165–73; I. Hahn, "Der Begriffe auf—*Phós*," *Sozialen Typenbegriffe* 4 (1981): 54–58.

49. See below, p. 26, n. 4.

50. See above, n. 36.

of a child in relation to its parents, or of a citizen in relation to the magistrates).[51]

In general, the word most frequently used is *oiketes* (*oikiatas* or *oikeus*), which, strictly speaking, denotes the slave in relation to his master, as a member of a family group (*oikos*), and—by extension—as the performer of the various tasks of everyday life or, in an even wider sense, simply as a concrete reality.[52] Hence it may also apply, particularly in the earlier writers (such as Herodotus) to any type of servant, whatever his or her status.

But when no precise indication of either origin or function is required, the ordinary slave may also, albeit more rarely, be called *therapon*, that is to say "servant" (the feminine *therapaina* is used the more frequently because the word *oiketes* has no feminine form); *akolouthos*, meaning "follower"; *hyperetes*, meaning "aide" (feminine: *hyperetis* or *hyperetria*); *pais*, meaning "child," a term of both affection and contempt, indicating a relationship of age rather than of kinship (although "boy" used in this way does not necessarily refer to a slave who is young)[53]; or even, still more neutrally, *anthropos* ("man") or *gyne* ("woman"). None of these terms makes the juridical condition of the subject clear beyond doubt.

From the fourth century onward, the terminology of slavery tends to become even less specific: the words *doulos*, *andrapodon*, and *oiketes* are in effect treated as synonyms or frequently supplanted by the common terms listed above or by the word *sôma* ("body," that is, "human being," which means "slave" only when that is clear from the context, as in acts of manumission), or by a series of diminutives of *pais* (*paidion*, *paidarion*, *paidiskos*, or *paidiske*). Contemporaries must have been more or less conscious of the ambiguity, since it is evident from the Ptolemaic papyri that the terms are used only in letters or notes addressed to people aware of the status of those in question; clearer labels (*andrapodon doulos*, *soma doulikon*) are used in documents destined for officials.

Then there are a few terms which are less widely used: *latris*, which may be applied to both paid work and slavery[54] and—more com-

51. The verb *douleuein*, in particular, can have a metaphorical meaning: cf. M.-M. Mactoux, "L'esclavage comme métaphore: *Douleuô* chez les orateurs attiques," *Index* 10 (1981): 20–42.
52. K. M. Kolobova, "The term *oiketes* in Thucydides" (in Russian), *Monde antique*, 187–203.
53. M. Golden, "*Pais* in Hipp. fr. 13 w," *Quaderni Urbinati di Cultura Classica* 41 (1982), 73ff.; H. Heinen, "Zum militärischen Hilfspersonal in *P.Med.* Inv. 69.65," in *Egypt and the Hellenistic World* (1983), 129–42.
54. See below, p. 101, n. 33.

mon—*amphipolos, prospolos* ("female companion") and *dmos* (feminine: *dmoe*), which were used frequently in the Homeric poems and reappear in later archaizing poetry (see below, p. 31).

The ambiguity of the terminology of slavery thus stems partly from the metaphoric extension of its specific meanings to the world of free men but above all from its being constituted from terms borrowed from traditional systems of dependency and solidarity (the household, the family, associations, clientship, and so on). It is consequently employed on a number of different levels that should be assessed in each case in relation to the context—for the choice of the word used is in principle explained by the particular aspect of the slave to be emphasized. The terminology seizes upon the slave in action, engaged in a network of relationships. It presents one selected aspect of the slave in question, but that should not obscure the fact that there are many others.

The problems of interpretation are no less delicate when it comes to nomenclature[55]—the importance of which is nonetheless crucial for, particularly in epigraphy, the proper name allotted to an individual is often the only clue to his juridical status.

The names of free men are normally followed by a patronym (in the genitive) and an adjective indicating either their place of origin (city or people) or else the subgroup to which they belong (deme, phratry, tribe, and the like). The names of slaves, in contrast, as a general rule appear either in isolation or else accompanied by the name (in the genitive) of their master (or, very exceptionally, of their father). Their place of origin is seldom indicated. But these general rules do not always apply, especially in funerary epigraphy, an essential source for the names of slaves. Thus, during the Hellenistic period, in certain regions (central Greece, the Ionian islands, Euboea, and the northern Peloponnese), the funerary monument of a citizen generally carried no more than the name of the deceased, whereas in Rhodes, Athens, and Thessaly it was customary to give his patronym as well. Neither in Athens nor in Rhodes, however, do epitaphs devoid of patronyms invariably refer to slaves: in Athens they may be memorials to metics, in Rhodes to foreigners. In Delos, where men of many different origins rubbed shoulders, it would be risky to presume that all stelae engraved with no more than one

---

55. O. Masson, "Les noms des esclaves dans la Grèce antique," *Colloque Besançon 1971*, 9–23. For names that appear in the acts of manumission, see L. Collins Reilly, *Slaves in Ancient Greece* (1978), and "The Naming of Slaves in Greece," *Ancient World* 1 (1978): 111–13, together with O. Masson's review in *Revue de Philologie* (1981), 326–28.

name are memorials to slaves,[56] particularly since slaves' stelae differed not at all, neither in size nor in decoration, from those erected to the memory of freed or free men. The same phenomenon has been noted in fourth-century Attica, where the iconography of slaves' stelae is identical to that used for free men. Hence the interest of research into nomenclature, which aims to determine with varying degrees of probability whether particular proper names should be associated with slaves and their specific spheres of geographical diffusion.

During the classical and Hellenistic periods, when it was evidently the master who fixed the identity of his slaves, it is clear that the latter might be given a variety of names: that of the master; one of more or less transparently ethnic character—connected with a particular people: Thratta, Carion, Phrygios, Lydos, Syros; a topographical name: Asia, Italia, Neilos; or a typically native one: Manes (Lydian), Midas (Phrygian), Tibios (Paphlagonian)—; names of historical figures (whether or not compatriots of the slave in question): Alexander, Cleopatra, Croesus, Amasis; certain divine names (Satyros, Hermes, Eros, but never Zeus, Apollo, or Poseidon) or names derived from them (Apollonius, Dionysius, Demetrius) or composed on the basis of them (Apollodorus, and others ending in -dorus); names relating to the situation, qualities, or defects of the subject (*Titthe,* the nurse; *Eirene,* Peace; *Pistos,* the dependable one; *Harpax,* the rapacious one), and many other auspicious names prefixed by *Eu-, Zo-, So-* or *Sos;* or a variety of titles (such as *Leon,* the lion; *Chrusos,* gold). Only a handful from all these names were reserved for slaves alone: those that clearly refer to barbarian countries, such as Thrace, Syria, central Asia Minor, or Calabria,[57] places which were particularly despised for being major suppliers of slave labor. For the rest, assumptions regarding even the most denigratory of names are extremely flimsy, even when they are based upon a general study of the characteristic nomenclature of a particular region or period.

We must recognize that very few of the apparently purely scholarly debates on this topic avoid, in one way or another, consciously or unconsciously, adopting a particular ideological perspective. Moreover, if we also recognize the inevitable interactions between these different levels of research, the hazards of a comprehensive study of slavery in ancient Greece become increasingly clear.

56. See M.-T. Couilloud, *Les monuments funéraires de Rhénée, Expl. arch. Délos* 30 (1974).

57. G. Nenci, "Kolabrizesthai (*Vet. Test.* Job, 5, 4)," *ASNP,* 3d ser., 12 (1982): 1–6.

Chattel Slavery

Contemporary historians and anthropologists are no more successful than the ancient authors in providing a clear and precise definition of slavery, distinguishing it from all other forms of exploitation similarly based on extra-economic constraints (that is, on direct use of force, not on the "free" play of the economy as in capitalist societies).[1]

The common-sense notion of slavery, which is confused and much governed by emotion, is dominated by the idea that slaves are *par excellence* foreigners who are bought and sold as though they were simply objects; it is an idea, influenced by Aristotelian theories and Roman law, inherited from recent practice in the European colonies and in the American South. Those historical models are not altogether identical; nevertheless, belonging as we do to Western civilization, we spontaneously if only approximately adopt the idea of "chattel slavery" as it existed, in particular, in classical Athens. It therefore seems natural to make Athens the starting point of our inquiry (particularly because, as is well known, it also happens to be our richest source of documentation).

This type of slavery, distinguished by these two characteristics, was certainly present earlier in Greece, in both the Mycenaean and the Homeric worlds. But, so far as we can judge from the documentation available, it appears to have incorporated different features in each of those two periods. A brief historical glance back at not so much the

---

1. See in particular *L'esclavage en Afrique précoloniale*, ed. C. Meillassoux (1975).

origins as the antecedents of the classical Athenian "model" will help
us to distinguish, by contrast, the particular socioeconomic features
that conditioned its formation.

"Mycenaean" Slavery

It is not and probably never will be possible to give a precise date
for the appearance in Greece of slavery (whatever the meaning given
to the term), for the simple reason that both the Neolithic Age (to
venture no further back) and the major part of the Bronze Age can
be known only through the mute testimonies to material conditions
of life unearthed by the archaeologists. Now, while such evidence
can certainly inform us about the growth of productive forces and
the progress of social differentiation, it tells us nothing of their
corollary, the concrete mode of exploitation. That still holds good
for the Crete of the first half of the second millennium: many traces
of its brilliant palace civilization remain (at Knossos, Phaestos, Mal-
lia, and elsewhere) but its system of writing, known as "Linear A" has
yet to be deciphered. We must therefore content ourselves with
selecting a still later starting point for our inquiry. It is determined by
the recent decipherment of "Linear B," the syllabic writing used in
the Mycenaean palace civilization of the fifteenth, fourteenth, and
thirteenth centuries.[2]
We are today capable of translating this archaic Greek language
introduced by Indo-European invaders at the beginning of the
second millennium, albeit with hesitations over points of detail.
Nevertheless, we must recognize the limitations imposed on our
information by the very nature of our documentation. Essentially,
this takes the form of simple clay tablets, accidentally preserved
because they were baked at the time of the final conflagration of the
palaces: Most were found in Pylos and Knossos, a few in Mycenae
and Thebes. They were designed to record the operations controlled
by the palace scribes over the current year and consequently provide
no more than a partial and randomly selective view of the situation
on the eve of the destruction.
Nevertheless, these written documents have opened up to historical knowledge a whole new economic, social, political, and cultural
universe, in which the royal palaces played an essential role at every

2. Of the recent works of synthesis, we should mention J. Chadwick, *The Mycenaean World* (1976).

level. The picture tallies with the overall impression already provided by the archaeological discoveries. But we now also learn that
this society, already known to be extensively differentiated and rigidly structured, included "slaves"[3]—or at any rate individuals referred to by the words *doero* and *doera,* later to reappear in the forms
doulos and *doule*[4].

In the documentation from Pylos, which constitutes our principal
source of information on this point, these words appear frequently:
more than one hundred and fifty instances have been counted. If,
however, we bear in mind that the same slave may be included in
several different series, we obtain an approximate total of one hundred and forty *doero/doera* specifically named as such (the maximum
number belonging to a single individual being thirty-two women).
We have, however, no means of calculating their percentage in
relation to the population as a whole, particularly as the exact meaning of the lists of those drawing rations which appear in the Pylos
series Aa, Ab and Ad and the Knossos series Ai, Aj and Ak is still a
matter of conjecture:[5] in the kingdom of Pylos the total comes to
about 450 mothers and grandmothers, 350 adult sons and an equal
number of adult daughters, 450 young girls and 350 young boys, as
well as 100 adolescents who were placed in the charge of supervisors.
Following most specialists, I am inclined to believe that it was so
evident that these people were slaves that it did not seem necessary to
make the point more than once:[6] they may have been refugees or
prisoners of war accompanied by their children, or alternatively
wives and children delivered into temporary servitude by the heads

3. M. Lejeune, "Textes mycéniens rélatifs aux esclaves," *Historia* 8 (1959): 129–44
(=*Mém. de philologie mycénienne,* 2d ser. [1971], 63–81); J. A. Lencman, *Die Sklaverei in
mykenischen und homerischen Griechenland* (1963 in Russian; German translation appeared in 1966), 95–202; P. Debord, "Esclavage mycénien, esclavage homérique,"
Revue des Etudes Anciennes 75 (1973): 225–40.
4. The etymology of the Mycenaean words is by no means established. Some
scholars believe it is impossible to trace an Indo-European origin for them and instead
regard them as borrowings from Carian or Lydian. Within the Greek language itself,
associations have been suggested with the verb *deo,* to bind; the verb *didomi,* to give;
the noun *leia,* the smaller livestock and booty, etc. The most convincing solution
derives them from the Indo-European root **dem-,* meaning both to build (a house)
and to tame or dominate, completed by the suffix *-e-lo* (**dm-s-e-lo*) or from another
root **dos* (*dos-e-lo*), enemy, barbarian, servant (A. Tovar, "Indo-European Etymology
of *do-e-ro,*" *Minos* 12 [1971]: 318–25; F. Gschnitzer, *Studien zur griechischen Terminologie der Sklaverei,* 2 [1976]: 2–8).
5. P. Carlier, "La femme dans la société mycénienne d'après les archives en linéaire
B," in *La femme dans les sociétés antiques,* ed. E. Lévy (1983), 9–32.
6. *Contra* A. Uchitel, "Women at Work," *Historia* 33 (1984): 257–82, who sees
simply a system of forced labor here.

of their families, in payment of debts, as sometimes happened in the East.

From a juridical point of view, the slaves named as such fall into two categories. Those in the first group, consisting of twenty-nine men and seven women, are simply referred to by the noun *doero/ doera*, which is generally preceded by the name of their master (an individual of variable rank, or occasionally, at Knossos, the community of the "people" as a whole). The second category, which is considerably larger, is composed of *teojo doero/doera:* that is, slaves of the god (perhaps Poseidon) or, in a few cases, slaves belonging to other deities (Artemis or Divia). In classical Greece (see below, p. 112), a similar distinction between private or public slaves and sacred slaves also existed, and there too they appear to have been recruited in the same manner as chattel slaves. First, many must have been captured in warfare or piracy (many of the slaves in Pylos have ethnic names connected with some locality outside the kingdom, such as Cythaera, Miletus, Cnidus, Halicarnassus, Lemnos, or Chios). A second factor would have been the natural increase in the slave population; a third, various operations in which property changed hands, attested in particular by two tablets from Knossos upon which it is stated that so-and-so bought (*qi-ri-ja-to*) so-and-so, the slave of so-and-so—the verb being preceded by the term *si-ra/si-ra-to*, the meaning of which escapes us.[7]

There can, however, be no question of assimilating Mycenaean slavery to classical slavery of the Athenian type, for quite apart from the fact that far smaller numbers appear to have been involved in Mycenaean slavery, many qualitative differences exist between the two.

Consider, in the first place, the juridical relations between slaves and nonslaves, as they emerge from the Pylos tablet An 60, which mentions thirteen *doera* who live in Metapa and are known by the mysterious name (possibly signifying their profession or status) of *doqeja*. Six of these women are the daughters of a slave father and a mother who may possibly have come from Cythaera; three of a slave father and a mother who was a slave of Divia; four of a slave mother and a blacksmith father. In all these cases their servile status appears to be inherited from whichever parent is first mentioned with the simple description of *doero/ra*, regardless of the status of the other parent. If we were certain that (as most specialists believe) these "people from Cythaera" and these "blacksmiths" were not them-

7. J.-P. Olivier, article for the *Festschrift J. Chadwick, Suppl. Minos* (forthcoming).

selves slaves, we could conclude that unions between slaves and nonslaves (in particular between male slaves and free women) were relatively common at this period. A series of tablets from Pylos (Es), containing a list of thirteen people who in all probability belonged to a religious brotherhood devoted to Poseidon, also suggests that slaves—those consecrated to a deity, at any rate—could enter into this type of association with nonslaves.

To judge by the size of the offerings mentioned, however, this same series of tablets indicates that the economic situation of these slaves must, for the most part, have been inferior to that of other members of the brotherhood. All the same, they were recognized to enjoy some rights to property. Tablet C 915 from Knossos indicates the existence of "ten ewes belonging to Apiqota and ten goats belonging to his slave," and tablet C 912 mentions sixty rams and forty ewes belonging to a slave. We also know that slaves could exercise the profession of blacksmith in a more or less independent manner, as is indicated by the Jn series of tablets from Pylos, which carry lists of the blacksmiths in each locality who have or have not received an allocation of bronze from the palace (about three hundred names in all, coming from sixteen different localities). The second of these categories mentions, together with the names of their masters, a dozen *doero* artisans, most of whom are weavers.

Even more interesting in this respect is the series of cadastral documents from Pylos which contains a list of the *onatere*, that is, the beneficiaries of allotments of land (*onato*) taken either from the "private" domains held by a small number of important personages (*tereta*) or from communal land belonging to the community (*damo*). In the first of these series (En and Eo), of 382 units allotted by the *tereta*, 297 were to slaves (181 to 11 *teojo doera* and 116 to 10 *teojo doero*)— the rest to 5 free people. In the second of these series (Eb and Ep), the slaves receiving allotments are again for the most part slaves of the god, with the exception of two slaves of the goddess, one slave of the *karawiporo* (a religious dignitary) and three slaves belonging to a certain Amphimedes: these six hold 86 units among them.

In order to form some idea of the different grades recognized among the Mycenaean slaves, we may resort to the evidence of the nomenclature. To judge from the sixty-three names in the inventory compiled in 1958, they do not seem to have differed fundamentally from those found among nonslaves, except that the former include a higher proportion of names indicating professions (the Shepherd, the Fire-keeper) or of ethnic origin (the Theban woman, the Corinthian woman, the Trojan woman) and virtually no composite names in the aristocratic style (such as Eri-bios, Eury-otos).

All this evidence indicates that a certain hierarchy existed within the servile group. There were distinctions between on the one hand the privileged slaves, devoted to a deity, whose individual personalities were more or less recognized (although we cannot go so far as to assume that their servitude was purely symbolic) and, on the other, the most deprived slaves, the anonymous mass who received nothing but a small ration of food.

In any event, one difference between Mycenaean slavery and chattel slavery of the classical type is that the former did not represent the polar opposite to liberty. The reason for this is not, as is sometimes suggested, the "primitive" character of Mycenaean slavery and the fact that statutory distinctions had not had time to develop; it is, rather, that even allowing for the particular nature of our evidence, the opposition between slaves and nonslaves does not appear to have played a major role in the structuring and differentiation of this type of society. What does appear to have constituted a determining factor is the situation of individuals vis-à-vis the palace.[8] That is proved by the fact that it is in relation to the palace that the notion of liberty is defined: in the context of the production of linen, the term *ereutero* (that is, *eleutheros,* free) is applied to the quotas that are exempted from being turned over to the palace, those that are not at the disposal of the administration. It is thus a term that connotes the space within which autonomy in relation to the palace is possible: autonomy for produce and perhaps also for men. Thus liberty is not identified with nonslavery, for the points of reference lie elsewhere. There is, in the last analysis, nothing to prevent a slave's product from receiving the privilege of freedom (although there is no evidence to suggest that it ever did). The whole mass of nonslaves thus appears to be normally situated in a state of dependency vis-à-vis the palace, a position which, from a modern point of view (or from that of the classical *polis*), would appear to lie somewhere in between slavery and liberty. In all these respects, this Mycenaean society resembles the contemporary despotic societies of the East.

Homeric Slavery

The absence of written documentation for the "Dark Ages" through which Greek history passed following the disappearance of

---

8. A. Mele, "Esclavage et liberté dans la société mycénienne," *Colloque Besançon 1973,* 115–55.

the Mycenaean kingdoms causes us to lose the thread of the story we are following. However, to judge by the relative poverty of the material remains archaeologists have discovered, it seems reasonable to suppose that the collapse of the palace economies and the disintegration of the sociopolitical structures intimately connected with them must have resulted in a considerable reduction in slavery. At the same time, a kind of resurgence of less centralized and less hierarchical forms of community organization appears to have taken place, prompted, it is generally believed, by the "Dorian invasions" of the end of the second millennium.

Whatever the extent and duration of this apparent recession, Greece eventually made a new start, which launched it on a perceptibly different path of development. As early as the tenth to ninth centuries BC, it appears to have been structured upon new bases and divided into small kingdoms of an aristocratic nature. The Homeric poems *The Iliad* and *The Odyssey*, probably composed during the eighth century, after an interval of two or three generations, bear witness to this evolution. They introduce us to the world of these aristocratic kingdoms, but by paths so devious and complex that modern historians even today continue to ponder about the era to which they refer. Rather than the Trojan War itself (mid-thirteenth century?) or the period of the poems' composition, do they not in truth lead us to some point situated chronologically in between, more or less contaminated both by the distant past and by the contemporary present, and also more or less sublimated by the poet's imagination and the rules of the epic genre—in truth, to what in many respects has become a utopia?[9]

In any event, so far as social structures and particularly slavery go, there is without doubt a certain discontinuity between the Homeric world on the one hand and both the Mycenaean and the classical worlds on the other, a discontinuity immediately detectable in the vocabulary.[10] In Homer, terms belonging to the *doero/doulos* family

9. See M. I. Finley, *The World of Odysseus*, 2d ed. (1977), and A. Mele, *Società e lavoro nei poemi omerici* (1968).

10. See G. Micknat, *Studien zur Kriegsgefangenschaft und zur Sklaverei in der griechischen Geschichte*, 1 (1954), rpt. in G. Wicert-Micknat, *Unfreiheit im Zeitalter der homerischen Epen* (1983); W. Beringer, "Studien zum Bild von unfreien Menschen in der griechischen Literatur von den Anfängen bis zum Ende des klassischen Dramas" (diss., Tubingen, 1956); Beringer, "Die ursprüngliche Bedeutung von *Doulosunen anechestai* in *Odysee* 22, 423," *Athenaeum* 30 (1960): 65–97; Beringer, "Zu den Begriffen für 'Sklaven' und 'Unfrei' bei Homer," *Historia* 10 (1961): 259–91; Beringer, "Der Standort des *oikeus* in der Gesellschaft des homerischen Epos," *Historia* 13 (1964): 1–20; and Beringer, "Servile Status in the Sources for Early Greek History," *Historia* 31 (1982): 13–32; Lencman, *Die Sklaverei*, 203–301; M. Gerard-Rousseau, "*Dmôs* et *dmôe* chez

are rare. The classical term *andrapodon* (in the form *andrapous*) appears in only one passage—which may be an interpolation (*Il* 5.475). As for the noun *oikeus*, it has the ambiguous meaning of "people of the household," denoting the servants in general, free and slave alike, or even the members of the family (in *The Iliad* at least; in *The Odyssey*, the noun does tend to apply to slaves alone). The most common word for slave is *dmos* (masculine), *dmoe* (feminine),[11] names which after Hesiod are rarely to be found, except in deliberately archaizing poetic language. To refer to female slaves who work close to the mistress of the house, *amphipolos* is frequently employed, a term that subsequently came to be used in the same manner as *dmoe*. Finally, in Homeric vocabulary, we find two terms which are applied generally to all individuals of inferior condition, whether they be slaves or not. The first is *gynaikes* (women), which in the plural form has a definitely derogative implication; the second *drester* (m) and *dresteira* (f), which derive from the verb *dran* (to do) and denote "those who do things."

The vocabulary thus testifies to certain differences between Homeric slaves and both their Mycenaean and their classical counterparts. But all that it tells us about the phenomenon of slavery in general is that it included many different types of concrete conditions—the more so since, in Homer, the adjective *eleutheros* (free) describes not the personal condition of nonslaves as a group but very specifically the independence collectively enjoyed by a city such as Troy before its capture, State liberty rather than liberty within the State; it stands in opposition to terms belonging to the *doulos* family, which denote membership of a foreign community that has been subjected and do not relate to the condition of the *dmoes* integrated into an *oikos*.[12] Consequently, our knowledge about Homeric slaves essentially depends on whatever the scenes of warfare in *The Iliad* and the adventures of the heroes in *The Odyssey* can tell us regarding the sources of slave recruitment and slaves' living conditions.

Homère," *Ziva Antika* 19 (1969): 163–73; Debord, "Esclavage mycénien"; G. Ramming, "Die Dienerschaft in der 'Odysee'" (diss., Erlangen, 1973).

11. Gschnitzer, *Studien zur griechischen Terminologie der Sklaverei*. According to most ancient lexicographers and modern philologists, these terms are derived from the verb *daman*, to tame, to take possession by force; but others believe them to be related to the term *domos*, house, or the Cretan word *mnoia*, which in the classical period designated a particular category of slaves (see below, p. 102). Yet others regard it as a word of foreign origin.

12. F. Cassola, "*Eleutheros*,' EREUTERO," *Synteleia V. Arangio-Ruiz* (1964), 269–79; K. Raaflaub, "Zum Freiheitsbegriff der Griechen," *Soziale Typenbegriffe*, ed. E. C. Welskopf, 4 (1981), 180–405.

In *The Iliad,* as a general rule the defeated are massacred forthwith, on the battlefield. But they may occasionally be spared: either to be used as a means of exchange, as in the case of Priam's numerous children whom "swift-foot Achilles took . . . and sent them over the barren seas for sale in Samnos or in Imbros or in smoke-capped Lemnos" (24.751–753); or to be freed in return for a large ransom, if they have managed to deflect the sword of death by evoking the treasures of bronze, gold, and wrought iron into which their father would dip without counting the cost as soon as he knew them to be "taken alive to the Achaean ships" (6.46–50); or to be used later as a sacrifice like the "dozen brave men, the sons of noble Trojans" whom Achilles massacres on Patroclus' funeral pyre (23.175–176). Women were much more likely to fall into the hands of their conquerors alive. Some would be returned in exchanged for a ransom, others might be offered as gifts, while the majority would be condemned to end their days in the house of whoever received them as a part of his share of the booty. As for children, they shared either their father's fate or their mother's, depending on the circumstances. In view of all this, it is easy to see why only female slaves are to be found in the Achaean camp set up on the Trojan shores. Most came from one or other of the twenty-three Aegean towns sacked by Achilles during the long, empty hours of the siege of Troy. Their principal task was to help ensure the material comfort of the heroes during their stay on Trojan shores and, later, in their palaces. Hector wonders what Andromache's fate will be when she is "dragged off in tears by some Achaean man-at-arms to slavery. I see you there in Argos, toiling for another at the loom, or carrying water from an alien well, a helpless drudge with no will of your own" (6.454–458). For prisoners of high rank who were young and beautiful (and the poet picks them out by name from the anonymous mass of slaves: Chryseis, Iphis, Diomedes, Hecamedes, Briseis), a different fate would of course be reserved. They would be required to enter the bed of their master, either as his concubine or as his legitimate wife.

Passing on from *The Iliad* to *The Odyssey,* we notice that here too most of the slave population appears to be of the female sex. In the households of both Alcinoos and Odysseus, the staff of servants is fifty strong, a number that can no doubt be regarded as conventional although in the second case at least it would seem on the whole justifiable, given the need to provide hospitality for one hundred and eight suitors. *The Odyssey* gives us a clearer picture of the tasks of slaves than *The Iliad* does. It was their duty to take care of the guest who, exhausted and covered in dust, crossed the threshold of the master's house, to bathe him, rub him with oil, and clothe him in a fine mantle and robe. They had to make ready for the banquet, under the orders of the housekeeper; prepare the beds, "put piles of bread in baskets" (1.147); "make up the fire which never quite died down in the hearth" (20.123); light and carry the torches, serve the food and drink and, later, clean the banqueting hall all over again. And the rest of the time they had to spin wool and make beautiful objects from it under the supervision of the mistress of the house. Meanwhile the humblest of all—twelve of them in Odysseus' palace—toiled in the mills "grinding the barley and the wheat into meal for the household bread which gives men strength" (20.108–9). This is not to mention the dozen who, ignoring the housekeeper Eurycleia's orders to abstain from lechery (23.423), found their way each night to the beds of the suitors.

Nonetheless, the greater number of woman than men among the slaves in *The Odyssey* is largely an optical illusion, which it is easy to correct if one remembers that most of the action takes place inside the royal houses, a domain reserved as the domestic female sphere. Out in the fields we catch glimpses of many male slaves, not so much in agriculture, where the poorest of the free men, who are called "thetes" are also employed, but herding the flocks. On Odysseus' estate, for example, the herds were guarded by about thirty men, most of them slaves, all placed under three more slaves: the master swineherd, Eumaeus, who had at least four swineherds under his orders; the master goatherd, Melanthius, with at least two assistants; and the master cowherd, Philoetius. If we add to these the slaves responsible for certain domestic tasks (such as the assembling and maintenance of carts) we are bound to conclude that there must have been almost as many males as females among the slave staff of the kings of *The Odyssey*.

This difference between *The Iliad* and *The Odyssey* in the composition of the servile group is in line with a certain change in the sources of slavery. In the later work, no more than a vague memory linked with the Trojan War remains of the capture of entire towns where men and goods alike fell as loot to the victor. The only way left for the exhausted and decimated race of heroes to increase their fortune and their glory too was to mount fruitful plundering operations in neighboring territories or on distant shores. So common were such activities at the time that Odysseus imparts a ring of truth to the fantastical stories he tells of his past when he declares that he himself has frequently indulged in them. Thus, he claims (17.42) that he at one time came to possess "thousands of slaves and plenty of all that one needs." In this domain, furthermore, the Achaeans had a number of redoubtable rivals (or valued collaborators) in the shape of the Phoenicians and the Taphians, who enjoy an equally high reputation as sea rovers in Homer (although in the former case that is a historical fact, in the latter simply a mythological fiction). We are afforded a glimpse of the Phoenicians at work on the island of Syros, where they capture and carry off the king's young son (who becomes Eumaeus, the swineherd), with the complicity of a slave-girl who had herself been carried off by Taphians as she was "coming in from the country, far from Sidon where they deal in bronze" (15.42).

Once captured, however, prisoners might pass from hand to hand in a peaceful fashion: either as gifts, as in the case of Odysseus himself who, having been overcome on Egyptian territory, was (if we are to believe one of his tall stories) "given to a man called Dmetor, son of Iasus, the undisputed king of Cyprus" (17.43); or as merchandise, like the Phoenician servant whom Eumaeus' father had bought from the Taphians, Eumaeus himself who was sold by the Phoenicians to Odysseus' father, Laertes, or the slave Mesaulius whom Eumaeus in his turn acquired from the Taphians. By the latter method it was easy to get rid of undesirable property: it could be sold "far from Ithaca," in Sicily to be precise, or even in Libya. In the formulaic style of the Homeric poems, it is taken for granted that a slave is sold for "a good price," although that price is seldom stated. The nurse Eurycleia, however, had been bought by Laertes "when she was still a girl, for the price of twenty oxen" (*Od.*, 1.431); Priam's son Lycaon was sold for the price of "one hundred oxen" by Achilles and was later "ransomed for three times as much" (*Il.* 21.78–80); the woman who was "skilled in fine crafts," offered as a prize in the games held to honor Patroclus' funeral, was valued at four oxen (*Il.* 23.705). The last of these three prices was probably the most usual. It corresponded to a third of that of "a great tripod for the fire" (*Il.* 23.703). However, it is also apparent that, depending upon a slave's skills and "rank," which are frequently taken into account, the prices might vary considerably (particularly in a world with no understanding of a market economy), sometimes increasing to three times as much as is mentioned above, to judge by Agamemnon's promise to allow Teucer "a tripod, a pair of horses with their chariot, or a woman to share your bed" as his share of the booty after the sacking of Troy (*Il.* 8.290–291). In any event, it seems clear from Homeric vocabulary that, at this period, slaves were regarded as objects of transaction of the first importance. Emile Benveniste writes: "The right which the captor has over the captive, the transfer of prisoners, the sale of men by auction: such are the conditions in which the notions of 'purchase,' 'sale' and 'value' emerge."[13]

One manifest reason why it is impossible to assimilate the Homeric slaves to the Athenian slaves of the classical period, despite the similarities in their recruitment, is the "patriarchal" nature of the relationships binding the former to their master within the *oikos*. As is well known, a strong sense of solidarity existed here: the slaves shared in the family joys and tribulations; slaves and family often worked side by side; the label *dmos* was, in itself, in no way derogatory and in some instances slaves are entitled to descriptions usually reserved for free individuals or for deities ("resembling the gods," "white-armed," "of the beautiful locks"). Equally, their living conditions were often similar to their masters'. For example, Laertes, on the estate to which he retires, "eats and drinks with his slaves on the farm" (*Od.* 16.140–141) and "he lies down in the winter time with the slaves at the farm, in the dust by the fire, and goes about in rags" (*Od.* 11.188–191). Then, conversely, there is the case of Eumaeus, the "divine" swineherd who, apart from the contingents of animals he was expected to deliver to the master's house, was apparently free to dispose of the produce from his herd as he wished and, indeed, had managed his affairs so well that he had saved enough to secure himself the services of a personal slave.

We should, however, beware of painting, as many authors have, an idyllic picture that would make us forget that "all-seeing Zeus takes half the good out of a man on the day when he becomes a slave" (*Od.* 17.323). The condition of a thete, which the dead Achilles declares he would prefer to that of a king in the Underworld, is no doubt simply the worst of the conditions reserved by the gods *for a free man.* (It is interesting to note, in this respect, that in Homer, although we find gods working as thetes in the service of others, there are no slave gods). We should therefore pay the greatest attention to the circumstances which gave rise to such situations: for example, to the fact that, in the case of Laertes, the poet's intention is to underline the decline of the former king of Ithaca (not the good fortune of his slaves); and above all to the fact that the majority of such marks of esteem and indications of easy living relate only to a privileged category of slaves: the favorites who enjoy the rank of concubines or wives and also the housekeepers and chambermaids, or the chief herdsmen responsible for the welfare of the flocks (such as Eumaeus and Philoetius, but not Melanthius, who betrays Odys-

13. *Indo-European Language and Society* (1973), 131.

seus). Those placed in such positions of responsibility had, for the most part, won the friendship of their masters early on, either through having brought them up, as in the case of Eurycleia, who had been Odysseus' nurse, or through growing up alongside them, as in the case of Eumaeus who "up to the age when love will have its way" had been the companion of the lady Ctimene, Laertes' eldest daughter (*Od.* 15.363–365). It is hardly surprising if the mass of slaves could not expect particular favors from such of their number who had "made it": Eurycleia tells Odysseus that she is ready to denounce some of them, while Eumaeus is more inclined to advocate submissiveness, for "servants do miss it mightily when they cannot talk face to face with their mistress, and find out all the news, and have a bite and a sup, and carry off a tidbit to the farm as well. That is the sort of thing that always warms a slave's heart" (*Od.* 15.376–379). Reading between the lines of such moralizing comments, which in their own way testify to the existence of a kind of slave "ideology," we can see that if their masters seemed "stupid" or incapable of imposing their authority, slaves might well either live in fear or sabotage their work. *The Odyssey* contains many episodes that testify to the disastrous consequences of Odysseus' absence in this respect. Among his slaves there are some who resent the cantankerous, arrogant, and demanding behavior of the suitors, one example being the frail woman whose "heart and knees were broken as she milled the flour" *Od.* 15.118–119), whereas others, "faithless girls" such as the Dark Melantho, daughter of the Cunning Dolios, milked the situation for all it was worth up until the day of reckoning, when "they held their heads out in a row and a noose was cast around each one's neck" and none were left alive "to remember their loves and the hours they stole in those young gallants' arms" (*Od.* 22.446–473).

Were the Homeric slaves treated kindly or harshly? That is not really where the problem lies, for their integration is simply the reverse side of the coin to their dependency. Rather, the problem stems from the uncertainty of the status granted them. In particular, in contrast to the thetes, the fact is that the individual position which the slaves acquired within such or such an *oikos* in varying degrees counterbalanced their low statutory state to the extent that they participated in the networks of aristocratic solidarity which provided the framework for Homeric society. Meanwhile the thetes, lacking all means of production, tended to link themselves to the nobles by entering into obligations through contracts of total prestation to such a point that Telemachus considers them to belong to him on virtually the same grounds as his slaves! The status of slaves was also ambiguous in relation to the free servants (*therapontes*) serving in the palaces, since the two groups found themselves relegated to the same side of the barrier that separated the nobility from the non-nobility, the aristocracy from the confused mass of people who existed simply to serve it. Thus Homeric slaves cannot—any more than Mycenaean slaves—be regarded as the direct ancestors of the chattel slaves of the classical period, although at the same time, that is no reason for disregarding their truly servile characteristics, as has sometimes been proposed, or for dramatically minimizing their numbers.

The Development of Chattel Slavery in the Archaic Period

Even in the Homeric poems, slavery is never quite presented as a royal monopoly. Out of one hundred forty-one mentions of slaves, ten are not linked with the royal milieus either directly or indirectly, and this ratio confirms what Hesiod's *Works and Days,* in the late eighth or early seventh century, tells us about the development of slavery in a little village in Boeotia. Hesiod's peasant starts out possessing no more than "a house, a woman and an ox for the plough" (l. 405), to which he soon adds "a brisk fellow of forty years" (l. 443), but it is not made clear whether the latter is a free man receiving a wage or a slave. Later, we find Hesiod's peasant with several slaves at his disposal, as well as a couple, of free status, who may be responsible for supervising them. But the juridical status of the *dmoes* is never specified.

Slaves also appear in the little that survives of the lyric poetry of the seventh and sixth centuries, from such writers as Archilocus, Hipponax, and Theognis. Now, however, they are referred to as *douloi* and in all likelihood should be identified with the chattel slaves of the classical type, to judge not only by the nomenclature applied to them but also from such glimpses as are afforded of their characteristics.

In Athens, one of Draco's laws on homicide dating from about 620 may already have mentioned slaves;[14] and, according to tradition, more certain evidence existed of legislation concerning them passed during the special magistracy assumed by Solon, probably in 594–593.[15] It was Solon, for example, who "wrote a law forbidding a slave

14. R. S. Stroud, *Drakon's Law on Homicide* (1968); E. Grace, "Status Distinction in the Draconian Law," *Eirene* 11 (1973): 5–30.
15. J. A. Lencman, "The slaves in Solon's laws" (in Russian), *Vestnik Drevnei Istorii* (1958), no. 4: 51–69; E. Ruschenbuch, SOLONOS NOMOI. *Die Fragmente des solonischen Gesetzeswerkes, Historia-Einz.* 9 (1966).

to practise gymnastics or have a boy-lover" (Plutarch, *Life of Solon*, 1.6), who "knew that sales of slaves are constantly taking place in the city," and decided that "any offenses or crimes committed by a slave shall be the responsibility of the master who owns him at the time" (Hyperides, *Against Athenogenes*, 22). He also legalized expeditions organized by individuals "for booty" (*leia*),—slaves, among other things. The first reports, by more or less late writers, of the presence of slaves of the Athenian type in certain archaic cities also refer to this period. Thus Herodotus (2.134–135) tells us that the Thracian courtesan Rhodopis, who "flourished in the reign of Amasis" (between 569 and 526) having been (along with Aesop) the slave of a Samian, "was brought to Egypt by Xanthes of Samos and, on her coming, was for a great sum of money freed for the practice of her calling by Charaxus of Mytilene, son of Scamandronymus and brother of Sappho the poetess." According to Nicholas of Damascus (FGH 90, fr. 58), Periander, the tyrant of Corinth said to have reigned from 627 to 587, "prevented the citizens from acquiring slaves and living in idleness and was always finding them work to do. If any was found resting in the public square, he had him arrested for fear lest he might be plotting against him." Finally, at Cyzicus we know of a decree of the seventh century which granted "Medikes, the children of Aisepos and their descendants exemption from taxes," except for a few such as the *andrapodonie*, which was probably a levy on the sale of slaves (Syll.³34).

It thus seems likely that in the city about which we know the most, namely Athens, slavery made, if not its appearance, at least considerable progress, during the time of Solon. This was exactly the time when the legislator was ensuring the liberty of the people as a whole (many of whom had until then lived in some kind of servitude, for reasons we shall be discussing later) and granting it a greater role in the government of the city. Moses Finley has compared the example of Athens to that of the town of Chios, about which a number of facts are known: (1) According to a passage in Book XVII of the *Philippica* of the historian Theopompus (probably written around 330) this was the first town in Greece to make use of chattel slaves ("barbarians purchased for money") at a date not determined but certainly not later than the Dorian invasions of the end of the second millennium. (2) According to a passage in Thucydides (8.40.2), at the end of the fifth century "the slaves of the Chians were numerous—and indeed the most numerous in any single city except that of the Lacedaemonians."[16] (We can believe the first of those statements without sub-

16. "Was Greek Civilization Based on Slave Labour?" *Slavery*, 71–72.

scribing to the second.[17]) (3) To judge from an inscription of the first half of the sixth century, the city of Chios had embarked very early upon a road leading toward a certain measure of democracy, which presupposes greater participation in government on the part of the citizens.[18] In the case of Chios as in that of Athens, it thus seems that as the concept of (political) liberty spread and became more firmly established, it had a twofold effect. It reduced the potential of exploitation within the civic community and thus increased both the number and the demands of the privileged. Meanwhile, this process was accompanied by an increase in chattel slavery, that is, by massive recourse to a foreign labor force entirely subject to the will of its masters and hence, from a statutory point of view, reduced to the polar opposite of liberty. It would seem that, to borrow Finley's felicitous expression, "one aspect of Greek history, in short, is the advance, hand in hand, of liberty *and* slavery."[19]

That the two ideas go together, that the affirmation of the freedom of some was connected with the definition of the slavery of others, is not in doubt. A more delicate question is that of identifying what sparked off this evolution. Two causal processes, resting on noticeably different bases, are conceivable. (1) Economic progress leads to the development of slavery, which leads to the progress of democracy; (2) the progress of democracy leads to the development of slavery, which leads to economic progress. In support of the first hypothesis as to the starting point, it is easy to refer to an extension of commercial and artisan activities accompanied by a reduction in the available labor force in Greece, following the surge of colonization from the eighth to the sixth centuries; there are also a number of indications of technological progress (in architecture, ceramics, and naval construction). For the second hypothesis, we may point to a reinforcement of the demos to the detriment of the aristocracy, in the course of a series of episodes of a tyrannical nature. There are

17. I. A. Sisova, "Slavery in Chios" (in Russian), *Escl. périph.*, 149–92.

18. Finley's conclusions here need qualification: the *Boule demosie* attested to in this inscription is not a "democratic council" but a "public council" representing the community as a whole. See C. Ampolo, "La *Boule demosie* di Chio: Un consiglio populare?" *PP* 213 (1983): 401–16.

19. *Slavery*, p. 72. A similar process eventually led to a clear distinction between metics and both slaves and citizens. But at the end of the sixth century in Athens, that process appears still to have been in progress, which may be why Aristotle (*Politics*, 1275b) can speak of "metic slaves," included by Cleisthenes in the list of tribes (cf. E. Grace, "Aristotle on the Enfranchisement of Aliens by Cleisthenes," *Klio* 56 [1974]: 353–68; G. Luzi, "Nuovi cittadini di Clistene [Aristot., *Pol.*, III. 1275 b]," *ASNP*, 3d ser., 10 [1980]: 71–78). However, Heraclitus' famous statement that "war . . . has made slaves of some and free men of others" (H. Diels and W. Kranz, *Die Fragmente der Vorsokratiker I*, 6th ed. [1951], 162, n.53) dates from the late sixth–early fifth century.

several possible reasons for this, some directly economic (the increasing importance of artisans and commerce). Another is the
growing demand for soldiers imposed by the adoption of hoplite
tactics from the early seventh century onward. Yet another is simply
a renewal of community vitality and a taste for political liberty,
accompanied by all the material advantages that went with the status
of a citizen. The fact is that we should probably take into account a
whole complex of possibilities (opened up by an increase in "productivity" and hence also in the surplus demanded) and necessities
(stemming from the numbers of members of the community strug-
gling to emancipate themselves); and we should bear in mind that it
all took place in a context in which private property had predominated since a very early date. There is also one other essential factor:
these developments were favored by a powerful surge in both the
military and the commercial sectors, a development that made it
possible for the Greeks gradually to acquire a position of hegemony
vis-à-vis a "barbarian" world overflowing with human livestock.[20]

The Juridical Status of Athenian Slavery

Although it was universally agreed that a slave was a human being
(*anthropos*), not an animal, the Athenian slave constituted first and
foremost a possession[21] and, as such, was transferable in the same
way as any other movable chattel, regardless of his own wishes.
Sometimes the transfer would be to the detriment of his owner (as a
result of some legal ruling), but more often it would be in accordance
with the owner's interests and desires (a gift given by one living party
to another, a bequest, or some kind of commercial transaction,
usually a simple sale). No particular restrictions affected such trans-
fers between the inhabitants of the same or of different cities.

In the vast majority of cases, a slave depended on a private owner
who was specifically known as a master (*despotes*) and who might be

20. I. Hahn, "Die Anfänge der antiken Gesellschaftsformation in Griechenland
und das Problem des sogennanten asiatischen Produktionweise," *Jahrbuch für Wirtschaftsgeschichte* 2 (1971), 29–47, in particular 31–36 (an article reprinted by H. G.
Kippenberg in his collection *Die Entstehung der antiken Klassengesellschaft* [1971], 68–
99).

21. On the various aspects of Athenian legislation relating to slaves, see L. Beau-
chet, *Histoire du droit privé de la république athénienne*, 2 (1897), 393ff.; more recently, A.
R. W. Harrison, *The Law of Athens* (1968), 163–80. On particular points see L. Gernet,
"Aspects du droit athénien de l'esclavage," *Archives d'Histoire du Droit Oriental*, 1950,
159ff. (=*Droit et société dans la Grèce ancienne* [1964], 151–72).

any free person—either a citizen or a foreigner more or less temporarily resident in the city—that is, who might or might not be included in the official list of metics. A relatively small number of public slaves, often known as *demosioi*, belonged, as might any other movable chattels or real estate, to the people, which collectively exercised over them the same rights as a private owner.

Being himself a possession, the Athenian slave enjoyed no rights to property of his own, not even to the savings he was often allowed to amass but could not use without the permission of his master.

In many other respects too, he was deprived of all juridical identity: thus, his family, whose existence was often tolerated,[22] had no legal standing and could at any moment be dispersed by his master. His name appeared on no official register except for inventories of possessions. In that sense, he was "an absolute foreigner" within the city, uprooted from his own native community and subjected to a concerted process of veritable deculturization (in particular, through the loss of his name and, in many cases, the replacement of his mother tongue by Greek). All of this plunged him into a kind of void and reduced him to the status of nonperson.

This situation was, however, subject to certain limits. Some stemmed from ancient family law which accorded to the slave, in his capacity as a servant, an embryonic personality as a human being ritually associated with his master's house. Here he received a new name, was welcomed, like a bride, with a showering of nuts and fruits, symbols of prosperity, and took part in the cult of the household gods. Other limits derived from the community's interest in not attracting the wrath of the gods through acts of immoderation (*hubris*) such as castration[23] or unjustified blows and injuries, as the orator Aeschines explains to his fellow-citizens: "It was not for the slaves that the lawgiver was concerned, but he wished to accustom you to keep a long distance away from the crime of outraging free men, and so he added the prohibition against the outraging even of slaves" (1.17). It was only thus that the slave could hope to enjoy a few guarantees as a person, meanwhile finding himself obliged in return to protect the group to which he belonged. If he was Greek by birth, he also retained a few religious rights, such as that of becoming an initiate of the Eleusinian Mysteries. Finally, especially from the fourth century on, it became necessary for practical reasons to adapt

22. I. Biezunska-Malowist, "La vie familiale des esclaves," *Colloque Camerino 1978*, 140–43.
23. See P. Guyot, *Eunuchen als Sklaven und Freigelassene in der griechisch-römischen Antike* (1980).

his juridical position to the economic functions entrusted to him, by granting him a measure of responsibility in commercial matters.[24]

These various factors give us some idea of the place of slaves in the legal context, which for its part is fairly well known not only through the Attic orators but also because of the legislation of Plato's *Laws*, a work largely inspired by the factual situation in Athens.

In the normal way of things, slaves could not enter into litigation, certainly not to claim their own liberty when they considered themselves unjustly deprived of it; in order to do so, they needed the intervention of a citizen who thereby exposed himself, in the event of losing the case, to having to pay an indemnity to the slave's owner and a fine of equal amount to the State. In a court of law, they were represented by their master, except in a few exceptional circumstances: (1) if they denounced a traitor to the city, or anyone guilty of sacrilege or corruption (as a result of which they would either be affranchised or put to death, depending on whether their denunciation was upheld); (2) if, as a result of their professional activities, they became involved in "commercial lawsuits" (*dikai emporikai*)—a type of lawsuit which, from the mid-fourth century onward, made it possible to settle within one month obligations concluded in or on behalf of the Athens marketplace; and (3) possibly also in the case of public slaves with a citizen guarantor (*prostates*) who would represent them.

In such cases as these, their evidence was as acceptable as that of a free man, just as when they were called, together with other members of the household, to testify against the murderer of their master. Otherwise, it was valid only if obtained under torture; and here the violence that constituted the basis of the relationship between slaves and free men is reaffirmed.[25] The torture (*basanos*) was administered either by the master, in private, to his own slave, or else at the request of the plaintiff, in which case the defendant had no means (no legal means at any rate) of opposing the request. The methods of torture employed were laid down in a kind of contract drawn up between the parties involved, which made provision for compensation to be paid to the slave's master if lasting disability resulted from the torture. The contents of such a contract are parodied by a character in Aristophanes' *Frogs:* "Pile bricks upon him; stuff his nose with acid; Flay, rack him, hoist him; flog him with a scourge of

---

24. E. Cohen, *Ancient Maritime Courts* (1973), 116–21.

25. See the recent summary by G. Thür, *Beweisführung von den Schwurgerichtshöfen: Die Proklesis zur Basanos* (1977), and also the stimulating article by E. Grace (Kazakevich), "'Word' and 'Deed' in the Athenian *Dikasterion*," *Monde antique*, 96–104.

prickly bristles . . . Torture him in any mode you please" (ll. 618–625). The plaintiff might himself undertake the operation in the presence of the defendant, or alternatively he might entrust it to specialists (*basanistai*).

It is hard to say how much credibility such "testimony" had. No doubt plenty in the eyes of those to whom it spelt advantage, as is explained by the Pseudo-Aristotle of the *Rhetorica ad Alexandrum:*

> When it is to our interest to strengthen such evidence, we must say that individuals take their proofs from evidence under torture in their most serious affairs, and cities in their most important business and that evidence under torture is more trustworthy than ordinary testimony. For it is often to the interest of witnesses to lie; but those who are under torture gain by telling the truth, for doing so will bring them the speediest relief from their sufferings.
>
> When you wish to discredit evidence given under torture, you must say in the first place that slaves who are being tortured become hostile to those who have delivered them up to be tortured and for this reason tell many lies against their masters. Secondly, you must say that they often make confessions to their torturers which are not the truth, in order to end their torments as quickly as possible. You must also point out that even free men have often before now lied against themselves under torture, to escape from the suffering of the moment. It is therefore much more likely that slaves should wish to avoid punishment by lying against their masters, rather than, when they are enduring great bodily and mental pain, deliberately refuse to utter a falsehood in order to save other people from suffering.

On the whole, however, it seems that confessions extracted from slaves under torture appeared eminently credible to the mass of the people: partly because they believed that an action exerted upon the *body* of the slave made it possible to reconstitute in its pure state *the fact* to which he had been a witness, and also because of the flimsiness of other proofs (since written evidence was on the whole very rare and almost invariably needed to be authenticated by witnesses who were known to be easy prey to corruption).

A master was held responsible for any damages committed by a slave belonging to him, whether directly or indirectly, that is, whether or not he had acted on the master's orders. Even in the latter case, an old law of Solon's was supposed to have stipulated that the master should pay compensation to the damaged party unless he preferred simply to abandon the guilty slave temporarily or definitively to him. (This is known as "noxal abandonment" in

Roman law.[26] Where physical damage had been done to free men, the master of the slave had to allow the injured party to exercise his right of punishment in person. If a murder had been committed, he was obliged to hand over the guilty slave to justice, which would make an example of him. Plato's *Laws* (9.872b) laid down that: "The public executioner of the State shall drag him in the direction of the tomb of the dead man, to a spot from which he can see the tomb and there scourge him with as many stripes as the prosecutor shall prescribe; and if the murderer be still alive after the beating, he shall put him to death." If it was the slave's own master who had been injured, corporal punishment was even more inevitable. It would take the form of flogging (the number of lashes being generally limited to fifty by the court), a prospect by which the slaves of comedy are haunted,[27] incarceration, confinement to the iron collar, or chains. However, neither the master of a slave nor, a fortiori, any third party had the right, for the reasons mentioned above, to strike or kill a slave without valid reason or without being accountable to the law.

Because there was in Greece no public authority responsible for automatically activating court proceedings, it was obviously up to the slave's master to intervene to seek reparation for bodily harm illegally inflicted upon a slave by a third party. If the slave had been wounded, it was his master's responsibility to bring a private action to obtain damages; if the slave died of his wounds,[28] a private action for murder could also be brought (not possible where only animals were concerned). In that case, the guilty party was brought before the Palladion court (as would be anyone who killed a citizen or a foreigner without premeditation). If the culprit was himself a slave, he risked the death penalty; if not, he got off with no more than a fine and the obligation to purify himself. Furthermore, in such cases anybody could bring a public action for outrageous behavior (which, according to Demosthenes, might lead to a death sentence) or for impiety against a murderer who neglected to purify himself; but the accuser risked a heavy fine if he did not win one fifth of the jury's votes. In circumstances such as these, it is not hard to understand why, if the guilty party was the slave's own master, the matter seldom

26. H. Meyer-Laurin, "Die Haftung für den *Noxa Non Solutus* beim Sklavenkauf nach griechischen Recht," *Symposion 1974* (1979), 263–82.

27. G. Glotz, "Les esclaves et la peine du fouet en droit grec," *Comptes Rendus de l'Académie des Inscriptions* (1908), 571–87.

28. G. R. Morrow, "The Murder of Slaves in Attic Law," *Classical Philology* 32 (1937): 210–27.

came before the courts; it would do so only if a third party took the risk of bringing a public action or if another member of the family assumed responsibility for a private action. A slave could not even plead legitimate self-defense to avoid a harsh sentence. According to Plato, that would not prevent him from being condemned to death if he had murdered a free man. If he was a victim of persecution, the only course open to him was to seek temporary asylum in the sanctuary of the Theseion close to the agora or at the foot of the altar to the Eumenides on the Areopagus, in the hope that the priests would recognize him to be in the right and accept his request to be sold to another master.

The Sources of Chattel Slaves

In classical Athens, very few exceptions were allowed to the principle that a slave could not be a former member of the civic body.[29] Two are known, both probably survivals from ancient family law; but such instances must have been so rare as to be negligible.[30] The exceptions were daughters who had committed adultery, who could be put up for sale by their fathers; and newborn infants "abandoned on the rubbish heap," who provided New Comedy with so many plots involving touching scenes of long-lost foundlings rediscovered. (Elsewhere, however, the exposure of infants was forbidden—in Thebes, for instance, where, on the other hand, poor citizens were allowed to hand their children over to the magistrates, who then sold them as slaves.) In the domain of debts, Solon's legislation, which forbade the acceptance of security in the form of a citizen-debtor's person, remained in force. Occasionally, however, there were exceptions to this rule: one was apparently a former prisoner of war. Demosthenes (*Against Nicostratos,* 11) tells us that "the laws enact that a person ransomed from the enemy shall be the property of the ransomer if he fail to pay the redemption money" (although we should note that the initial enslavement here was perpetrated by a foreigner). The rule did not always apply if the debt was owed to the State or to the gods.[31] Finally, an exile who reentered the country illegally could also be reduced to slavery.

In all these cases, either the figure concerned is marginal to the

29. E. Lévy-Bruhl, "Théorie de l'esclavage," *Slavery,* 151–69.
30. L. Germain, "L'exposition des enfants nouveaux-nés dans la Grèce ancienne," *Recueils de la Société Jean Bodin* 35, 1: *L'enfant* (1975), 211–46.
31. See below, pp. 88–93.

civic body, or else the delinquent is eventually sold outside the State; so it is indeed fair to say that enslavement on the spot for full citizens was excluded. The only penalties applicable to them were fines, political disqualifications (*atimia*), imprisonment, exile, or death. Obviously bastards (*nothoi*) with one non-Athenian parent, and free foreigners, whether visiting or resident (metics), did not enjoy the same guarantees.[32] In Athens, such people could be reduced to servitude on the spot for reasons of external politics or for contravention of the particular laws to which they were subject (usurping citizens' rights, marrying a member of the civic body, refusing to pay the *metoikion* tax or to choose themselves a guarantor from among the citizens or, in the case of freedmen, manifesting ingratitude toward a former master).

Almost without exception, slaves were imported from outside the State. Indeed, on principle, they were supposed to be barbarians, that is to say non-Greek speakers, ignorant of the political institutions and cultural characteristics of life in the city. This equivalence, firmly established at a theoretical level (as we shall see), does appear to have corresponded to reality, even if there is no way of proving that statistically.

Slaves were drawn from all the peoples who bordered on the Greek world, in proportions that varied from city to city and from one period to another. At first, most probably came from Scythia, especially Thrace,[33] brought by way of the Greek towns of the Black Sea and the northern Aegean. According to some authors, the mother of Archilochus (the Parian poet of the second half of the seventh century) was a Thracian slave—as was the courtesan Rhodopis and also, it was said, the mother of Themistocles. Following the Persian Wars, increasing numbers came from outlying areas around the Greek cities of Asia Minor, now liberated from Persian domination; of these most were Carians. In the last third of the fifth century, at the time of the Peloponnesian War, these two ethnic groups probably accounted for the greater part of the slave population of Athens, to judge by Aristophanes' comedies and by the stelae which carry lists of goods confiscated from the "*Hermocopidai*" found guilty

32. G. D. Rocchi, "Considerazioni a proposito della schiavitù come pena nell'Atene del v–iv secolo," *Acme* 28 (1975): 257–79.
33. M. I. Finley, "The Black Sea and Danubian Regions and the Slave Trade in Antiquity," *Klio* 40 (1962): 51–59; M. F. Vos, *Scythian Archers in Archaic Attic Vase-Painting* (1963); V. Velkov, "Zur Frage der Sklaverei auf der Balkanhalbinsel während der Antike," *Etudes Balkaniques* 1 (1964): 125–38; Velkov, "Thracian slaves in the ancient Greek cities from the sixth to the second centuries B.C." (in Russian), *Vestnik Drevnei Istorii* (1967), no. 4:70–79.

of having mutilated the *hermes* in the agora in 415:[34] of the thirty-three slaves whose origins are mentioned here, twelve are Thracians and seven Carians, i.e. 60 percent overall. Later the proportion of slaves from all over Asia Minor (Lydians, Cappadocians, Mysians, etc.) further increased while the number of northerners diminished. On the funerary stelae of the Hellenistic period in Rhodes, only one third of the slaves mentioned are natives of countries in the Black Sea area, in Delphi no more than one fifth of the freedmen whose origin is recorded. Also characteristic of the Hellenistic period is the increasing, although always limited, number of Blacks imported, along with monkeys and ostrich feathers, from deepest Africa. But, as goes without saying, at every period slaves from all barbarian regions in the neighborhood of the Greek world are to be found everywhere, in varying proportions.

Some of these barbarian slaves were delivered over to the Greek merchants by their own fellow-countrymen: it was a way for the latter to remedy demographic surpluses, as the Thracians did, according to Herodotus, no doubt also to settle a number of internal old scores, whether social or political (to the advantage of the local aristocracy, usually), and, above all, to make a profit on the prisoners captured from some neighboring community. Others the Greeks procured directly by force of arms, but their numbers were probably smaller than the historians would have us believe, for this could not explain how it was that the Greek cities received such regular supplies of barbarian slaves from regions unaffected by warfare.

However, among the slaves were also some who were of Greek origin. This was not so much for the reasons mentioned above as a result of the "rules" of warfare, which were theoretically the same whoever the adversary was.[35] Whether or not they had participated in the fighting and regardless of sex, age, and juridical status, prisoners, like any other moveable chattels or real estate, were considered the victor's property, unless, that is, other stipulations were made in the agreement governing the cessation of hostilities. The victor could consequently dispose of them howsoever he wished, in the furtherance of his own interests: either release them, thereby

34. R. Meiggs and D. M. Lewis, *Greek Historical Inscriptions* (1969), no. 79.
35. See H. Volkmann, *Die Massenversklavungen der Einwohner eroberter Städte in der hellenistisch-römischen Zeit, Abh. Ak. Wiss. Mainz*, 1961, no. 3; P. Ducrey, *Le traitement des prisonniers de guerre dans la Grèce ancienne* (1968); I. A. Sisova, "The enslavement of prisoners of war in Greece in the fifth–fourth centuries B.C." (in Russian), *Escl. périph.*, 42–92; A. H. Jackson, "Some Recent Works on the Treatment of Prisoners of War in Ancient Greece," *Talanta* 2 (1970): 37–53; Y. Garlan, "War, Piracy and Slavery in the Greek World," in *Slavery and Abolition* (special issue).

turning them into allies or tributaries; keep them in captivity, later to grant them a merciful release by exchanging or ransoming them; reduce them to slavery; or put them to death. The decision would depend on a large number of factors: the circumstances of the victory, the grievances and intentions of the victor, the composition of the armies, and the status of the vanquished—far more than on the development of abstract notions of humanity in philosophical thought.[36] It has been possible to establish statistically that enslavement took place in about one quarter of the cases mentioned by the historians. That does not enable us, however, to estimate the number of individuals concerned. The total varies considerably in each instance—from a few dozen to several or even tens of thousands—depending on whether a pitched battle or the capture of a city is involved and on whether or not particular treatment is meted out to different categories of prisoners (for example, the fate of adult citizens might be better or worse than or just the same as that of their slaves, their families, and the foreigners in the city).

Sources of slaves, in addition to conventional warfare, were brigandage on land and piracy at sea, the effects of which are hard to gauge but must have been serious in some regions and at certain periods at least.[37] Although all Greeks were perfectly capable of resorting to such behavior in times of war or under cover of the paralegal exercise of the right of reprisal, some peoples, as it were, specialized in such practices: first and foremost the Phoenicians and Tyrrhenians (Etruscans), but also the Cretans, the Aetolians, the Illyrians, and other marginal peoples whose range of operations depended on the degree of sophistication of their military techniques and their sociopolitical structures. In the mid-Hellenistic period, these groups were joined by the Cilicians and other mountain peoples of the southern coast of Asia Minor. The great powers of the day regarded them either as out-and-out enemies or as more or less declared accomplices, depending upon whether they were suffering or profiting from the predatory operations. That explains, in particular, the prosperity enjoyed by the Cilician pirates in the second half of the second century. Strabo reports as follows (14.5.2):

> The exportation of slaves induced them most of all to engage in their evil business, since it proved most profitable, for not only were they

36. As is mistakenly believed by F. Kiechle, "Zur Humanität in der Kriegführung der griechischen Staaten," *Historia* 7 (1958): 129–56.
37. See H. A. Ormerod, *Piracy in the Ancient World* (1924); A. H. Jackson, "Privateers in the Ancient Greek World," in *War and Society*, ed. M. R. D. Foot (1973), 241–53; Y. Garlan, "Signification historique de la piraterie grecque," *DHA* 4 (1978): 1–16; P. Brulé, *La piraterie crétoise hellénistique* (1978).

easily captured but the market, which was large and rich in property, was not extremely far away, I mean Delos, which could both admit and send away myriads of slaves on the same day; whence arose the proverb, "Merchant, sail in, unload your ship, everything is for sale." The cause of this was the fact that the Romans, having become rich after the destruction of Carthage and Corinth, used many slaves and the pirates, seeing the easy profit therein, bloomed forth in great numbers, themselves not only going in quest of booty but also trafficking in slaves.

Although the figures mentioned by Strabo are clearly exaggerated (even if the recent identification of the "Agora of the Italians" in Delos as a slave market does tend to support his text),[38] it would thus appear that at this period the Cilician (and Cretan) pirates were making up for the relative inactivity of the Roman armies in this part of the Mediterranean, which had been supplying the Italians with not only many of their slaves but those most highly prized since the early second century. If, from around 100 B.C., the Romans took to opposing these Eastern pirates with increasing vigor, it was probably less on humanitarian grounds than because they now judged it possible and necessary to do without this source of supply in slaves. For the persistence of the pirates was undermining the more "rational" forms of exploitation the Romans were adopting in the new "provinces" and, at the time of their wars against Mithridates at the beginning of the first century, was even compromising Roman domination in the East. Simultaneously, moreover, there are signs that the pirates' objectives may have been changing. They appear to have become less concerned with capturing all and sundry who could be turned into slaves and more interested in individuals of rank, such as the youthful Caesar, who could fetch them a fine ransom. It was at this point, when it was seen as no longer contributing to the slave economy but instead reduced to a simple phenomenon of parasitism, that piracy became the target of a "common war" and for a time disappeared. These changing fortunes of piracy during the late Hellenistic period afford us a glimpse of its structural links with the practice of slavery.[39]

Given the frequency of the conflicts that opposed one Greek city to another and the numbers of their inhabitants who fell victim to the pirates, one would expect them to have supplied a large proportion of slaves. But, as we have seen, that is far from corresponding to the

38. See F. Coarelli, "L"agora des Italiens' a Delo: Il mercato degli schiavi?" *Opuscula Instituti Romani Finlandiae* 2 (1982): 119–39.

39. Cf. M. H. Crawford, "Republican *Denarii* in Romania: The Suppression of Piracy and the Slave-trade," *JHS* 57 (1957): 117–24.

general picture of servile stock which has emerged or to the (admittedly quite rare) individual cases in which it is possible to deduce the slave's ethnic origins (and these cases are all the more rare since even a barbarian slave might be described as "coming from" such and such a Greek town where he had previously been living, or might even be known by an ethnic name relating to it).[40]

The fact is that, whatever they may have said and done in particular circumstances, the Greeks did feel a measure of repugnance at the sight of certain of their own compatriots living in slavery.[41] Not only were the latter likely to show insubordination but also, and above all, Greeks had a feeling of solidarity and were concerned to distinguish themselves collectively from the barbarian world. Herodotus already implies as much in a passage where he declares, in connection with Arisba, a city on the island of Lesbos, that "its people were enslaved by the Methymnians, even though they were of their own blood" (1.151); and so do some of Euripides' tragedies relating to the Trojan War (*The Trojan Women, Andromache, Hecuba*), in which the emphasis is laid on the lamentable nature of the fates of these captives of noble origin.[42] But in the fourth century, with the intensification of pan-Hellenic feeling directed against the Persians, these feelings tended to grow stronger. Even in the work of Xenophon, where the paramount rights of the victor are affirmed in the most trenchant fashion, we find placed in the mouth of Socrates a number of declarations aimed at legitimizing enslavement only in the case of a city which is "unjust and hostile" (*Memorabilia*, 4.2.15), as well as several anecdotes with similar implications in his historical accounts. One such example is the declaration made by Agesilaus, king of Sparta, to the effect that "the Greek cities ought not to be enslaved, but chastened" (*Agesilaus*, 7.6); another is the Spartan Callicrates' reply to his allies, telling them that "while he was commander no Greek should be enslaved if he could help it" (*Hellenica*, 1.6.14). Plato, much concerned to reinforce the separation between free men and slaves in the constitutions of his *Republic* and his *Laws*, naturally chimed in, stipulating that in clashes between Greeks, which he assimilated to civil wars, the vanquished should not be chastised "with a view to their enslavement or destruction" (*Republic*, 5.471a), in other words, only "the goods of the vanquished fall into the hands

40. H. Klees, "Beobachtungen zu den Sklaven Xenophons," *Annali del Istituto Italiano per gli Studi Storici* 1 (1967–68): 89–112.

41. I. A. Sisova, "The ideas of the ancient Greeks regarding the reduction to servitude of Hellenes" (in Russian), *Escl. Périph.*, 7–23.

42. See H. Kuch, *Kriegsgefangenschaft und Sklaverei bei Euripides* (1974).

of the victors" (*Laws*, 1.626b). All of which explains the embarrass-
ment of Aristotle when, as we shall see (below, p. 125), he set out to
provide some theoretical justification for the presence of Greeks
among the slave population.

Hence the unanimous condemnation (in principle, at least) of
pirates who molested Greeks. Hence too the intensity of the po-
lemics that followed the enslavement of entire cities at the conclusion
of regular wars—for example, the enslavement of Thebes by Alexander the Great in 335, or of Mantinea by the Achaeans in 223. Both
the victors and the vanquished would claim to be on the side of
justice, or rather that justice lay on their own side.

Hence, too, the frequent and diverse practical attempts made to
encourage the liberation of Greeks reduced to slavery. Their relatives were under obligation to provide for buying them back, if
necessary with the aid of free loans, while their other compatriots
were offered powerful incentives to do so, such as promises of
honorific rewards and individual assurances that they would subsequently recoup their outlay. A friendly city, acting either officially or
through the intermediary of private citizens, might also undertake to
buy back Greek slaves, either spontaneously or in accordance with
official diplomatic agreements such as those concluded around the
mid-third century B.C. between Miletus and a number of Cretan
cities notorious for their involvement in piracy. Here is an extract
from one of them: "A Knossian shall not buy a Milesian nor a
Milesian a Knossian if he knows him to be a free man. Whoever buys
such a one knowingly shall lose his outlay and the person shall be
freed; if he buys the person in ignorance, he shall return the latter
and recover the entire sale price."[43] It even sometimes happened
that an entire city, having been reduced to slavery and dispersed to
the four corners of the Greek world, would be collectively restored to
freedom through the intervention of a third party acting out of
generosity or, no doubt more often, in his own conscious interest.
thus, in 316: "summoning from all sides those of the Thebans who
survived, [Cassander] undertook to reestablish Thebes, for he assumed that this was a most excellent opportunity to set up once more
a city that had been widely known for its achievements and for the
myths that had been handed down about it; and he supposed that by
this benevolent act he would acquire undying fame"—which could
well have been useful to him, as one of Alexander the Great's

---

43. Brulé, *La piraterie*, 5–12; I. Hermann, "Zum Rechtshilfevertrag zwischen Milet
und Gortyn," *ZPE* 17 (1975): 127–39.

successors, in winning the favor of the Greek cities (Diodorus, 19.53.2). In exceptional circumstances the victor himself undertook to make the reparation, as did Philip II for instance: "The city of Stageira . . . of which Aristotle was a native and which he had himself destroyed, he peopled again and restored to it those of its citizens who were in exile or slavery" (Plutarch, *Alexander*, 7.3). Such practices, whose importance seems to me often to have been underestimated, would not usually adversely affect the economic interests of the victor. Nor did they render the threat from enemies and pirates any less menacing, for nobody could ever really be sure of recovering his freedom in the end. Nevertheless, that is certainly the explanation for the discrepancy we have noted between the number of Greek captives condemned to slavery and the number of those who were actually enslaved. (Similar cases involving captives of barbarian origin were certainly much rarer, for among them only an elite held any hope of escaping from slavery in this way.)

Finally, one other variable source of slavery was the natural increase in the servile population—to which the slaves' masters would sometimes contribute in person. (The child of a free man and a slave, in Athens and probably in most other cities too, would inherit the status of its mother.) This type of slave farming was more or less encouraged, depending on the availability of supplies from other sources.[44] At the beginning of the fourth century, in his *Oeconomicus* (9.5), Xenophon called attention to the drawbacks of the practice, drawbacks both economic (the temporary unavailability of the mother for work, the incidence of infant mortality) and also psychological (the formation of links of solidarity within the servile class), and he accordingly recommended that the women's quarters be kept "separate by a bolted door from the men's, so that nothing which ought not to be moved may be taken out, and that the servants may not breed without leave." On the other hand, the Pseudo-Aristotle's *Oeconomica*, at the end of the century, advised ensuring the loyalty of slaves by sometimes making it possible for them to breed (1.5.6). Elsewhere, for example in Ptolemaic Egypt, where prisoners of war were in short supply after the middle of the third century, and possibly in the Hellenistic world generally, the proportion of slaves "born-in-the-house" appears to have been higher, although it varied from one region to another. Thus, in the commercial center of Rhodes, so active in the early second century, they made up no more

---

44. The "natural" incapacity of the population to reproduce itself is, as is well known, simply a myth. See, for example, M. I. Finley, "The Significance of Ancient Slavery," *Acta Antiqua* 9 (1961): 285–86.

than one eighth of the known number of slaves, whereas at the same period they accounted for one quarter of the affranchised slaves in Delphi.[45] Admittedly, in this part of central Greece, the self-sufficient way of life was more common. (But the higher proportion here is also in part a result of masters' being more inclined to grant affranchisement to this type of slave.) These slaves presented a double advantage: not only were they in principle more loyal but furthermore they could be apprenticed at an early age and thus acquire a particular skill.

The Slave Trade

Apart from the born-in-the-house slaves and the few captives (quite rare, it would seem) whom the fighting men brought home "in their luggage," servile stock thus tended to be bought. This conclusion altogether tallies with the Greeks' own preconceived idea of the situation, although not with what might be supposed from the sparse documentation relating to this type of trade (which, we should remember, not only had a bad name, acquired from its many shady deals but above all was essentially based upon private intitiative—not a subject of great interest to the majority of our informants).

It is significant in this respect that the slave merchants best known to us are those who followed in the wake of the armies or those who worked hand in glove with the pirates. They were ready to buy cheaply and resell far from the main theater of operations the masses of captives whom the conquerors sought to be rid of as soon as possible (either because they were engaged in a long expedition or because they needed further financial resources). Special commissioners presided over these transactions, in the course of which the prisoners were all paraded publicly, sometimes in the nude, and occasionally branded.

On the other hand, virtually nothing is known of the activities of the merchants who trafficked with the barbarian world. Yet it is they who must have been principally responsible for providing regular supplies for the large slave markets we guess to have existed: at Tanais at the mouth of the Don, Byzantium, Ephesus, Pagasae in

45. Their percentage among slaves of known origins was to increase during the last two centuries B.C., as K. Hopkins (in collaboration with P. J. Roscoe) shows in "Between Slavery and Freedom: On Freeing Slaves at Delphi," *Conquerors and Slaves* 1 (1978): 139–41: 11 percent between 201 and 153; 44 percent between 153 and 100; 46 percent between 100 and 53; 36 percent between 53 and 1.

Thessaly, and on the main trade routes (at Chios, Delos, Corinth, Aegina, Rhodes, and also Athens, where a slave market was held every month at the new moon, in the "Circles" of the agora), not to mention those which lasted no longer than the duration of a festival in sanctuaries such as that of Apollo at Actium[46] or Zeus of Baitokake in northern Syria (during the Hellenistic period). The local authorities would normally levy a tax on the transactions.

Apart from this, all that we know is that the seller was in principle supposed to warn the buyer of any "hidden vices" the slave had (the same applied in the case of an animal).[47] Such an obligation is noted, in particular, in Plato's *Laws* (11 916a):

> If a man sell a slave who is suffering from phtisis or stone or strangury or the "sacred disease," as it is called [epilepsy], or from any other complaint, mental or physical, which most men would fail to notice, athough it be prolonged and hard to cure—in case the purchaser be a doctor or a trainer it shall not be possible for him to gain restitution for such a case, nor yet if the seller warned the purchaser of the facts. But if any professional person sell any such slave to a lay person, the buyer shall claim restitution within six months, saving only in the case of epilepsy, for which disease he shall be permitted to claim within twelve months. The action shall be tried before a bench of doctors nominated and chosen by both the parties; and the party that loses his case shall pay double the selling price of the slave.

A similar stipulation has been found in a contemporary inscription in the town of Maronea in Thrace. In Plato, and also in a Cretan law of the early fifth century, similar reservations were made concerning any slave who was a murderer or guilty of a crime that made him liable to be delivered over to his victim.

The price of slaves varied considerably according to sex, age, professional skills, and perhaps above all—although this is even more difficult to gauge—the local relations of supply and demand. In his *Memorabilia* (2.5.2), Xenophon writes: "One servant, I suppose, may be worth two minas [two hundred drachmas], another less than half a mina, another five minas, another no less than ten. Around the beginning of the Peloponnesian War, Nicias, son of Niceratus, is said to have given a whole talent (six thousand drachmas) for a manager of his silver mine." In his *Ways and Means* (4.23),

46. T. Blavatsky, "Ueber den Sklavenmarkt am Aktion," *Klio* 56 (1974): 497–500.
47. See I. Triantaphyllopoulos, "Les vices cachés de la chose vendue d'après les droits grecs à l'exception des papyrus," *Scritti in onore di E. Volterra* 5 (1971), 697–719.

the same author estimates the average price for slaves working in the Laurium mines at 180 drachmas but puts it at 173 for the slaves confiscated from those who, in 415, had mutilated the *hermes* in the agora of Athens and parodied the Mysteries.[48] Two or three artisans in the knife-manufacturing workshop bequeathed to Demosthenes by his father were worth five to six minas each, while others were valued at not less than three. Thanks to Zeno's papyri, we also know that the price of the slaves he bought in Syria around 260, on behalf of Apollonius, Ptolemy II's minister of Finance (*dioecetes*), ranged from 20 drachmas for a small boy to 300 drachmas for a woman. The only statistics available to us that reveal any continuity come from the many Delphic acts of manumission during the second and first centuries B.C.[49] The table given below (p. 81) shows in particular that in the course of this period, on an average the sums paid for unconditional liberation (which are likely to correspond most closely with the real value of the slaves) rose appreciably. The increase was probably not because of any proportional rise in the cost of living but was no doubt a consequence of a coincidental slump in supply, accompanied by a rapid rise in demand from Italy.[50] To form an approximate idea of what the sums invested represented, we should note that in the classical period the price of a slave was about the same as that of a mule and half that of a war horse; that at the end of the fourth century a skilled worker employed on public building sites could earn almost two drachmas a day; and that at the beginning of the second century 400 drachmas was the equivalent of the average price of 3,500 kilograms of wheat (which would last a family with modest needs for over three years).

The Diffusion of Chattel Slavery of the Athenian Type

I have already shown that slavery of the Athenian type was extremely widespread in the Greek world of the classical and Hellenistic periods, and nothing would be gained by listing more examples at this point—particularly as many more will be found in our subsequent discussion. Let us for the moment limit ourselves to noting

48. W. Kendrick Pritchett, "The Attic Stelai," *Hesperia* 25 (1956): 276–77; N. B. Kliacko, "The *Hermokopidai stelai*: as a source for slavery in the fifth century B.C." (in Russian), *Vestnik Drevnei Istorii* (1966), no. 3: 114–27, summarized in *Biblioteca Classica Orientalis* 13 (1968): 281–82.

49. See below, p. 76. Cf. the article by R. P. Duncan-Jones, "Problems of the Delphic Manumission Payments, 200–1 B.C.," *ZPE* 57 (1984): 203–9.

50. In particular, if we judge by the stability of the sums paid for conditional liberty.

that the extent of the diffusion of this type of slavery remains unclear only in regions where other forms of exploitation already existed. We must therefore examine these before attempting to come to any conclusion on the matter, at the end of Chapter 2.

Are we in a position to gauge the strength of slavery of the Athenian type at least in areas where it encountered no competition? Most of our general information on this subject is provided by the ancient authors included in Book 6 of the *Deipnosophists* of Athenaeus of Naucratis, a compiler of the second century A.D. It relates to three towns: Corinth (at an unknown date, probably the end of the archaic period); Athens (under the tyranny of Demetrius of Phalerum, probably in 317–316; and Aegina (at an unknown date, possibly in the early fifth century). "In the third book of the *Histories*," we are told, "Epitimaeus [a name applied to the Hellenistic historian Timaeus] has said that the city of Corinth was so rich that it had acquired 460,000 slaves. . . . Ctesicles [also of the late Hellenistic period], in the third book of his *Chronicles,* says that at Athens, during the one hundred and seventeenth (?) Olympiad, a census of the inhabitants of Attica was taken by Demetrius of Phalerum, and the number of Athenians was found to be 21,000, of metics 10,000, of slaves 400,000. . . . Aristotle, in the *Constitution of Aegina* says that even among the Aeginetans there were 470,000 slaves" (272b–d).

The first question raised by this passage of Athenaeus is that of its authenticity, that is, the conformity of the original text with the text reproduced, which is known to us only from a single manuscript from the late ninth century A.D.[51] There is really no serious reason to doubt it, however, given that these figures, which reappear in a summary (*epitome*) by Athenaeus quite independent from this manuscript, tally perfectly with the relevant circumstances and given also that one of the figures reappears in a scholium to Pindar (*Olympian Odes,* 8.30) that is in all probability directly inspired by Aristotle's own text.

Second, we must raise the question of the honesty and trustworthiness of this late compiler. But on this point no more than a qualified answer can be made. Athenaeus undeniably committed a number of

---

51. See in particular R. L. Sargent, *The Size of the Slave Population at Athens during the Fifth and Fourth Centuries B.C.* (1925); A. W. Gomme, *The Population of Athens in the Fifth and Fourth Centuries B.C.* (1933); Gomme, "The Slave Population of Athens," *JHS* 56 (1946): 127–29; W. L. Westermann, "Athenaeus and the Slaves of Athens," *Harvard Studies in Classical Philology, Suppl., 1941,* 451–70 (=*Slavery,* 73–92); A. Dreizehnter, "Die Bevölkerungszahl in Attica im Ende des 4. Jahrhunderts v.u.Z," *Klio* 54 (1972): 147–51; L. Gallo, "Recenti studi di demografia greca (1970–1978)," *ASNP,* 3d ser., 9 (1979): 1595–1608.

blunders in the rest of his work (in particular, his personal estimates relating to the Roman world, in Book 6, must be recognized to be totally fantastic); however, it is also clear that his citations as a whole are, on the face of it, reliable—to judge, for example, by what he tells us about the number of slaves in the possession of the Athenian Nicias, which tallies with the report given in the manuscripts of Xenophon's *Ways and Means*.

Hence there are two possibilities. Either Athenaeus accurately reproduced the numerical information provided by Timaeus, Ctesicles, and Aristotle; or else he involuntarily distorted them, having misunderstood the system of numeration used in his sources. And if we adopt the first of these two hypotheses, we must go on to ask whether a similar misunderstanding may not have occurred in the transcription of the statistical data either independently, by Timaeus, Ctesicles, and Aristotle (which is highly improbable) or by the author who collected all this information, probably none other than Polybius.[52] Modern historians have considered each of these latter hypotheses. But we are bound to admit that none of them carries conviction.

Modern historians are not even in agreement over the meaning of the figures. In the eyes of some, who seek to inflate them with a view to discrediting them, they all have a military significance and relate only to men of an age to bear arms. For others, that is true only of the citizens and metics, not of the slaves, who were bound to be counted head by head, like livestock. According to the latter hypothesis it would be the case, if we are to believe Athenaeus, that Athens at the end of the fourth century, for example, numbered 400,000 slaves, 21,000 mobilizable citizens (implying a total civic population of about one thousand people) and 10,000 mobilizable metics (who, for obvious sociological reasons, in all probability represented a major proportion of this group, say, one third).

The second—and only other—overall estimate that we possess is that of the orator Hyperides, in a fragment of the *Against Aristogiton* delivered soon after 338, in which mention is made of liberating "slaves both from the silver mines and up and down the country, more than a hundred and fifty thousand in number." But this piece of information has also been a subject of controversy. It has been claimed that the late compilation from which it is an extract (the *Suda*) does not provide sufficient guarantee of its authenticity and that the figures given could very well, like those mentioned above,

52. L. Canfora, "Polibio e la schiavitù greca," *Index* 10 (1981): 55–65.

have been distorted in the manuscript tradition. Furthermore, interpretation of the information is also a delicate matter. We do not
know, in the first place, whether it refers to the servile population as
a whole or only to men of an age to take part, alongside citizens and
metics, in the defense of Attica against the Macedonians. Second, we
do not know whether the town of Athens itself should be included in
"up and down the country." Depending on which hypothesis is
adopted, it either is or is not possible to make this text of Hyperides
tally with that of Athenaeus.

Despite the fact that the two texts are beyond question from a
philological point of view[53] and furthermore appear to be altogether
compatible, most modern historians have attached little importance
to them, making use of arguments based on plausibility similar to
those put forward in 1752 by David Hume, in his essay *The Population of Ancient Nations*. They claim, for example, that it is improbable
that the island of Aegina, which had 8,000 inhabitants in 1920,
should have had more than 500,000 on the eve of the Persian Wars,
and that in Attica at the end of the fourth century, a force of 400,000
slaves should have allowed themselves to be dominated by 31,000
free men of an age to bear arms, without ever attempting to revolt,
and so on.

Attempts have therefore been made to replace the ancient "statistics" with others which relate to the population of Athens as a whole
and which consequently make it possible, by subtracting the citizens
and metics, about whose numbers we are better informed, to gain at
least an approximate idea of the total number of slaves. Some authors, for example, have endeavored to estimate the number of
inhabitants in Athens at the beginning of the fourth century by
assuming that, as Xenophon states in his *Memorabilia* (2.7.2; 3.6.14),
the area enclosed by the walls contained 10,000 houses, each inhabited by a maximum of fourteen people. Others have attempted to
calculate the consumption of wheat in Attica at the time of Demosthenes: 400,000 *medimnoi* locally produced, if we are to credit the
sum of tithes paid to the goddesses of Eleusis in 329–328, supple-
mented by twice (perhaps three times) as much from imports, according to Demosthenes. That is enough to feed at the most 270,000
people, hence fewer than 100,000 slaves. Yet others have argued on
the basis of the fact that the total wealth of the Athenians, which
happened to be assessed for tax in 378–377 and 354–353, was
estimated at between 5,750 and 6,000 talents. This represents ap-

53. L. Canfora, "Il soggetto passivo della *polis* classica," *Opus* 1 (1982): 33–51.

proximately the value of 180,000 slaves (taking no account of the other forms of wealth assessed!). All these calculations would suggest that we should challenge the figure mentioned by Athenaeus and considerably reduce it, by at least half if not four fifths—if, that is, the calculations did not themselves rest upon the flimsiest bases. For the truth is that any estimate of either the size of the population of the town of Athens or that of the cereal production in Attica or of the real (not simply fiscal) value of the wealth of the Athenians is bound to remain a controversial matter. Even if they tend to affirm our own initial feeling, it is tempting to agree with David Hume (p. 248) that "many grounds of calculation proceeded on by celebrated writers are little better than those of the emperor Heliogabalus, who formed an estimate of the immense greatness of Rome from ten thousand pounds weight of cobwebs which had been found in the city."

Even less reliable are the estimates based upon the number of slaves belonging to such and such an individual or working in such and such a sphere of production for, as we shall soon see, in this area it seems possible to bicker on forever. Here is a single example of the way historians have been crossing swords on the subject for more than two centuries. Partisans of a major reduction in the estimate of the slave population have often made much of a passage in Demosthenes' speech *Against Timocrates* (197), in which the orator reproaches him for his violent requisitioning raids on many citizens' homes, "demolishing their front doors, dragging their bedclothes from under them and laying distraint on a man's maidservant, if he possessed one. . . . "In fact, though, the text should be understood quite differently, for the verb translated here as "possess" in this particular context means "possess" in the sexual sense—[54] a delicate situation that can hardly have arisen on the occasion of each and every raiding operation!

We should remember that the number of Athenian slaves certainly did not remain stable throughout the classical period (it must have been on the increase up until 431, declined during the Peloponnesian War, then made a slow recovery over the first three quarters of the fourth century). So it is not surprising that, on the basis of documentation such as this, estimates have varied widely: from 20,000 to 400,000, with many historians favoring a figure of around 100,000, that is, a proportion of roughly one to three in

54. P. J. Bicknell, "Demosthenes 24,197 and the Domestic Slaves of Athens," *Mnemosyne*, 4th ser., 21 (1968): 74, and also "Some Missing Slaves," ibid., 18 (1965): 187–88.

relation to the population as a whole or, say, an average of three or four slaves per household. In this way one arrives at a percentage at least as high as that for the American South around 1860, but in Athens slavery was more widely diffused, since in the Old South three quarters of the free did not own slaves.

Clearly we are even less well placed to pursue such speculations in connection with Hellenistic Athens and the rest of the Greek world. But then, that is really not where the most important point lies. What we ought to try to assess is the role played by slaves in productive work, especially in accumulating *the surplus* that made their masters' social existence possible.

The Work of the Slaves

It is only from Athenian society in the classical period that we can form a fairly precise idea of the various activities pursued by the chattel slaves. In general, they seem to have had no truly professional qualifications: these are the slaves whom we find living alongside their masters, performing household tasks—domestic slaves, as we call them. In daily life they are everywhere. For Aristophanes, their presence is so natural that neither the gods, nor the city in *Birds*, nor the ideal world depicted in *Plutus* can manage without them. They are also taken for granted in the speeches of fourth-century orators: by Demosthenes, who asks each of his listeners, in the speech *Against Stephanus* (86) to think of the servant "he has left at home" and whose "master" he is; by Lysias, who declares in *For Callias* (5) that "everybody" has some; and, finally, also by Aristotle, who considers in his *Politics* (1253b) that "the household in its perfect form consists of slaves and free men."

In reality, however, in this respect a certain inequality existed among citizens, as is shown by the measures contemplated in the utopian world of Aristophanes' *Ecclesiazusae* (l. 593) to rectify a situation in which one man has "hundreds of servants," another "none at all." The fact is that some of the poorest lacked the means to own slaves. There were artisans unable to "buy servants to relieve them of work," as Xenophon's *Memorabilia* (2.3.3) puts it, peasants like the *autourgos* in Euripides' *Electra*, who worked on their own in their fields and for whom, as Aristotle said (*Politics*, 1252b, 15), "the ox serves instead of a servant." Men as "poor" as these, Aristotle goes on to say (1323a, 5–6) "having no slaves, are forced to employ their women and children as servants," which in Aristophanes' *Wasps* is precisely the position of the judges of popular courts, who were so poor that they had to rely on their own children to light their way through the streets. It does not, however, seem feasible to conclude that a high proportion of free men—as many as half the civic body, according to Eduard Meyer—found themselves in such a situation. To the doubtful examples mentioned above, which we should be unjustified in exploiting to make that point, let me add that of the invalid mentioned by Lysias, whose trade gave him "but slight assistance": he complains not of having no servants at all but of being unable to "procure someone qualified to take over" the business from him (24.6).

At any rate, if one was in or above the census class of the zeugites, who could afford to arm themselves as hoplites, as a general rule one did own domestic slaves, probably mainly of the male sex. That fact is clearly attested in Aristophanes' comedies, on the basis of which it is even possible to draw up a list of minimum figures:

Play	Date	Master	Social class	No. of slaves	Men	Women
Ach.	427	Diceopolis	average peasant	4	2	2
Knights	426	Demos	average peasant	4	4	?
Clouds	425	Strepsiades	average peasant	2	1	?
Wasps	422	Bdelycleon	rich	7–8	6	1–2
Peace	421	Trygaeus	peasant	2	2	?
Peace	421	Choristes	peasant	3	1	2
Frogs	405	Pluto	rich	5–8	4–7	1
Eccl.	392	Chremes	peasant(?)	3	2	1
Plutus	388	Chremyles	peasant	3	1	?

This list suggests that "average" peasants, who made up the social backbone of Periclean democracy, owned on average at least three slaves.[55]

The "rich" belong to the "knight" and *pentacosiomedinoi* classes. Ischomachus, the hero of Xenophon's *Oeconomicus*, was certainly one of their number. However, on the subject of the female slaves who assisted the mistress of the house (males appear to have worked only in the fields), all we know is that they were numerous enough to need to be placed under the direction of one of their number, promoted to the position of supervisor. Legal speeches sometimes allow us to calculate how many of this type of servant would belong to a single household. Thus, we learn from Antiphon (6) that an Athenian of the late fifth century who was in a position to pay for the

55. The table is reproduced from E. Lévy, "Les esclaves chez Aristophane," *Colloque Besançon 1972*, 33.

training of a chorus of fifty youths for a religious festival used probably no more than ten slaves in his home. Isaeus (8) tells us that in 375 one Ciron, whose fortune amounted to about two talents, owned two female servants and a young slave-girl; that at the same period Demosthenes' father, who, with his fourteen talents, was one of the wealthiest Athenians of his day, was attended in his home by ten or so slaves (27). In the wills of the most prosperous of the great Athenian philosophers, Diogenes Laertes found comparable figures: five for Plato, more than thirteen for Aristotle, nine for Theophrastus, six or seven for Strato, twelve for Lycon. This is a far cry from the veritable herds of slaves who afforded the Roman aristocracy of the late Republic a lifestyle of the utmost refinement.

As a general rule, Athenians were thus not in a position to employ the members of their domestic staffs as Democritus advised, "like the limbs of their bodies, each with a different purpose" (Stobaeus, 62.45). Far more typical would be those like Molière's Harpagon, who called his only servant by a whole string of different names so as to impress his guests. Apart from those with specialized skills present in the greatest houses—nurses, pedagogues, janitors, housekeepers, female (or occasionally male) cooks (assisted for large banquets by teams of slaves hired for the occasion: valets, cooks, dancers, citharists, and courtesans)—slaves were, in most cases, simply general dogsbodies. Today their essential tasks would fall into the "service" category: the stocking of supplies, shopping for food and other errands, milling grain, preparing meals, various forms of cleaning, attending to the physical well-being of their masters (a number of eunuchs were to be found in the women's quarters in the fourth century, and they sometimes acquired considerable influence in the royal courts of the Hellenistic period). Slaves might sometimes accompany their masters on their outings in town or on their travels, but always in small numbers. The Greeks, unlike the Romans, never sought to swell the size of their train with a view to boosting their own prestige. (According to Plutarch (*Phocion*, 19.3), the wife of the general Phocion always went out accompanied by a single servant; and according to Demosthenes (31.157 and 159), the wealthy Midias required only three or four valets to escort him.)

These service-category activities cannot, however, be disassociated from the strictly productive work to which domestic slaves devoted part of their time within the traditional framework of the family economy, more often than not alongside the master or mistress of the house—that is, outside the market sphere so that the product of their labor could never be assessed by itself. From this point of view, their relative importance in overall production should not be under-estimated, even though it probably did tend to diminish from the fourth century onward, as family self-sufficiency declined. In any event, there are grounds enough for not proceeding, without more ado, to classify domestic slaves as nonproducers; in particular, the term *oiketes* does not justify the assumption that such slaves' activities were strictly domestic in character.

In the case of the men, agriculture was bound to hold first place among these productive tasks.[56] At the time of Pericles, most Athenian citizens owned one or more allotments of land, of varying dimensions, naturally, but unlikely to exceed about thirty hectares. Even after the ravages of the Peloponnesian War, it seems that fewer than five thousand citizens, that is, a quarter or a fifth of the civic body, possessed no real estate at all and, in the view of most specialists today, that proportion did not increase significantly during the fourth century. There were also the citizens who farmed public land and freedmen and metics who rented private land. The landowners and tenant farmers, assisted by their families and domestic slaves, were probably able to make a profit from these holdings, which would have ranged between three and five hectares, at the end of the classical period. They would no doubt also draw upon the seasonal labor of hired workers, either freedmen or slaves. Such is the picture that emerges, in particular, from the works of Aristophanes and Menander, where it is virtually impossible to distinguish between purely domestic slaves and those who devoted themselves exclusively to agriculture.

Such a degree of specialization probably existed only on those small or medium-sized properties where the owner happened not to live on the spot and, primarily, on large estates under direct exploitation such as that of Ischomachus, in Xenophon's *Oeconomicus* (even though its exact area is unknown). Here, a number of slaves (several dozen, apparently: 20.16) worked full time under one or more foremen and the ultimate supervision of their master, who visited the estate every day. There is no mention of free workers, not even seasonal ones. Admittedly, this type of exploitation does not appear to have been very common, in reality. It was probably followed, however, at the end of the fifth century on Alcibiades' estates, which covered an area of twenty-six hectares; on those of Pericles, which were placed under the control of a slave manager; and, around 330,

---

56. M. H. Jameson, "Agriculture and Slavery in Classical Athens," *Classical Journal* 73 (1977–78): 122–45.

also on the two estates of Phainippus, which together probably amounted to less than one hundred hectares (even though their combined perimeters measured over seven kilometers).

But we should not underestimate the number of agricultural slaves.[57] If many did not exist, it would be hard to see the purpose of a book such as the *Oeconomicus,* a handbook on the management of a family estate—and certainly no utopian one. It would also be hard to see why, in Aristophanes' *Ecclesiazusae,* Praxagora should think of equating the ownership of a large estate with that of large numbers of slaves (ll. 592–593). Similarly, if livestock in the form of slaves had been rare in the countryside, it would be hard to see why Plato, in the *Laws* (6.761a) should advise the land-stewards and phrourarchs, (watch captains) stationed in the countryside, to construct defenses, making use of "the beasts of burden and servants in each district, employing the former and supervising the latter, and choosing always, so far as possible, the times when these people are free from their own business." Nor could one understand why the normal fate reserved for Greek prisoners of war in the *Rhesus,* attributed to Euripides, should be to work on the land (ll. 74–75, 176–177). All these allusions would have been incomprehensible to readers or listeners unaccustomed to rural slavery. Nor is it significant that there were very few agricultural workers among the slaves who, in about 330, dedicated *phialoi* to the goddess Athena on the occasion of their manumission, since the chances of such slaves being freed were much lower than those of domestic or artisan slaves. It would be mistaken to conclude, as many do, that slaves played no more than a minor role in Attic agriculture, for we should not forget that, quite apart from the slave labor force necessary to run the "large" estates, the small farming landowners, who constituted a definite majority in classical Athens, would not have been able to manage without the help of their domestic slaves.

On the other hand, however, there can be no doubt that as artisans slaves also played an important, if not essential, role in Attica. Thanks to the figurative representations of Greek pottery and, above all, to the orators of the fourth century, we can be certain that there were very few artisans who did not have at their disposal at least a small number of slaves to assist them and that many of the wealthy owned quite large workshops (*ergasteria*),[58] all of which were staffed

57. As is done, in particular, by C. G. Starr, "An Overdose of Slavery," *Journal of Economic History* 18 (1958): 17–32 (=*Essays on Ancient History* [1979], 43–58). Cf. the justified criticisms of C. N. Degler, *Journal of Economic History* 19 (1959): 271–77.
58. Cf. J. K. Davies, *Wealth and the Power of Wealth in Classical Athens* (1981), 41–43.

exclusively by male slaves. Timarchus employed a dozen in his leather works and Kerdon thirteen in his cobbler shop (Aeschines, 1.97). Demosthenes had inherited two workshops from his father: the one employed thirty-two or thirty-three cutlers, the other twenty constructors of beds (27.9–11). The former slave Pasion was the proprietor of a shield factory that employed about sixty workers (Demosthenes, 36.11) while the workshop belonging to the metic Lysias and his brother had over a hundred (12.8 and 19). It should not, however, be imagined that the men worked on a production line. As in the workshops of the ancien régime, the introduction of concentrations of workers had, in practical terms, prompted virtually no development in the division of labor. In the records relating to the construction of the Athenian Erechtheum in 408–407,[59] as in those that relate, later, to Epidauros, Delphi, Eleusis, and Delos, a certain percentage of slave workers is again mentioned among the teams assembled by the contractors: among the eighty-six workers on the Acropolis whose origin is known, twenty-four were citizens, twenty-four metics, and twenty slaves. The slaves worked either as masons or as carpenters. It should also be pointed out that in such documents, which in the main refer to highly difficult work that was rated as particularly honorable, the servile workforce is certainly underrepresented.

In Athens, the artisan sector of the slave economy appears to have developed in particular from the mid-fifth century on, at first simply as a sideline to the agricultural (or even commercial) activities of the *oikos*, and subsequently in an increasingly autonomous fashion. Concurrently, the discredit affecting the "nouveaux riches" who had made their fortune out of such slaves diminished. In Old Comedy it is strongly marked, with the "new politicians" such as the "tanners" Cleon and Anytos, the "lamp-maker" Hyperbolos, and the "lyre-maker" Cleophon, who had, if not acquired, at least increased their fortunes in this way, all held up to ridicule. But by the fourth century, the theme seems to have practically disappeared: for example, the family of Demosthenes whose wealth, with virtually no basis in real estate, stemmed essentially from workshops manned by slaves and from moneylending, suffered no ridicule.

It was above all in the mines—especially in Athens, in the silver-bearing lead mines of Laurium which, since the end of the sixth century, had been producing the metal necessary for its large quan-

---

59. R. H. Randall, "The Erechtheum Workmen," *American Journal of Archaeology* 57 (1953): 199–210.

tities of minted coins—that servile labor was predominant.[60] Slaves were employed here in every capacity, as workers or foremen, in the processes of mining the ore, and in the processing mills and foundries, working alongside a small minority of free men taking part in the exploitation of their own claims. But the only available documentation on which to base an estimate of the numbers involved is incomplete and not easy to interpret. Thus, it is not clear how many of the slaves who escaped after the Peloponnesian occupation of Decelia in 413—over twenty thousand, a large proportion being artisans (*cheirotechnai*), according to Thucydides (7.27.5)—really came from the Laurium region or what porportion of the overall slave population they represented. Xenophon's treatise *Ways and Means*, dating from just before the middle of the fourth century, meanwhile tells us that between 430 and 420 some wealthy Athenians, Nicias, Hipponicus and Philemonides, had hired out to the mining concessionaries one thousand, six hundred, and three hundred slaves respectively. The author suggests that the city should solve its financial difficulties by following their example: it should begin by acquiring twelve hundred slaves, then use the profit made from hiring them out to increase their number to ten thousand or more "until there are three for every Athenian," that is to say, at the lowest estimate, seventy-five thousand—which provides some idea of the numbers of slaves, if not actually employed, at least theoretically employable. Clearly, the actual figures would depend on the richness of the seams under exploitation and also the prevailing political and economic circumstances. Siegfried Lauffer has taken all these considerations into account in order to produce the accompanying graph, but, needless to say, it remains, for all that, highly hypothetical.

Merchants of all categories, both those who operated locally (*kapeloi*) and those who traded internationally (*emporoi*), as well as ship owners (*naukleroi*), were also assisted by their slaves.[61] Indeed, the practice of entrusting the management of commercial ventures abroad to slaves is clearly attested by the fourth-century Attic orators and from then on by a large number of decrees granting tax exemptions to both merchants and their servants (*therapontes*). A letter written on a lead tablet, discovered on the island of Berezan, near the

60. S. Lauffer, *Die Bergwerkssklaven von Laureion, Abh. Ak. Wiss. Mainz, 1955*, no. 12, and *1956*, nos. 11 (2d ed. 1979 in the *Forsch. ant. Skl.* 2, with fifty or so extra pages).

61. E. Erxleben, "Die Rolle der Bevölkerungsklassen im Aussenhandel Athens im 4. Jahrhundert v.u.Z.," *Hell. Poleis*, 460–520.

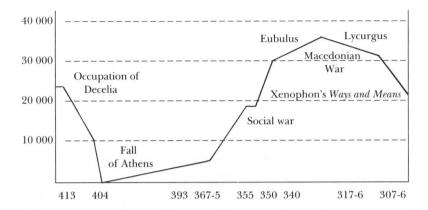

estuary of the Dnieper and the Bug, even suggests that this practice began as early as the start of the fifth century.[62]

It is once again the Attic orators of the fourth century who suggest that slaves, together with metics, also played an essential role in banking activities.[63] The great majority of employees of every rank in this domain appear to have been slaves, probably for two reasons. In the first place, during law suits, the banker could more or less control the evidence slaves gave in court; and second, in a profession that for a long time was much despised, this type of subordinate position held no attractions for citizens. Frequently, it was even a slave who, having been freed, inherited the business, in some cases together with his deceased master's widow or daughter. In Athens, between the end of the fifth century and the middle of the fourth, we know of several banking "dynasties" drawn from among slaves. The most famous was founded by Antisthenes and Archestratus, who were followed by Pasion (a little before 395), Phormion (in 371), and then an association consisting of Xenon, Euphraios, and Callistratus, all of whom, at the time they took over the bank (in 364–363), were still slaves of Pasion's sons. And the situation was similar for their major rivals, Socrates and Satyrus, Socles and Timodemus. For them, this was the starting point for upward social mobility, which

62. R. Bravo, "Une lettre de plomb de Berezan: Colonisation et modes de contact dans le Pont," *DHA* 1 (1974): 149–54; Bravo, "Remarques sur les assises sociales, les formes d'organisation et la terminologie du commerce maritime à l'époque archaï-que," *DHA* 3 (1977): 1–59.

63. R. Bogaert, *Banques et banquiers dans les cités grecques* (1968); E. Erxleben, "Das Kapital der Bank des Pasions und des Privatvermögen des Trapeziten," *Klio* 55 (1973): 129–30.

we shall be examining when we come to consider the position of freedmen. We should, however, beware of regarding these examples as anything but exceptional success stories, and their incidence, furthermore, seems to have been very much on the wane during the Hellenistic period; in the Delos market, banking was the preserve of free men, sometimes citizens but more often foreigners, from excellent families in some cases.

As well as these slaves who contributed in varying degrees and more or less directly to material production, there were others engaged, outside their master's house, in purely "service"-type activities: prostitutes of varying reputations, sometimes assembled in special "houses," as well as banqueting companions such as dancers and cithar players; and slaves who assisted their masters in the exercise of a "liberal" profession (doctors' assistants, for example). Finally, there were also many public slaves.[64]

The latter certainly included a number of manual workers under the orders of magistrates or commissioners. In Athens, they were used in the workshops where coins were minted, as laborers employed by five "road constructors" or on public building sites, under the supervision of an *epistates*. (According to Aristotle [*Politics*, 1267b, 17–18], all the workers at Epidamnus were of slave status.) But most were engaged in administrative tasks. Some, under the direction of the "Eleven," made arrests, acted as guards in prisons or sometimes as executioners. Some were ushers in the courts and popular assemblies, others staffed the offices of the various commissions and magistracies, in particular the Council (*Boule*), or attended to the archives kept in the Metroon. Some kept charge of the official weights and measures or, as is shown by a recently published inscription dating from 375–374,[65] were employed in checking the authenticity of coins used in the agora of Athens, in the Piraeus, and so on. Between the Second Persian War and the beginning of the fourth century, the city of Athens also employed a group of Scythian slaves, numbering initially three hundred, later one thousand.[66] These had policing duties at meetings of the people's assembly, the Council and the Areopagus. They were grouped into military units known as *lochoi* and equipped with whips, swords, and bows (they are generally known as "the Scythian archers"). They were stationed at first on the

64. O. Jacob, "Les esclaves publics à Athènes," *Musée Belge* 30 (1926): 57–106; Jacob, *Les esclaves publics à Athènes* (1928).
65. R. S. Stroud, "An Athenian Law on Silver Coinage," *Hesperia* 43 (1974): 157–88.
66. A. Plassart, "Les archers d'Athènes," *REG* 16 (1913): 151–213; Vos, *Scythian Archers*.

agora and later on the hill of the Areopagus. Aristophanes gives a grotesque representation of them in his comedies (the *Lysistrata* and the *Thesmophoriazusae*).

The Various Forms of Exploitation of Slave Labor

The State provided public slaves with a food allowance (*trophe*) which in Eleusis, around 320, amounted to three obols a day: probably just enough to keep up their strength to work.

As for private slaves, most worked directly for their master, receiving nothing but their keep and retaining nothing from the product of their labor apart from the odd bonus to put toward their savings. Here, in the private domain, as soon as there were enough slaves to make the organization of their work too complex and to qualify their master to devote much of his time to the political and cultural activities expected of a citizen, it became necessary to proceed to the delicate business of appointing a housekeeper to supervise the domestic staff and a steward (*epitropos*) to set in charge of the smooth running of affairs.[67] In the *Oeconomicus* (9.11–13), Xenophon describes the selection of such a person:

> In appointing the housekeeper, we chose the woman whom on consideration we judged to be the most temperate in eating and in wine-drinking and sleeping and the most modest with men, the one too who seemed to have the best memory, to be the most careful not to offend us by neglecting her duties, and to think most how she could earn some reward by obliging us. We also taught her how to be loyal to us by making her a partner in all our joys and calling on her to share our troubles. Moreover, we trained her to be eager for the improvement of our estate by making her familiar with it and by allowing her to share in our success. And further, we put justice into her, by giving more honour to the just than to the unjust and by showing her that the just live in greater wealth and freedom than the unjust.

The ideal for a steward was that he should be loyal, careful, sober, active, chaste, motivated, honest, and a good leader. The best example is Evangelus who, according to Plutarch (*Pericles*, 16.4 and 6) "kept strict order in Pericles' house" and "was either gifted by nature

67. See E. L. Grace, "What is a slave and the art of administrating?" (in Russian), *Vestnik Drevnei Istorii* (1970), no. 1: 49–67; G. Audring, "Ueber den Gutsverwalter (*epitropos*) in der attischen Landwirtschaft des 5. und des 4. Jh.v.u.Z.," *Klio* 55 (1973): 109–16.

or trained by Pericles so as to surpass everybody else in domestic economy." It was probably he who was entrusted with the responsibility of selling "his annual products all together in a lump and buying in the market each article as it was needed." According to the Pseudo-Aristotle's *Oeconomica* 1.6.4,): "in estates managed through stewards, inspections must be frequent. For in stewardship as in other matters there can be no good copy without a good example; and if the master and mistress do not attend diligently to their estate, their deputies will certainly not do so." Ischomachus, in Xenophon's treatise, makes a point of visiting his estate every day and likewise advises his young wife to keep a close watch on her servants' domestic activities and even to take part in them herself (see below, p. 143).

An alternative to engaging in this type of direct exploitation was for a master to hire out his slaves to a third party, either for continuous periods or from time to time (when there was no work for them at home) and either collectively (for example, a whole workshop) or individually.[68] If necessary, each morning he would send them off to the markets where slaves could be hired, which were usually held in the Anakeion, a sanctuary of the Dioscuri situated on the northern slopes of the Acropolis. In exchange, he would receive in their name a wage (*misthos*) which would vary according to the service rendered, and the hiring contractor would also be responsible for the welfare of his employee and for the risks of accident or escape for the duration of the contract. Thus, according to Xenophon's *Ways and Means* (4.14), Nicias hired out one thousand of his slaves to a concessionary of the Laurium mines known as Sosias the Thracian,— probably the very slave whom we have encountered earlier (p. 54), for whom he had paid a "good price" and apparently later freed. Nicias made the condition "that Sosias should pay him an obol a day per man net and fill all vacancies as they occurred."[69] Sometimes, too, a master who had signed a contract for work on a public building project would include a percentage of slaves in his work team and for them would be paid the same wage as free men would have received: about one drachma a day, according to the account relating to the Erechtheum in 408–407.[70]

Somewhat different was the position of Athenian slaves whose

68. See E. Perotti, "Contribution à l'étude d'une autre catégorie d'esclaves attiques: Les *andrapoda misthophorounta*," *Colloque Besançon 1973*, 179–94.

69. See, for this work as a whole, P. Gauthier, *Un commentaire historique des 'Poroi' de Xenophon* (1976); on this passage, 137–42.

70. Randall, "Erechtheum Workmen."

master allowed them to work independently, on their own account, and in many cases also to live with their families outside his own house.[71] Perhaps it was they who, for that reason, were known as *choris oikountes* ("those who live apart"), or possibly they were included, with the preceding group, in the category of *misthophorountes*, ("salaried" slaves). We cannot be sure. What is certain, however, is that they paid their master fixed dues (*apophora*), the amount of which must have varied according to their skills and earnings. Thus Timarchus, a contemporary of Demosthenes, received two obols a day from each of a dozen leather-workers and three obols from the foreman of their workshop (Aeschines, 1.97), which was considerably less than one might expect to make out of, for example, a highly rated courtesan.

These two forms of servile exploitation in all likelihood became increasingly common. That would explain, for example, the noticeable increase, between the end of the fifth century and the end of the fourth, in agreements relating to public works, in the proportion of slaves who worked on their own, without a master. It would also explain why, on the *phialoi* consecrated by freed Athenian slaves around 330, their demes of residence differ from those of their masters.[72] Hence too, perhaps, the increasing concern to have young slaves taught a skill,[73] so that they would eventually bring in higher dues (the practice is well attested in the Egyptian papyri of the Hellenistic period[74]). All this would seem to suggest that the monetary economy was exerting an increasing influence upon relations of slave production; and also that more flexible forms of exploitation were evolving even if these still involved no essential alterations in the relations of property. There are, in particular, still no grounds for speaking of an erosion of the slave-holding system as a result of any humanitarian tendencies.

Nevertheless, might one not suppose that considerations of "economic profitability" to some extent prompted these developments? It is a problem posed at two different levels.

First, on the question of the relative profitability of slave labor and

71. E. Perotti, "Les esclaves *choris oikountes*," *Colloque Besançon 1972*, 47–56.

72. *IG* II² 1553–1578; see, most recently, A. Kranzlein, "Die attischen Aufzeichnungen über die Einlieferung von *phialai exeleutherikai*," *Symposion 1971* (1975), 255–64.

73. See C. A. Forbes, "The Education and Training of Slaves in Antiquity," *TAPA* 86 (1955): 321–60.

74. I. Biezunska-Malowist, "Les esclaves payant l'*apophora* dans l'Egypte grécoromaine," *Journal of Juristic Papyrology* 15 (1966): 65–72, and "Quelques formes non typiques de l'esclavage dans le monde antique," *Monde antique*, 91–96.

free labor, not only can we not give any kind of answer based on statistics, but we must recognize this to be a false problem anyway. In truth there was no real alternative nor, except in a few specific cases, any material basis for making a choice. The simple reason is that, in this type of society, employment in the service of others was bound to be a last resort for a free man because it affected his very quality as a free man and conferred a certain servile character upon him. Consequently, given that no labor market unaffected by social values as a whole existed, it was not feasible for such factors of profitability to be taken into consideration. (They very seldom are, anyway, in economic systems dominated by the production of use-values.) There is no evidence of any discrimination in the pay for slaves on the one hand and free men on the other on public building sites (in particular on that of the Erechtheum of Athens in 408–407), nor is there any sign of competitiveness between the two groups when it came to being hired.[75] So even if, as we shall see later, slaves did not always show much enthusiasm for their work, we are bound to recognize that it did not occur to anybody to suggest that they be systematically replaced by free men on that account. Nor was any serious doubt felt about the profits that they brought in for their masters (provided, of course, that they were given tasks that were productive or some kind of lucrative activity). On this last point, that is, the profitability of servile labor *to* free men rather than as compared to the labor of free men, we do possess a body of telling evidence. In Xenophon's *Memorabilia*, Socrates asks the courtesan Theodote whether her wealth is based upon her ownership of fields, houses, or artisans (3.11.4), and elsewhere (2.7.6) he cites the heads of four Athenian families who have become rich because "they buy foreign slaves and can force them to make what is convenient" (they make flour, bread, cloaks, and coats).

Several attempts have been made to quantify the degree of the profitability of slave ownership as compared with other forms of investment.[76] If we compare the price paid for slaves with the income that they produced in the form of *misthos* or *apophora*, we find the annual rate of profit to be about 33 percent for those hired out to

75. G. Nenci, "Il problema della concorrenza fra manodopera libera e servile nella Grecia classica," *ASNP*, 3d ser., 8 (1978): 1287–1300.

76. See the calculations of L. Casson, "The Athenian Upper Class and New Comedy," *TAPA* 106 (1976): 35–41; W. E. Thompson, "The Athenian Investor," *Rivista di Studi Classici* 16 (1978): 16, 407–12. In a different context, see A. I. Pavlovska, "The profitability of slave labor in Hellenistic Egypt" (in Russian), *Vestnik Drevnei Istorii* (1973), no. 4:136–44.

the contractors working the Laurium mines, and 20–25 percent for those owned by Timarchus. These are higher profits than the 14 percent that Demosthenes appears to have made from his two slave-manned workshops (this time taking into account his necessary outlay for materials). In none of these cases, however, do the calculations include the sums needed to renew the slave workforce, despite the fact that at least in some sectors such as the mines, life expectancy cannot have been very high. It is, in my own view, thus not possible either to quantify the real level of the profitability of slave labor in the artisan sector or to conclude with certainty that it was less profitable when exploited directly than when exploited indirectly, or yet that to own slaves was more advantageous than to own real estate. Even if that was the case, it is still unlikely that, when it came to choosing how to invest one's wealth, such considerations should in general have carried more weight than the whole combination of values which shaped the course of economic life (the security and regularity of incomes and the politico-ethical implications of various forms of ownership).

The Practice of Manumission

The practice of manumission is attested from the end of the sixth century, certainly in Chios which, as we have noted, was the scene of an early and massive increase in chattel slavery.[77] But it probably appeared even earlier, in the archaic period, in an essentially oral context, with no official agreements drawn up. In some Greek cities such informal procedures continued to be followed for a long time. To guard against the possibility of the manumission being subsequently contested, the master's declaration would be made in circumstances that afforded the greatest measure of publicity: during court proceedings, a religious festival, or the performance of a play.[78] Such customs—banned in Athens toward the middle of the fourth century because of the uproar that they invariably provoked—continued to be followed elsewhere until the third century

77. A. Calderini, *La manomissione e la condizione dei liberati in Grecia* (1908), has still not been superseded. See, however, H. Raedle, *Untersuchungen zum griechischen Freilassungswesen* (1969), and *Rechtsprobleme in den Freilassungen der Böotier, Phoker, Dorier, Ost- und Westlokrer* (1978). Many acts translated into French may be found in R. Dareste, B. Haussouillier, and T. Reinach, *Recueil des inscriptions juridiques grecques* 2 (1898).

78. H. Raedle, "Freilassung von Sklaven in Theater," *Revue Internationale des Droits de l'Antiquité* 18 (1971): 361–64.

at least: in Epidaurus and in Oinaidai in Acarnania, for example, where the beneficiaries would inscribe their names on the steps of the theater; and at Delos and Thera, during the festivals of the Dionysia and the Carnea.

Although the epigraphical evidence is slight for the classical period, there are indications, especially in Attic literature, that manumission became increasingly common from the fourth century on. Writers such as Xenophon and Aristotle regard it as the best stimulus for a slave, while other writers are beginning to denounce its abuse. This impression appears to be confirmed by the proliferation of acts of manumission recorded in stone inscriptions during the later Hellenistic period although, admittedly, most crop up outside the major centers of classical slavery. In Delphi,[79] for example, about nine hundred have been discovered, dating from the first and second centuries B.C. (in particular, on the polygonal wall supporting the terrace of the temple of Apollo). Dozens have been found in other sanctuaries (Dodona, Bouthrotos, Lebadaea, Cos, and others) and varying numbers in other Greek cities (particularly in Thessaly and Boeotia), although one is not, even given the most striking cases (Delphi, for instance), justified in extending the significance of the numbers provided by the epigraphical material of any individual site to apply to the Greek world as a whole. Nevertheless, this mass of documentation, which is quite exceptional in ancient history, does make it possible to establish a relatively solid basis for a juridical study of the various modes of manumission.

In the vast majority of cases (that is, unless the State intervened: see below, p. 83) the decision to affranchise a slave appears to have been freely taken by his master, who might be either a citizen or a foreigner. In most cases the master would be a man, but with increasing frequency in the Hellenistic period it might be a woman, acting with or without the authorization of a guardian. It might be an adult or, in exceptional cases, a minor (invariably assisted by one parent or the other), or it might be a group of individuals. Among the slaves freed individually or in small groups (and known as *apeleutheroi* or *exeleutheroi*), the number of women[80] appears overall barely to exceed that of men (61 percent), so we should not exaggerate the influence stemming from the sexual relations that existed between

79. Texts in H. Collitz, *Sammlung der griechischen Dialekt-Inschriften* 2, nos. 1684–2342, and in a number of volumes of Book 3 of the *Fouilles de Delphes*. A new publication has been undertaken by D. Mulliez (see a few preparatory articles in the *Bulletin de Correspondance Hellénique*).

80. C. Wayne Tucker, "Women in the Manumission Inscriptions at Delphi," *TAPA* 112 (1982): 225–36.

many of them and their respective masters. With very few exceptions, the slaves appear in the official documents simply as items of property, themselves possessing neither initiative nor any juridical personality. Finally, one last feature characterizes these private acts of manumission: except where they are declared to be free, they always impose a price (sometimes specified, sometimes not) for the repurchase of liberty, a price that presumably corresponded roughly to the market value of the slave. This sum would either be drawn from the savings of the slave himself, lent by his master, or advanced by an association (*eranos*)[81] of individuals constituted for that very purpose (such as the *eranos* formed for the liberation of Neaera by her former lovers: Demosthenes, 59.29–32). For the rest, the more or less prolix formulas employed vary principally according to the mode of manumission adopted: religious or civil or something in between the two, as in the cases of a large number of intermediary examples which, for want of a better term, we will call "mixed."

The religious mode (where the deity plays an active role in the slave's liberation) has often been considered the most ancient, being seen as a progressive development from sacred slavery or the right of asylum. However, nothing could be more uncertain.[82] In some regions and at certain periods, the sanction of religion could equally well be applied to palliate the weakness of the State. In any case, there is no documentary evidence to support such an evolution.

A slave who acceded to freedom in this way might be consecrated to one of the major gods of the Greek pantheon (Zeus, for example, at Olympia and Dodona; elsewhere Apollo, Artemis, Athena, or Poseidon) or, alternatively, to one of the healer gods around whom cults sprang up during the Hellenistic period (Asclepius, and also the Egyptian deities Isis and Serapis). This procedure appeared in the fourth century at Olympia (and possibly as early as the end of the fifth in the sanctuary of Poseidon on Cape Tenarum in Laconia, if it is true that these are indeed acts of manumission rather than of the consecration of actual sacred slaves), and it was to remain current right down to the Roman period.[83] Usually it implied that the priests

81. J. Vondeling, *Eranos* (1961); H. Raedle, "Selbsthilfeorganisationen der Sklaven und Freigelassenen in Delphi," *Gymnasium* 77 (1970): 1–5.

82. F. Bömer, *Untersuchungen über die Religion der Sklaven in Griechenland und Rom*, 2, *Abh. Ak. Wiss. Mainz, 1960*, no. 1. The act from Beroia in Macedonia, which dates from 225, has nothing to do with religion; on the subject of this act, see H. Raedle, "Der Selbstfreikauf griechischer Sklaven im Lichte der Inschrift SEG, XII, 1953, 314 aus Beroia," *Zeitschrift der Savigny-Stiftung für Rechtsgeschichte* (*Röm. Abt.*) 89 (1972): 324–33.

83. For example at Chaeronea, where the acts of manumission are all consecrations, generally to Serapis, occasionally to the Mother of the Gods, the Great Mother or Athena Elithia (P. Roesch and J. M. Fossey, *ZPE* 29 [1978]: 123–37).

would guarantee the rights of the affranchised slave and would receive at least a proportion of the fines inflicted upon those who infringed them.

Otherwise, in central Greece and particularly at Delphi, from the second century on, the manumission might take the form of a resale of the slave to the deity, which undertook to free him. In the sanctuary at Delphi, it was Apollo, more often than Artemis or Athena, who concluded the business (through the intermediary of one of his priests). Most of the manumission certificates specify that the slave (or his mother, if he was a minor) had paid the full sum of the ransom to the god and had "entrusted" the purchase to him;[84] that the master had been duly paid (and sometimes the circumstances of the payment are mentioned: on the square in front of the temple, before such or such an altar . . .). Like all official commercial documents, they also give the name(s) of the guarantor(s) of the transaction and those of the witnesses (magistrates or private individuals): in the event that the vendor was a foreigner, half would be chosen from among his compatriots, half from among natives of Delphi. It would also be recorded that the original document had been deposited in the temple archives and sometimes also that copies had been presented to the magistrates or to private individuals.

Where a deity played no part in the proceedings (even if the inscription recording them is subsequently exhibited in a sanctuary), the manumission is known as "civil."

The simplest type of civil manumission is that in which everything mentioned was the wish of the master, sometimes expressed in his will. But the State could also be an involved party, either because its representatives played the role of guarantors or witnesses and were made responsible for protecting the affranchised slave, or even if their only task—admittedly an essential one—was to register the act and make it public (sometimes in an individual but more often in a collective form, as in Thessaly, where numerous lists of names arranged in alphabetical order have been discovered). In exchange, the freedman was expected to pay the State a lump sum (of 15 staters in Thessaly) quite apart, clearly, from the payment due to his master.

A clear distinction between the religious and the civil modes of manumission was by no means always made. Often enough we come across "mixed" manumissions in which the slave, liberated at the wish of his master and sometimes also under the control of the

84. H. Raedle, "Finanzielle Aspekte der Freilassung von Sklaven in Delphi," *Historia* 19 (1970): 613–17.

authorities, is furthermore placed under the protection of the deity. Either the latter may simply be invoked by name, or the act may be validated in the deity's temple or in the presence of its priest or, then again, the priest may also be responsible for seeing that the manumission is respected and for receiving the fines imposed on those who contravene it. But in such cases the deity simply provides a supplementary guarantee with which it is possible to dispense without fundamentally diminishing the authority of the act. Thus, at Dodona, people sometimes would and sometimes would not take the precaution of soliciting the protection of Zeus Naios or Dione, at Bouthrotos that of Asclepius.[85]

In some acts, the rights and obligations of the freedman are defined only by reference to the "laws on freedmen." More often, though, they are listed, in varying degrees of detail, in the acts themselves. Most such acts, whether religious, civil, or mixed, appear to grant the former slave unconditional liberty, entailing the right to go and live wherever he chooses, to do as he pleases, and to dispose of his possessions as he will. To prevent all arbitrary attempts to reduce him to slavery again, it was laid down that the master who freed him, or his heirs or guarantors specifically designated by name, or sometimes simply some other individual of good will, should have an obligation to intervene, generally on pain of the payment of a fine. In Delphi such fines varied between one-and-a-half to six times the slave's ransom, and they were paid half to the god, half to the victim. To guard against unlawful moves against the person of the freedman on the part of his former master's heirs, the act sometimes also notes their approval (*eudokesis*) or, as in Thessaly,[86] cooperation (except where the liberating master is declared to be unmarried and childless).

As time passed, however, acts in which the liberty of the freedman is explicitly limited became increasingly common. First, he was obliged to have a patron, known as a *prostates,* who was often automatically his former master or the master's heir (as in Athens), occasionally another member of the master's family or, in Thessaly, the slave's own father if he happened to be a free man. Through this *prostates,* the freedman was able to go to law. But he also had to fulfill

---

85. P. Cabanes, "Les inscriptions du théâtre de Bouthrotos," *Colloque Besançon 1972,* 105–209; Cabanes, *L'Épire de la mort de Pyrrhos à la conquête romaine* (1976), 397ff.

86. A. Babacos, *Actes d'aliénation en commun d'après le droit de la Thessalie antique* (1966). This may also be the meaning of the law of the "*ateknoi*" in manumissions in Epirus; cf. P. Cabanes, *Symposion 1977* (1982), 197–213.

various duties toward his former master (such as arranging for his burial, and choosing him as his heir if he had no legitimate children), and he had one more demanding obligation, which modern historians refer to as the *paramone*.[87]

The *paramone* obliged the freedman to "stay," "remain" (*paramenein*) with his former master, the latter's children, or whatever other individual was named in the act, for a limited period of time (sometimes fixed in advance as so many years, but increasingly determined by the death of the beneficiary). As a general rule, however, the freedman could liberate himself before the appointed time on payment of a certain sum or if he provided a slave to take his place—that is to say, by paying a price even higher than the one he was required to pay anyway when his period of service came to the end in the normal fashion. More precisely, the *paramone* in some cases meant that the former slave had to follow the beneficiary wherever he went and could himself move from one place to another only if he had the latter's authorization. He had to serve and so far as possible obey every order of the beneficiary, work for him, and provide him with a certain income, pay his debts and, in some cases, hand over a number of children to him, etc. If the freedman did not fulfill his obligations, the beneficiary of the *paramone* could beat him, chastise him, put him in irons, or hire him out to a third party, although he was supposed to proceed with moderation, always bearing in mind that he was now dealing with a free man. In extreme circumstances, the beneficiary could even reduce the delinquent to the status of slave once more, by having the act of manumission annulled. Where disagreement arose between the two parties, it was possible to have recourse to arbiters chosen by common assent.

Modern historians hold a number of different views on the status of these affranchised individuals submitted to *paramone*. Are they still slaves, truly free men, or is theirs a status somewhere in between slavery and liberty?

The rights and duties implied in this type of manumission are in fact somewhat ambiguous, for our documentation comes from a variety of sources and appears to be totally unsystematic. There are on the one hand good reasons for regarding these people as free: their liberty and the rights that stemmed from it (particularly the right to property), together with the security clauses attached to it (similar to those to be found in "simple" acts of manumission), do not in principle appear to be affected by the limited obligations that stem

87. A. E. Samuel, "The Role of *paramone* Clauses in Ancient Documents," *Journal of Juristic Papyrology* 15 (1965): 221–311.

from the *paramone*. They are endowed with a juridical personality vis-à-vis their former masters; they may not be reduced to slavery without the annulment of the act of manumission; their children (unless specifically designated to serve as slaves or to be similarly subject to a *paramone*) are born free; and finally, the contemporary Ptolemaic papyri contain many examples of free men similarly subjected to a *paramone*. On the other hand, it could be argued that the restrictions affecting movement, the limitations imposed on the use of possessions, and the infliction of corporal punishment are hardly compatible with liberty and also that the freedman, whose servile origin is clearly indicated by his having to bear his patron's name, in many cases continues to be regarded as a slave. That some were so regarded is proved by many examples provided by the Attic orators, where the term *doulos* is applied to a freedman, and by a remark of Chrysippus, a philosopher of the third century, who states quite categorically that "the affranchised are still slaves" (Athenaeus, *Deipn.*, 6.267b). Thus, even if the duties laid upon the freedman do not, in principle, affect the liberty granted to him by the act of manumission, nevertheless they do to a large extent perpetuate his exploitation by his master. The juridical situation is confused, and the concrete circumstances belong somewhere in between slavery and liberty, evidence that manumission never ceased to be considered as a *de facto* as well as a *de jure* matter.

This uncertainty is probably the principal reason for the large number of restrictive clauses introduced in the later periods. There is every reason to suppose that the apparently unconditional liberty granted in the "simple" acts was always (unless specifically stated otherwise) more or less limited by obligations comparable to those we find recorded in the inscriptions of later periods. Simply, the master did not always consider it necessary to mention in the act itself what either had previously been voluntarily agreed between both parties or was laid down either by law or by custom. In Athens, for example,[88] it is known that there existed "laws on freedmen." We can form some idea of their content from those (certainly more rigorous) which Plato establishes in his *Laws*[89]:

A man may arrest also a freedman if in any case he fails to attend, or to attend sufficiently, on those who have freed him; and such tendance shall consist in the coming of the freedman three times a month to the

88. L. M. Gluskina, "The legal status of Athenian freedmen in the fourth century B.C." (in Russian), *Vestnik Drevnei Istorii* (1965), no. 1:51–61.

89. H. Raedle, "Platons Freigelassenengesetze als Ausdruck attischer Standespolitik des 4. Jahrhunderts," *Gymnasium* 79 (1972): 305–13.

home of the man that freed him, and there undertaking to do those
duties which are both just and feasible, and in regard to marriage also
as may seem good also to his former master. The freedman shall not be
permitted to be more wealthy than the man who freed him; and if he is,
the excess shall be made over to his master. He that is let go free shall
not remain in the country more than twenty years, but shall depart, like
all other foreigners, taking with him all the property he owns—unless
he gains the consent of the magistrates and also of the man who freed
him. And if a freedman or any other foreigner acquire property exceeding in amount the third valuation, within thirty days from the day
on which he acquires this excess, he shall take his own property and
depart, and he shall have no further right to request from the magistrates permission to remain; and if he disobeys these rules and is
summoned before the court and convicted, he shall be punished by
death and his goods shall be confiscated. [11.915a–c].

In view of all this we should perhaps ponder the evolution evident
from the series of Delphic acts I have summarized in the table
below.[90] It shows an increasing proportion of conditional manumissions; expiration of the *paramone* taking place less and less frequently
at a fixed date and increasingly at the death of the master *and*
mistress; and increases in the sums to be paid for unconditional
manumission, in contrast to stability in the tariffs applicable for
conditional manumission. Perhaps what it indicates is not so much a
further degradation in the juridical condition of freedmen as rather
a reinforcement in the measures stipulated by masters in order to
forestall the effective emancipation of their former slaves at a time
when the Roman occupation was affording the latter more oppor-
tunities for "taking off," and making it more difficult for the masters
themselves to replenish their slave livestock.

The status of freedmen in the Greek world is all the more difficult
to gauge given that in public law it was, if not identical, at least very
similar to that of foreigners and even more to that of metics,[91] and it
consequently appears relatively seldom specified as such. In Athens
(where, it is true, the resemblance seems greater than in other Greek
cities), freedmen and foreigners alike were excluded from political
life since they were excluded from the deliberations of the people's
assembly and were ineligible for all magistracies. The ownership of
land in Attica, which went along with citizenship, was forbidden to

90. Drawn from the various tables presented by Hopkins, "Between Slavery and
Freedom."
91. On this subject see D. Whitehead, "The Ideology of the Athenian Metic,"
Proceedings of the Cambridge Philological Society, Suppl. 4, 1977.

Years	201–153	153–100	100–53	53–1	1–47	48–100	Total
Number of acts	411	303	93	96	45	26	974
Number of freedmen	495	378	123	128	63	50	1237
Percent children	8	18	27	30	39	14	17
Percent women among the adults	61	63	64	59	75	77	63
Percent slaves "born in-the-house"	11	44	46	36	41	18	29
Percent conditional freedmen	30	25	37	52	61	40	32
Percent definitive liberations at the deaths of master *and* mistress	11	24	35				
Percent definitive liberations at a fixed date	13	8	0				
Average cost of ransoms (in drachmas):							
Adult males	403	510	566	641			
Adult females	376	428	470	437			
Average cost of ransoms for unconditional manumission (in drachmas):							
Adult males	405	532	641	827			
Adult females	390	440	500	485			
Average cost of ransoms for conditional manumission (in drachmas):							
Adult males	396	422	(300)	433			
Adult females	337	372	367	383			

them, as were mortgage loans. Their marriages were legally recognized but, the children of them, even if one spouse was a citizen, were from the mid-fifth century on denied citizenship. Later such alliances were even prohibited, on pain of the freedman's being returned to slavery. Each year freedmen had to pay a personal tax, a fairly light one, known as a *metoikion,* and at the same rates as citizens, they had to make the contributions levied in times of war (*eisphorai*), undertake liturgies (to finance triremes, tragic choruses, and so on), and also donate the voluntary gifts (*epidoseis*) expected from the wealthy. Again depending on the size of their fortune, the men were bound to serve in the army either as hoplites or as light-armed infantrymen (in principle, only in defense of the territory) and, above all, in the navy, as oarsmen. From a legal point of view they, like all foreigners, came under the authority of the archon-polemarch, who assigned cases to various juries of citizens. The murderer of a freedman was usually brought before the Palladion tribunal where, other things being equal, his sentence was proportionate to the status of his victim: more severe than that for the murder of a slave but less severe than for that of a citizen. Like all the metics, freedmen participated extensively in religious life: they took part with citizens in associations devoted to the cult of foreign gods and in most of the sacrifices, banquets, mysteries, and festivals celebrated in the Pan-Hellenic sanctuaries or in honor of the gods of the city; they probably also had a place in the procession of the Panathenaea depicted by Phidias on the walls of the Parthenon.

Nonetheless, the situation of freedmen was not identical on all counts to that of metics. It was more precarious. Freedmen ran the risk of having their liberation challenged or of being condemned for the way they acquitted themselves of their obligations toward their former masters. In most of the Greek world, they were then liable to arrest and able to avoid it only by bringing into play the guarantees laid down in the act of their manumission. In fourth-century Athens, the State, which was responsible for enforcing the "laws on freedmen," might then make a legal ruling. If the freedman's status was what was challenged, he or she might, as we saw (p. 42), avoid arrest through the support of a third party who was prepared to bring a lawsuit against the person claiming to be the freedman's master and, if the suit was lost, to pay the latter a heavy fine (known as a *dike aphaireseos*). If, instead, the issue was one of reviewing the freedman's relations with his former master ("if they leave them, have another inscribed as their patron or fail to do what the laws demand": Harpocration), a lawsuit could be brought against him "for defection" (*dike apostasiou*). For the freedman, the outcome of such a situation would either be reduction to slavery once more or liberation from all obligations toward the former master. In the latter case it appears to have been customary, in Athens between about 340 and 320, to consecrate a commemorative *phialos* in the sanctuary of Athena on the Acropolis.

The (small number of) former slaves affranchised by the State for exceptional services—generally with the agreement of their masters, who were then paid compensation—found themselves in a less dependent position. In Athens, this was the reward granted in individual cases to slaves who denounced an act of treachery, sacri-

lege, seizure of public funds, or a violation of the regulations governing wheat supplies. In Thasos, too, according to a law dating from
the end of the fifth century, such was the reward (in addition to a
grant of 100 staters) for anyone "who denounces a revolutionary
movement stirred up against Thasos and whose statements turn out
to be correct,"[92] and in Ilium for whoever "killed the tyrant or leader
of an oligarchy or the author of an aggression against democracy"
(*OGIS*, 218). In the *Laws,* Plato uses similar deterrents against theft
of buried treasure and disrespectful behavior by children toward
their parents. But in quite exceptional circumstances such measures
were also occasionally applied collectively: when, as we shall see
(pp. 155–76), what was at stake was the safety of the community or
that of one faction in a civil war.

Normally, however, the chances of a freedman's acquiring citizenship on top of liberty were extremely slim. It is probably not true
that, as Dio Chrysostom (15.17) claims, a law existed in Athens
declaring that the "natural slave" could not be promoted to citizenship. But the examples of the bankers Pasion and Phormion, who
both did receive that favor at the end of their lives, should not
mislead us. All the indications are that Athenian freedmen who were
individually favored with citizenship by decree of the people's assembly, or who were even granted the privilege of the *atelia* (dispens-
ing them from payment of the *metoikion*) were rare indeed. As Philip
V of Macedon pointed out to the people of Larissa in Thessaly in
215, in this respect the Greeks lagged behind the Romans "who,
when they affranchise slaves, receive them into the city and grant
them access to the magistracies, thanks to which not only have they
made their own country grow but they have furthermore sent out
colonies to some seventy places" (*Syll.*³,543,1.31–34). It is a clumsy
comparison, as has been demonstrated,[93] since for anyone possessing neither wealth nor influence, the *civitas Romana* brought chiefly
civil rights (as did the condition of metic, in Greece) and very little
political power, this being monopolized by the aristocracy. The
Greek *politeia* in contrast, even in the Hellenistic period and whatever the form of government, essentially implied participation in
deliberative and judiciary power, with accompanying economic advantages. So the Greeks had good reasons for the niggardliness that
they displayed in this matter (and, as early as the fourth century,

---

92. J. Pouilloux, *Choix d'inscriptions grecques* (1960), 118–21, n.31.
93. P. Gauthier, "Générosité romaine et avarice grecque sur l'octroi du droit de
cité," *Mélanges d'histoire ancienne offerts à William Seston* (1974), 207–15.

there were even some who, scandalized at any exceptions to the rule, would have preferred more niggardliness). To set against this, it must be said that a freedman was much less easy to trace in Greece than in Rome and that his descendants, merging with the mass of metics, became totally indistinguishable.

[2]

Between Liberty and Slavery:
Communal Servitude

My decision to give pride of place in my study to chattel slavery of the classical Athenian type rests on obvious reasons of convenience. This form of slavery is not simply the one best known to us. It also presents not only the clearest image of the servile phenomenon, but the image which conforms most closely with that bequeathed to us by Western humanism, shaped as this is by both Roman law and modern colonialism.

But this "model" by no means covers all the forms taken by the exploitation of nonfree labor in the Greek world. If we reject all theoretical approaches of an exaggeratedly reductionist nature, we are bound to recognize that, as we have already seen, chattel slavery is not directly in line with the Mycenaean and Homeric forms of slavery, even if these share some of its fundamental characteristics. Furthermore, as we shall see, it should not be confused with other contemporary types of dependency, despite the fact that the Greeks themselves were prone to lump them all together in the concept of *douleia*.

The unilinear schema of the evolution of humanity, which postulated the existence of a single type of slavery in Greece (in the same way that, as it were, there might exist a single type of socialism), is thus demolished. But having seen it out by the door, might we not find it returning through the window in the form of a theory according to which chattel slavery is the "normal" manifestation of a process that, here or there and at one period or another, became "arrested" at an "archaic" stage, in an "incomplete" form?[1]

At the beginning of the last chapter, I showed that the history of chattel slavery is linked with a whole *complex* of particular historical conditions, among others a particular concept of liberty in terms of its opposite. So I have already begun to put forward a negative answer to the question just raised. It follows that all other forms of dependency must be equally inseparable from the whole network of social structures within which they are incorporated and that chattel slavery of the classical Athenian type is no more solely (and ultimately) descended from them than man is from the monkey.[2] Generalizations on this subject should beware of "mistakenly" isolating particular aspects of the phenomenon to the exclusion of others. They ought, on the contrary, to take into account all the essential features of the mode of production in all their specific diversity: especially the juridical status of the exploited and the mechanics whereby the surplus was appropriated, both of which, in precapitalist societies, are bound to vary in accordance with the nature of the superstructures that determine the impact of extra-economic constraints.[3]

So should we say that in ancient Greece we find, alongside chattel slavery, a multitude of forms of exploitation all radically different from one another? To confer a certain unity upon them, many modern historians are prone to group them all together under the concept of "dependency." That may be a useful concept to mark out their difference from chattel slavery but it does not help to define their nature, since it lacks an anchorage and a framework and lends a bogus, purely nominal unity to institutions that sometimes differ as

---

1. This is still the main tendency in Soviet historiography. See, for example, I. M. D'jakonov, "Slaves, Helots and Serfs in Early Antiquity," *Acta Antiqua* 22 (1974): 45–78: ancient relations of exploitation are more or less rigorous and resemble slavery more or less closely depending on what degrees of extra-economic constraint are technically possible (depending in essence on the techniques of armament and combat which make it possible for the dominant class to develop its forces of production).
2. An expression used by J. Ducat in "Aspects de l'hilotisme," *Ancient Society* 9 (1978): 19, with which I am largely in agreement.
3. I. Hahn, "Die Anfänge der antiken Gesellschaftsformation in Griechenland und das Problem der sogenannten asiatischen Produktionweise," *Jahrbuch für Wirtschaftsgeschichte* 2 (1971): 41–42 (=*Die Enstehung der antiken Klassengesellschaft*, ed. H. G. Kippenberg [1977], 68–99). Cf. D. Lutze, "Tributverhältnisse in einigen vorfeudalen Gesellschaften," *Caucasica-Mediterranea* 1980, 121–27; "Varianten der Produktionsweise in der griechischen Landwirtschaft der archaischen Periode," *Produktivkräfte und Gesellschaftsformationen in vorkapitalistischer Zeit*, ed. J. Herrmann and I. Sellnow (1982), 303–11.

much one from another as they do from chattel slavery.[4] That is why another solution, also one which many scholars have already considered,[5] is to use a formulation that offers the advantage of respecting the individuality of each differing form of exploitation while at the same time assigning them common points of reference. The formulation is "between free men and slaves" (*metaxu eleutheron kai doulon*), which adopts the terms used by Pollux, an Alexandrian Greek of the secondary century A.D. in his *Onomasticon*. (Pollux had himself borrowed the expression from the Hellenistic scholars.) It is used to label several social categories which were often lumped together as *douloi* but which also went by specific names: the Helots of the Lacedaemonians, the *Penestai* of the Thessalians, the *Clarotai* and the *Mnoitai* of the Cretans, the *Dorophoroi* of the Mariandynians, the *Gymnetes* of the Argives, the *Korynephoroi* of the Sicyonians—clearly not an exhaustive list.

But this representation of a comprehensive "spectrum" of social statuses ranging from liberty through to slavery[6] also presents certain drawbacks to the extent, first, that it takes as its points of reference two normative concepts ("liberty" and "slavery" in the Athenian sense) which are external to the reality that they are claimed to encompass; and, second, that its points of reference are limited to two, as if we were dealing with a homogeneous whole that can be expressed as a linear series. As has been pointed out, what is not viable is not the conceptual pair liberty-slavery itself, but the integration within a single category of statuses that belong to different places and different times.[7]

In order to mark the diversity of such statuses and at the same time their distinctness as a group in relation to chattel slavery, I suggest that we regard them as so many forms of "communal servitude," that is, a plurality of states of dependency which the ancient Greeks were apt to assimilate to chattel slavery but which are different from it essentially because they are constituted within a community framework rather than stemming from the misfortune of individuals torn from their own native collectivities. Whether it be a matter of intracommunity servitude (servitude within one community, for exam-

4. See the definition provided by M. I. Finley in his *Ancient Economy*, p. 69.

5. The success of this formula has been assured by two basic works, D. Lotze, *Metaxu eleutheron kai doulon* (1959), and M. I. Finley, "Between Slavery and Freedom," *Comparative Studies in Society and History* 6 (1964): 233–49.

6. This theme has been extensively developed by M. I. Finley, in particular in studies he produced during the 1960s.

7. Ducat, "Aspects de l'hilotisme," 23.

ple, as a result of debts) or intercommunity servitude (servitude of one community in relation to another, such as that of the Helots), the subjected individual does not cease to be regarded as belonging to a community, whether that of his exploiter or a different one. Highly significant in this respect is a prohibition which appears to have existed in all these cases, namely that against detaching an individual from the community and selling him or her beyond the State frontiers.

Intracommunity Servitude

Let us start by examining the simplest of the types of servitude which differ from chattel slavery (the simplest purely in the sense that it develops within the framework of a single community): servitude that results from an internal differentiation within the collectivity.

The reason Solon, at the beginning of the sixth century (as we have seen: p. 45), prohibits the acceptance of debtors' persons as security is that servitude for debts was the scourge that afflicted the Athens of his day. Our information comes, essentially, from three texts. The first is Aristotle's *Athenian Constitution* (2.2): "The poor themselves and also their wives and children were actually in slavery (*edouleuon*) to the rich; and they were called clients (*pelatai*) and sixth-part tenants (*hektemoroi*) (for that was the rent they paid for the rich man's land which they farmed, and the whole of the country was in a few hands) and if they ever failed to pay their rents, they themselves and their children were liable to arrest; and all borrowing was on the security of the debtors' persons down to the time of Solon." Our second text comes from Plutarch's *Life of Solon* (13.2): "All the common people were in debt (were *hypochreos*) to the rich. For they either tilled their land for them, paying them a sixth of the harvests (whence they were called *Hektemoroi* and Thetes) or else they pledged their persons for debts and could be seized by their creditors, some becoming slaves at home, and others being sold into foreign countries." Our last is a fragment from Solon's own *Elegies* (reproduced by Aristotle, *Athenian Constitution*, 12.4):

> But what did I leave unachieved, of all
> The ends for which I did unite the people?
> Whereof before the judgement seat of Time

The mighty mother of the Olympian gods,
Black Earth, would best bear witness, for 'twas I
Removed her many boundary posts implanted:
Ere then she was a slave but now is free.
And many sold away I did bring home
To god-built Athens, this one sold unjustly,
That other justly; others that had fled
From dire constraint of need, uttering no more
Their Attic tongue, so widely had they wandered,
And others suffering base slavery
Even here, trembling before their masters' humours,
I did set free.

These three texts overlap only partially and even contradict one another on some points—a fact that has given rise to endless controversies over details among modern historians, controversies which seem to me in many cases impossible to resolve.[8] Should the *hektemoroi* in fact be identified with the thetes (who, following Solon's reforms, were to constitute the lowest census class) and with the *pelatai* (a term which etymologically denotes "those who are close by" and which was later to be applied to the Roman "clients")? Why did the *hektemoroi* have to hand over one sixth (a much more likely proportion than five-sixths) of their harvests to the wealthy? In other words what was the "juridical" status of the land they cultivated? In what sense might these be called "slave" lands? Were they perhaps sold conditionally to the *hektemoroi*? If so, this might explain why they sometimes appear to belong to the *hektemoroi*, sometimes to the rich. Among those who could be reduced to slavery either on the spot or abroad, should not a distinction be made between *hektemoroi* who failed to fulfill their obligations and insolvent debtors? Does not the verb *douleuein*, as used in these texts, denote a lack of liberty far more than a particular form of slavery? And so we could continue. . . .

We must remember that there are two competing views of the process leading to servitude in pre-Solonian Athens. Modern historians were long content to set against a background of liberty the process of indebtedness described by Aristotle. Some have even simplified that picture; that is to say, they have assumed that a proportion of the peasants of Attica slipped from the status of free men into that of slaves (in the classical sense of the term) purely as a

8. See M. Sakellariou, *Colloque Besançon 1974*, 99–113; C. Mossé, "Comment s'élabore un mythe politique: Solon, 'père-fondateur' de la démocratie athénienne," *Annales*, 1979, 425–37.

result of economic forces that directly affected the conditions of their exploitation. As a result of land being divided up among a number of heirs upon a father's death, the productivity of the poorest would decline to less than a "vital minimum" level. The peasants would then run up debts to the wealthy and would soon find themselves obliged to surrender one sixth of their harvests. Meanwhile, the land would become covered with posts bearing witness to the obligations contracted by the owners. With their income thus reduced, the debtors would rapidly find themselves incapable of fulfilling their obligations and would be forced to fall even further into debt, now offering their own persons as security. Finally, when they fell behind with their repayments, they would be sold as slaves.

However, this type of explanation (of which there are many variants on points of detail) fails to account for some of our documentation, in which the process leading to servitude seems to have relatively little to do with running into debt. Let us distance ourselves from Aristotle, who had clearly read Solon's *Elegies* with the eyes of a fourth-century Athenian obsessed by the question of debts, and instead attempt, following Moses Finley,[9] to interpret the pre-Solonian crisis in the light of an overall analysis of the phenomenon of dependency. What becomes apparent is that, in archaic societies, control of the forces of production (the land and, even more important, those who cultivated it) and the establishment of particular social relationships are objectives considered more important than profit in the form of interest. In circumstances such as these, "debt" incurred between unequal parties serves rather to legitimate, to give material expression to, to provide a sanction for, and to codify a relation of dependency, rather than bring that relation into being. This means that the subjection of one of the parties may be a presupposition rather than a consequence of his indebtedness. In view of all this, we are bound to wonder whether it is legitimate to assume that, at the beginning of the evolution that culminated in the pre-Solonian crisis, there truly did exist free and independent peasants who, for a variety of reasons, became increasingly impoverished and fell into debt to the point where they found themselves forced to relinquish control of both their land and their persons. Should we not rather suppose that for many years in Attica there had already existed a class of members of the community—known as "those who stay close" (*pelatai*) and/or "sixth-portioners" (*hektemoroi*)—who, for

9. "La servitude pour dettes," *Revue Historique de Droit Français et Etranger*, 4th ser., 43 (1965): 159–84.

reasons that are not clear (but which do not appear to have anything to do with conquest) were forced into a form of subjection analogous to (but not so clearly defined as[10]) the form that affected, for example, the Helots of Laconia at this same period? Of course, this is not to deny that debt for purely economic reasons certainly did culminate, at the end of the seventh century, in a crisis, in which the dependent, and even a section of the free, peasantry was forced into a decline leading to chattel slavery. This brought about a dangerous deterioration in the community fabric which Solon, in quite exceptional historical circumstances, is supposed to have remedied by liberating the entire *demos* and importing a massive force of foreign slaves.

The decisions taken by Solon in Athens, however, should not lead us to conclude that throughout the Greek world citizens could not be reduced to servitude by their fellow countrymen, in particular for debt. We know of a number of such examples during the classical period, notably in Crete. In this region which, as we shall see (pp. 100–101), accommodated all kinds of dependants of native origin, the Gortyn code,[11] in about 460, mentions two categories of debt-bondsmen: the *katakeimenoi* (either free men who had pledged their own persons or slaves who had been offered as security), and the *nenikamenoi* (who had been condemned for debt by the courts). Both were in some respects still a part of the family and political structures, and their rights consequently fell between those of free men and those of slaves. They could be seized, but probably not in order to be sold abroad; they were awarded a portion of any fines imposed upon those who wronged them; and the slaves were not known by the same name as the master.

The best examples of debt-bondage come from Ptolemaic Egypt, although they have given rise to many discussions bearing as much on the precise nature of the sentences passed as on the circumstances in which they were applied. The first mention comes in 260 in Ptolemy II's statute relating to Syria and Phoenicia (PER 24552 gr), in which it was forbidden to purchase free natives (*laoi*) or to accept their persons as security, except where the director of revenues in Syria or Phoenicia had given permission for them to be used as security or for their persons to be seized. The exception is attested to

10. P. Vidal-Naquet, "Economie et société dans la Grèce ancienne: L'oeuvre de Moses I. Finley," *Archives Européenes de Sociologie* 6 (1965): 129: "Because there was no tradition of servitude through conquest, an Athenian peasant was much more Athenian than a Helot was Lacedaemonian."

11. See R. F. Willetts, *The Law Code of Gortyn* (1967); M. Bile, "Le vocabulaire des structures sociales dans les lois de Gortyne," *Verbum* 4 (1981): 11–45.

have applied to State debtors throughout the Ptolemaic kingdom and throughout its history. These could be sentenced to temporary servitude or even to be sold into permanent slavery. Where only private debts were involved, in contrast, although it is clear that failure to discharge them could occasion the physical seizure and imprisonment of the debtor, there is no evidence at all of this leading legally to true slavery (except, clearly, where it had been stipulated that the guilty party should be treated "as if it were a matter of royal business"). On the basis of many sources of evidence, admittedly all fairly ambiguous, some historians have in fact concluded that such a penalty, temporary or permanent, could be imposed by the courts right down to the beginning of the second century and continued to be applied in temporary form until the end of the Ptolemaic period.[12] Exemptions were made for certain special categories, however: citizens of Alexandria, for example, or those whose liberty was deemed necessary to the proper functioning of the royal economy. Furthermore, this type of "slave" was very seldom sold by the creditor and in any event, never outside Egypt. Other historians, in contrast, maintain that in such cases it was only a de facto servitude, taking the form of a contract for services, and no loss of liberty was implied (even if the victims did tend to be treated just as though they were slaves).[13] At least in the Eastern countries such as Egypt, where debt-bondage had been widespread in the past,[14] falling into debt in the Hellenistic period thus remained the source of numerous types of dependency, ranging from quasi-slavery to a limited commitment to perform services which retained all the formal characteristics of free labor.

The fact that in Hellenistic Egypt dependency frequently resulted from some contractual commitment sheds retrospective light for us on the free man's attitude to working for a wage in classical Athens.[15] Only with no other source of income and no alternative would he agree to such a course (unless it was a matter of serving the State or the gods, on public building sites). In particular, he was loath to place himself at the disposal of another for any length of time, as we know from a pasage in Xenophon's *Memorabilia* (2.8) in which Eutheros, who occasionally resigns himself to manual labor in return for a

---

12. I. Biezunska-Malowist, *L'esclavage dans l'Egypte gréco-romaine*, 1 (1974).

13. J. Modrzejewski, "Servitude pour dettes ou legs de créance?" *Recherches de Papyrologie* 2 (1962): 75–98.

14. For the Egypt of the Pharaohs see B. Menu, "Les rapports de dépendance en Egypte à l'époque saïte et perse," *Revue Historique de Droit Français et Etranger*, 4th ser., 55 (1977): 391–401.

15. Y. Garlan, "Le travail libre en Grèce ancienne," in *Non-Slave Labour in the Greco-Roman World*, ed. P. Garnsey, *Cambridge Philological Society*, Suppl. 6 (1980), 6–22.

wage, refuses to accept a permanent post as overseer, exclaiming that it would amount to "tolerating slavery." (Nor do we find any examples of free men working for wages as servants or as employees in artisan workshops in classical Athens). Why did the security of employment, nowadays considered so desirable, then seem so degrading? Free men appear to have feared that, by relinquishing the guarantee of freedom afforded by hiring out their labor on a temporary (daily?) basis, they might be reduced to the state of "client." To put it another way, it is as if contractual labor commitments ran the risk of being gradually transformed into habitual obligations of total commitment, with a more or less extra-economic basis. I do not think that such beliefs stemmed so much from the idea that this condition was contaminated by that of the slaves, who constituted the majority of those who did this type of work. Rather, they may be explained by the very nature of paid work in ancient Greece, as it is defined by, for example, Plato in *The Republic* (2.371e): wage-earners or *misthotoi* are those who sell "the use of their physical strength . . . , calling the price wages (*misthos*)." As Claude Mossé points out, the consequence of that definition is that "what they sell in return for a wage is not their labor, an abstract concept which can have a value set upon it only in a principally market-oriented system, but their body, or rather the physical strength that this body represents. In other words, they, free men, sell a part of themselves, thereby placing themselves in the kind of position of dependency which creates a relationship of service."[16] At this stage in human development, the worker was as yet incapable of selling himself as a pure unit of labor, something independent of himself; he consequently remained inseparable in his person from his labor.[17]

The degradation of free labor into dependent labor, which was detectable (but to a large degree unrecognized) in classical Athens, was accentuated in places such as Egypt where it was not contained by the polarization of social relations. In these circumstances it gave rise, in a process that was the reverse of affranchisement, to various forms of *paramone* that certainly fell in between liberty and slavery.

Intercommunity Servitude of the Helot Type

It is important both to compare and to contrast to this intracommunity servitude the forms of servitude I have described as inter-

16. "Les salariés à Athènes au IVᵉ siècle," *DHA* 2 (1976): 97–101, in particular 100.
17. In the famous chapter of the *Grundrisse* now generally known as the *Formen*, Marx studies how this "separation of free work from the objective conditions of its realization" came about.

community: those that result from the subjection of an alien community and constitute one of the more or less drastic solutions to the
interstate conflicts of the ancient world.[18] These solutions ranged
from the occasional looting foray into an enemy territory to the
extermination or dispersion of all inhabitants there and included
occasional or regular demands for tribute (of various kinds), in other
words, the imposition of an exploitative relationship through the
payment of tribute. Such a relationship had many points in common
with intercommunity servitude, as is proved by the use of the same
terms in both cases to refer to the surplus extorted (*phoros,* or even
suntaxis or *dasmos*)[19] and also by the use of the ambiguous label
perioikoi.[20] That word was generally used in Laconia to apply to the
inhabitants of the peripheral cities politically subject to Sparta, but
authors such as Plato, Isocrates, and Aristotle were prone to extend it
to all kinds of rural peoples reduced to servitude.

It is, however, not possible to extend this inquiry to take in the
whole of international life. My research is directed only toward
personalized (although not necessarily individualized) forms of exploitation. In the present work I am concerned only with such forms
as are directly employed within a single, (at least artificially) superior
community and which thus result from the personal status of those
involved. I shall therefore leave aside those implemented through
the mediation of two State systems which were separate (even if one
was necessarily subordinated to the other), quite independently (in
principle) from the forms of property and relations of production
which existed within each of the two communities.[21]

18. See Y. Garlan, *War in the Ancient World* (1975), 34–77, and more particularly the
interesting study by F. Gschnitzer, *Abhängige Orte im griechischen Altertum* (1958),
which, however, takes little account of the relations of exploitation.

19. I know of no general study of the terms relating to the surplus demanded of
communities or individuals. Confusion in the vocabulary relating to debt has also
been noted by J.-P. Olivier de Sardan, "Captifs ruraux et esclaves impériaux de
Sanghay," in C. Meillassoux, *L'esclavage dans l'Afrique précoloniale* (1975), 124: "The
reality of relations of production to the countryside cannot appear at the level of the
political superstructure, since the latter is connected not so much with the content of
internal social relations with the groups that it dominates as with those groups'
production of the surpluses which are indispensable to it."

20. For instance, we may wonder about the nature of the *perioikoi* who, in the same
way as citizens, sometimes initiated the decrees voted by certain Lycian towns: see M.
Wörrle, *Chiron* 8 (1978): 236–46.

21. The distinction has been clearly drawn in an illuminating article by A.-M.
Chazanov, "Les formes de dépendance des agriculteurs par rapport aux nomades
antiques des steppes eurasiatiques," *Colloque Besançon 1974,* 240–41 (cf. "Caractère de
l'esclavage chez les Scythes," *Rech. int. 1975,* 110–28). In fact, this dividing line was
probably ignored sometimes, and contaminations may have taken place between the
two systems: for example, in 427 the people of Lesbos were obliged to pay, instead of

Within this limited framework, let us begin by studying the serfs of the Helot type, that is to say, all those social categories Pollux situates in between liberty and slavery, as well as a few others that ancient authors often compare or assimilate to the Helots—rightly compare, but wrongly assimilate, since they are by no means identical on all points, as is immediately indicated by the wide variety of names applied to them. Some of these names are ethnic in character (the Thessalian *Penestai,* the Killyrians of Syracuse, and probably the Helots themselves). Others reflect their mode of work (the Cretan *Clarotai,* who are attached to a *kleros* or allotment of land), their obligations toward their master (the Mariandynian *Dorophoroi* or "gift-bearers"), or the conditions of their servitude (the Cretan *Mnoitai* who, etymologically, could be linked with the Homeric *dmoes*). Yet others emphasize that they do not belong to the military community of free men (the *Gymnetes* or "naked ones" of Argos, the *Korynephoroi* or "stave-bearers" of Sicyon). Finally, some have spatial or cultural connotations (the Cretan *Perioikoi,* the *Katonakophoroi* or "pelt wearers" of Sicyon, and the *Konipodes* or "dusty feet" of Epidaurus).

Helots were defined first as a native population.[22] But modern historians are even less in agreement among themselves than the ancient historians when it comes to being precise about their ethnic origin and the circumstances in which they were reduced to servitude. They are generally believed to be peoples, either free or already in servitude, established in Laconia in the Mycenaean period before the arrival (toward the end of the second millennium) of the Dorian invaders, who included the Spartans. But some scholars regard them as Dorians or as a mixture of Dorians and pre-Dorians, which would explain why, in the classical period, they were distinguished from the Spartans neither by their language nor by their religion. As for the circumstances in which they were reduced to servitude, the hypothesis of conquest predominates. It was first introduced by Hellanicus of Lesbos at the end of the fifth century

tribute, two minae per year to each of the three thousand Athenians manning the garrison on the island. The sum was to be taken from the produce of the three thousand allotments of land that they continued to cultivate themselves, under conditions about which nothing is known (Thuc. 3. 50. 2; cf. P. Gauthier, "Les Clérouques de Lesbos et la colonisation athénienne au Ve siècle," *REG* 79 [1966]: 64–88; E. Erxleben, "Die Kleruchien auf Euboa und Lesbos und die Methoden der attischen Herrschaft im 5. Jh.," *Klio* 57 [1975]: 83–100).

22. See P. Oliva, *Sparta and Her Social Problems* (1971); "Heloten und Spartaner," *Index* 10 (1981): 43–54; P. Cartledge, *Sparta and Laconia* (1979), 160–77; Ducat, "Aspects de l'hilotisme."

(prompted by the contemporary revolts or by the fashionable slaveholding theories of the day), and it presents Helotism as the result not so much of the Dorian invasion itself as of the expansion of the Spartan city after (presumably many years after) its foundation, that is, between the tenth century and the end of the eighth. This theory incidentally makes it possible to account for the name, Helots, which is supposed to derive from that of the town of Helos, held to be the center of the native resistance, and also to explain the presence of the *perioikoi* communities situated on the outskirts of Spartan territory. The *perioikoi* are supposed to have obtained from their conquerors the right to continue to lead an autonomous existence under the latter's political supervision. We are told, however, by a contemporary of Hellanikos, Antiochus of Syracuse, that those Lacedaemonians who out of cowardice refused to fight in the first Messenian War in about 725 "were adjudged slaves and were named Helots" (Strabo, 6.3.2). Is this an altogether different tradition, presenting Helotism as the result of an internal evolution in the civic community or is it, in this text, simply a matter of reducing a number of bad citizens to a preexisting condition?[23] Whichever of the two solutions is favored, it remains possible, despite the absence of any ancient evidence, to maintain either that Helotism emerged from a process (perhaps an economic process) of social differentiation or (reconciling the two views) that it was initially the product of conquest but later developed more fully as the result of an internal process. . . . Of these two traditions, the first has been and still is the more successful because it is altogether in line with what is known of the origin of other serfs of the Helot type and also of one category of Helots in particular, those domiciled in Messenia. In the case of the latter, it is quite clear that it was following a first and then a second war (in about 675?) that the inhabitants of the central plain, who were if not Dorians at least invaders related to them, were in their turn reduced to servitude by the Spartans.

The Helots lived in family groups on the parcels of land (*kleroi*) which were allocated to the Spartiates or Equals, the citizens with full-rights, whose numbers decreased over the centuries from about ten thousand to a few hundred. The Helots' principal obligation was to hand over to the "master" of the allotment they farmed a propor-

23. P. Vidal-Naquet, "Réflexions sur l'historiographie grecque de l'esclavage," *Colloque Besançon 1971*, 32–36 (=*The Black Hunter* [1986], 168–89); *contra*, P. Lévêque, *Colloque Besançon 1974*, 115.

tion of the harvests, usually know as *apophora*. According to the poet Tyrtaeus, who lived at the time of the second Messenian War, this amounted to one half of the produce; according to Plutarch (*Lycurgus*, 8.7), it consisted of a fixed quantity of cereals "with a proportionate amount of fruit and vegetables," that is, it was an amount of dues calculated per head of the Spartans, not the Helots, and could not be exceeded with impunity. The second of these possibilities seems the more likely, or perhaps both situations obtained at different times or in different localities. In either case, the Helots were allowed to keep the remainder of the harvests for themselves and could consequently amass a certain personal fortune, probably transferable to their heirs, while the Equals, for their part, (without—in principle, at least—bothering to obtain the maximum profit possible from their estates) were thus provided with whatever they needed to feed their families and could devote themselves solely to war and politics. Such a system presupposes the granting of allotments of civic land, and we do not know whether this was practiced or what forms it may have taken before the famous reforms attributed to Lycurgus. Even these are difficult to date between the conventionally accepted mid-eighth century and the mid-sixth century, the point at which the Spartan constitution was definitively established.

The Helots were also encumbered with other obligations, some toward their masters, whose personal servants they were also expected to be, even in the town of Sparta itself, and for whose profit they had to work as artisans and in trade. Alternatively, they might be obliged to work for the State: in workshops and on public building projects, as policemen or as haulers of heavy equipment to the army, perhaps also in magistrates' "offices" as well as by discharging special duties in the event of a king's funeral. If they were in a position to fulfill such obligations as these, it follows that they cannot have been too closely bound to the land.

On whom exactly were they dependent? Were they regarded as the private property of those who held the allotments of land or as the collective property of the Spartan community? Many texts testify to a personal link between the master and his Helots. According to Pausanias (3.20.6), though, they were "the slaves of the Lacedaemonian State." Strabo is less categorical (8.5.4): he believes they were considered "State slaves, in a way." It was certainly as members of the civic community that Spartans on the one hand qualified for the allotment of land to which the Helots were attached and, on the other, dominated the subject collectivity to which they belonged.

This double relationship of ownership may be expressed as fol-lows:[24]

In circumstances such as these, individual property could not be considered private property. It was inevitably encumbered by community obligations. Each Spartan was expected to hold his Helots at the disposal of the State or even of any other member of the community who ran into serious difficulties. Equally, the State alone was empowered to alter the status of a Helot, to affranchise him, usually as a reward for services rendered to the community, by allowing him to enter one or other of the many intermediary categories about whose particular privileges and duties we know very little:[25] the *aphetai* (the "liberated" ones), the *adespotoi* ("those without masters"), the *erukteres* (some kind of policemen?), the *desposionautai* (connected with the navy) and, above all, the *neodamodeis* (positioned in the garrisons set up along the borders of the territory and required to serve as hoplites alongside the Equals, but without sharing their political rights). It also seems likely that the *mothakes* or *mothones* included not only the bastards of Spartiates and the children of *hypomeiones* (free men with no *kleros* or political rights) but also children born from a Spartan and a Helot woman: these young men were educated alongside the young Spartans and thus acceded to certain political and military functions when, as adults, they entered the category of the *hypomeiones*. (At the end of the fifth century, it seems that some of their number were even recruited as *harmostai*, set in command of garrisons established outside the State.) Meanwhile, from the other point of view, the status of a Helot stemmed from his dependence on a *kleros* and his membership of one of the native communities subject to the Spartans. Consequently, by virtue of the, as it were, contract concluded at the moment of their collective reduction to servitude, they could not pass from one master to another nor could they be sold outside the State, for once beyond its frontiers they would automatically be regarded as free.

24. Ducat, "Aspects de l'hilotisme," 16.
25. As well as Oliva, *Sparta*, 163–79, see U. Cozzoli, "Sparta e l'affrancamento degli iloti nel V e nel IV secolo," *Miscellanea Greca e Romana* 6 (1978): 213–32; G. B Bruni, "Mothakes, neodamodeis, Brasideioi," *Colloque Bressanone 1976*, 21–31; D. Mendels, "Sparta in Teles' *Peri phugès*," *Eranos* 77 (1979): 111–15.

A number of other social categories that Pollux situates in between liberty and slavery are also to be found in these Dorian areas. So far as we can judge, however, their status appears to have differed somewhat from that of the Helots. In Sicyon,[26] we should perhaps add the *katonakophoroi* (those who wear sheepskins") to the *korynephoroi* mentioned by Pollux. Theopompus (Athenaeus, 6.271d) describes the *katonakophoroi* as "*douloi* who are analogous to the *epeunaktoi*" (the Helots who are supposed, during the Messenian wars, to have taken the place of the dead husbands of Spartan women and to have been made citizens for doing so); in other words, he knew very little about them. In sixth-century Megara, there was also a group of individuals clad in animal-skins who, to the disgust of the poet Theognis, had contrived to rise to the ranks of the "good ones" (1.58–59). At Epidaurus, the status of the *konipodes* is not much illuminated by a text of Plutarch's (*Aet. gr.*, 1), which states that they constituted the category that cultivated the fields of the citizens. The *Gymnetes* of Argos are equally mysterious.[27] It is not known whether they should be identified with the inferior classes referred to as *douloi* by Herodotus (6.83) and as *perioikoi* by Aristotle (*Politics*, 1303a, 7). These constituted the group to whom the citizens, after their serious defeat at the hands of Cleomenes I of Sparta in the late sixth or early fifth century, reluctantly entrusted the government on a temporary basis, until such time as the sons of the dead citizens became old enough to assume power. From its foundation in 426 until its dissolution in 394, the Spartan colony of Trachinian Heraclea also imposed a status similar to Helotism upon a pre-Greek people of central Greece, the Kilikranes, whose operations of brigandage Heracles was said to have repressed in times past.[28]

In Crete, finally, despite the relative abundance of our documentation, the situation remains extremely confused. The most ancient relevant text is a long inscription from the town of Gortyn, dating from about 460.[29] It consists of a collection of laws relating to the status of persons and possessions and is known as the Gortyn code, despite the fact that it is by no means systematic. Beneath the free men, some of whom enjoy full civic rights, some of whom do not, we

26. D. Whitehead, "The Serfs of Sicyon," *Liverpool Classical Monthly* 6 (1981): 37–41.

27. D. Lotze, "Zur Verfassung von Argos nach der Schlacht bei Sepeia," *Chiron* 1 (1971): 95–109.

28. D. Asheri, "Eracle, Eraclea e i Cylicranes: Mitologia e decolonizzazione nella Grecia del IV a.c.," *Ancient Society* 6 (1975): 33–50.

29. See Willetts, *Law Code*.

find two lower categories: on the one hand debt-bondsmen, whom I have already mentioned, on the other *douloi* and *oiketes* whom it seems reasonable to identify, even if it is not clear why they should be known by two different names.[30] These "slaves," who could be bought and sold, belonged to a master (*pastas*) who carried civil responsibility for their crimes and could dispose of their children as he saw fit. But they also enjoyed considerable privilege: they could take the oath to plead their own own cause in a court of law; they could enter into a more or less legal marriage with a spouse of equal or superior status (their children being recognized as free if only the mother was a slave); they could challenge any arbitrary moves by their master with their own rights of "possession" over the house in which they lived, their herds, and probably other goods of a similar kind. In about 330, Aristotle, in his *Politics* (1264a, 21–22) also noted the privileged situation that the Cretan "slaves" enjoyed. According to him, they differed from free men only insofar as they were prohibited from frequenting gymnasia and from owning weapons. It is, however, none too clear exactly who these "slaves" were. The literary sources from the fourth century onward provide us with a complex catalog which (as well as "subject" communities and servants "bought for money") includes: *Mnoitai*, who appear to have been native peoples, reduced collectively to servitude, who worked on the land or in the public services; *Amphamiotai* or *Aphamiotai*, apparently peasants of native extraction who belonged privately to citizens who possessed a land-holding (*apamia*), that is, a kind of allotment (*klaros*) and who may on that account also have been called *Clarotai*.[31] It was probably either one or both of these last categories that Aristotle described as *perioikoi* (whom he assimilated to the Helots of Sparta),[32] while other authors compare the *perioikoi* either to the *Mnoitai* or to the *Amphamiotai-Clarotai*. In fact there is reason enough to wonder whether the richness of the nomenclature might not to a large extent be explained simply by historical evolution and the wide range of local variations! In any case, Aristotle mentions only one type of serf when he compares the communal meals of

30. M. I. Finley, "The Servile Statuses of Ancient Greece," *Revue Internationale des Droits de l'Antiquité*, 3d ser., 7 (1960): 168–69; *contra* Willetts, *Law Code*; "The Servile System of Ancient Crete: A Reappraisal of the Evidence," *Geras G. Thomson* (1963), 257–71; *Ancient Crete: Social History* (1965), 95–109; Bile, "Vocabulaire"; H. van Effenterre, "Le droit et la langue à propos du code de Gortyne," *Symposion 1979* (1981): 115–25.

31. H. van Effenterre, "Terminologie et formes de dépendance en Crète," *Rayonnement grec: Hommages à Ch. Delvoye* (1982), 35–44.

32. J. A. D. Larson, "Perioeci in Crete," *CPhil* 31 (1936): 11ff.

Sparta to those of Crete: in Crete "the system is more communal, for out of all the crops and cattle produced from the public lands, and the tributes paid by the *perioikoi*, one part is assigned for the worship of the gods and the maintenance of the public services, and the other for the public mess-tables (*syssitia*), so that all the citizens are maintained from the common funds, women and children as well as men" (*Politics*, 1272a, 17–21). As well as these, situated in between the serfs and the citizens with full rights, we should mention the *apetairoi*, that is, all those who, although in no sense slaves, were for one reason or another excluded from the *hetairia* and in particular from the communal meals.

Outside the Dorian cities, the same phenomenon is to be found in central Greece. According to the Galaxidi bronze, the allotments of land to the colonists installed in the early fifth century in western Locris, at Naupactus, by the eastern Locrians were peopled by *woikiatai*.[33] The *Penestai* of Thessaly, above all, were frequently associated with the Helots.[34] Like the latter, they were believed to be the descendants of a local people of Achaean origin (as were the neighboring *Magnetai* and *Perrhaeboi*) who had been defeated around the end of the second millennium by a northwestern Greek tribe from Thesprotie, near Epirus. Although the ancient writers thought that the term *peneste* was derived either from the adjective *penes*, meaning "poor," or from the verb *menein*, meaning "to remain," today it is believed, rather, to be an Illyrian word denoting a people reduced to servitude (on account of the Illyrian suffix *-st-* and the existence of an Illyrian tribe known as the *Apenestai*). According to Archemachus (Athenaeus, 6.264ab), the natives (whom he believed to be Boeotians) "gave themselves up as slaves (*douleuein*) to the Thessalians according to a stipulation by which the latter were neither to carry them out of the country nor to put them to death, while they themselves were to till the land for the Thessalians and render them the contributions due." Their condition thus certainly appears to have been analogous to that of the Helots: they enjoyed certain guarantees; they were responsible for cultivating the fields, which were divided into vast allotments; and they handed over a proportion of their produce—which implies that they could themselves

33. P. Vidal-Naquet, "L'esclavage et gynécocratie dans la tradition, le mythe, l'utopie," *Recherches sur les structures sociales dans l'Antiquité classique* (1970), 71 (=*The Black Hunter* [1986], 213).

34. I. A. Sisova, "The status of the *Penestai*" (in Russian), *Vestnik Drevnei Istorii* (1975), no. 3:39–57; J. N. Corvisier, "A mi-chemin entre l'esclavage et la liberté, un cas peu connu: Les Pénestes thessaliens," *Information Historique* 43 (1981): 115–18.

dispose freely of the remainder and must have enjoyed some proprietorial rights over movable goods. (Archemachus even reports that, at a no doubt quite late date, many *Penestai* were more wealthy than their masters.) Some (known specifically as *latreis?*)[35] also performed domestic services for which they received a payment. The main difference between them and the Helots must have resulted from the peculiar sociopolitical situation in Thessaly. There, the existence of huge estates belonging to a number of "clans," the absence of any centralized State, and the competition for power among rival aristocrats were all factors from which the *Penestai* no doubt profited. They were not faced with such a unified and well-organized body of masters as that of the Spartans.

The Tribute-Paying Serfs in the Colonies

The great movement of archaic colonization (eighth to sixth centuries) also saw the introduction of analogous systems in a number of Greek cities established in immediate proximity with the "barbarian" world.

Herodotus (7.155) tells us that in Syracuse, founded by Corinth around 733, the *gamoroi,* or large landowners, in the early fifth century had slaves who were called Killyrians (or, according to later lexicographers, Kallikyrians or Killikyrians). They were supposed to outnumber their masters by far.[36] In other towns of Sicily (Gela) and in Magna Graecia (at Tarentum, Sybaris, and Epizephyrian Locris), similar rural slaves also probably existed, although nothing formally attests to their presence.[37]

A few decades after the foundation, in about 560, of the Boeotian-Megarian colony of Heraclea Pontica, on the Anatolian coast, a little to the northeast of the Bosphorus,[38] its inhabitants similarly intro-

35. Sisova, "Status," 48–50; see also G. Steinmayr, "Sviluppi semantici della base *latro* in Grecia e in Roma," *Atti Acad. Verona* (1955–56), 151–63.

36. I. S. Sifman, "Slavery in Sicily and Magna Graecia" (in Russian), *Escl. périph.*, 222–24; E. D. Frolov, "The *Gamoroi* and the Killyrians" (in Russian), *Vestnik Drevnei Istorii* (1982), no. 1:27–41.

37. E. Lepore, "Geografia del modo di produzione schiavistico e modi residui in Italia meridionale," in *Società romana e produzione schiavistica*, ed. A. Giardina and A. Schiavone, 1 (1981), 79–85.

38. A. A. Nejchardt, "Slavery in the Greek towns of the southern coast of the Black Sea" (in Russian), *Escl. périph.*, 135–48; D. Asheri, "Ueber die Frühgeschichte von Herakleia Pontike," *Forsch. an der Nordküste Kleinasiens* 1 (1972): 17–23; S. M. Burstein, "A Political History of Heraclea Pontica to 281 B.C." (diss., Univ. of Calif., 1972), in particular 6–30; "Heraclea Pontica: The City and Subjects," *Ancient World* 2 (1979):

duced a "contract" of servitude (whether by force or not is not known) with the neighboring people, the Mariandynians (of more or less Thracian origin). According to the Stoic Poseidonius, the Mariandynians "promised to serve them continually so long as the Heracleots provided for their needs, though they stipulated in addition that there should be no selling of any of them beyond the Heracleot territory but that they should stay right in their own territory" (Athenaeus, 6.263d). According to Callistratus, followed by Pollux, these were the people who "were called tribute-bearers (*dorophoroi*), to take away the sting in the term slave (*oiketai*)" (Athenaeus, 6.263e) and to whom Aristotle applies the name *perioikoi* which, as we have seen, he also often uses to refer to rural peoples reduced to servitude (*Politics*, 1327b, 12).

Heraclea was not the only Greek colony in the Black Sea region to use an agricultural labor force of this type.[39] According to the historian Phylarchus, who lived around the end of the the third century, "the Byzantians exercised mastery over the Bithynians as the Spartans did over the Helots" (Athenaeus, 6.271bc). These are probably the same Bithynians who are referred to as *laoi* in a text of Polybius' (4.52.7) reporting on one of the clauses of the treaty concluded in 220 between the city of Byzantium and King Prusias of Bithynia. It prescribed that Prusias "is to give up to the Byzantines the lands, the fortresses, the people, and the slaves (*laoi*) taken from the enemy, free from ransom." In a decree from Olbia of about 230 in honor of Protogenes (*Syll.*[3] 495), we are told that the Galatians have destroyed the entire rural *oiketeia* (a term which is elsewhere applied to Cretan slaves). A decree from Istros at the beginning of the second century, in honor of Agathocles[40] tells us that when the city was being attacked by enemies who were also laying waste the surrounding countryside, this benefactor, who had been elected as *strategos* with discretionary powers, managed to set up a force of volunteers recruited from among both the citizens and the "barbarians" who had come to the city to shelter from the enemy threat. In times of peace, those "barbarians" were very likely employed in cultivating the territory. There must have existed a dependent peas-

25–28; A. Avram, "Bemerkungen zu den Mariandynern von Herakleia am Pontus," *Studii Classici* 22 (1984): 19–28.

39. D. P. Kallistov, "Slavery in the north of the Black Sea, V–IIIth centuries B.C." (in Russian), *Escl. périph.*, 193–221; and above all D. M. Pippidi, "Le problème de la main-d'oeuvre agricole dans les colonies grecques de la mer noire," *Problèmes de la terre en Grèce ancienne*, ed. M. I. Finley (1973), 63–82.

40. L. Moretti, *Iscrizioni storiche ellenistiche*, 2 (1976), no.131.

antry in the kingdom of the Bosphorus too (fifth to fourth centuries). As we shall see below (p. 189), this was probably the group responsible for the temporary success of the revolt led by Saumacus against Pairisades V, in the last decade of the second century: alongside Scythians, we here find Tauri, who are referred to as *paroikoi* (a term close to *perioikoi*). None of these texts provides grounds for certainty; but on the other hand there are none that attest the existence of large numbers of chattel slaves engaged in agriculture in these Greek colonies. The colonists probably did not introduce a new system; the more or less Hellenized indigenous societies of these border lands were familiar with similar modes of exploitation: for example, tributary relationships also existed between the various Scythian tribes.[41] According to Theopompus (Athenaeus, 10.443bc), an Illyrian people known as the Ardians owned "300,000 bondsmen (*prospelatai*) who are like Helots";[42] according to Agatarchides of Cnidus (Athenaeus, 6.272d), the Dardani, another Illyrian people, had at their disposal a host of "slave" cultivators who must in reality have been dependants of some kind, since they followed their masters into battle (see below, p. 175), and the *oiketai* of the Dacians were probably in a similar position (*Suda*, IV, p. 517 Adler).[43]

It is in the East that we can observe most clearly the correlation between indigenous social structures and the nonslave (in the Athenian sense) forms of exploitation which the Greek colonists adopted overseas, at least for the cultivation of their territories.

The Greek presence on the western and, to some extent, southern coasts of Anatolia was essentially the result of an extensive and lengthy migration of Aeolians, Ionians, and Dorians, which took place around 1,000 B.C. From the archaic period on, the cities of Asia enjoyed a great prosperity that stemmed largely from the use made of chattel slaves. But it is clear that they also derived part of their agricultural revenue from subjected local peoples.[44] One example, in Caria, are the Leleges, said to be the earliest inhabitants of the

41. Chazanov, "Formes de dépendance."

42. Some modern historians believe that it was, rather, the Autariates who were concerned: see A. Mocsy, "Zu Theopompos fr. 39–40," *Rivista Storia dell' Antichità* 2 (1972): 13–16. The tradition is rejected, in my opinion without much justification, by P. Cabanes, *L'Epire de la mort de Pyrrhos à la conquête romaine* (1976), 481–85.

43. D. M. Pippidi, "A propos de l'esclavage chez les Daces," *Contributii la istoria veche a Romậniei* (1967), 519–23.

44. E. S. Golubcova, "Sklaverer und Abhängigkeit im hellenistischen Kleinasiens," in T. V. Blavatskaja, E. S. Golubcova, and A. I. Pavloskaja, *Slaves in the Hellenistic states in the third to first centuries B.C.* (in Russian, 1969; in German *Die Sklaverei im hellenistichen Staaten im 3.–1. Jh.v. Chr.*, 1972), 107–70; P. Debord, "Populations rurales de l'Anatolie gréco-romaine," *Colloque Gargano 1975*, 43–69.

area. In his treatise *On the Carians and the Leleges*, Philip of The-angela, "after giving an account of the Lacedaemonian Helots and the Thessalian penestae, says that the Carians have used the Leleges as slaves (*oiketai*) both in times past and today" (that is, around the mid-fourth century) (Athenaeus, 6.271b). Elsewhere we find more or less clear indications of an analogous situation: for example at Cyzicus which, according to Strabo (12.8.10), was surrounded by Doliones and Mydonians; at Tralles, where the Greeks appear to have subjugated the Leleges and Minyae (Plutarch, *Quaestiones Graecae*, 46); perhaps also at Colophon at the end of the seventh century, where the civic body was essentially composed of large landowners; at Teos, where the citizens seem to have included owners of village properties as well as of farms (*Syll.*[3], 344); and above all at Miletus where, according to Heraclides of Pontus (Athe-naeus 12.542ab), men of "the populace" (*demota*), known as Gergi-thes, rose in revolt against the wealthy in the archaic period. These Gergithes were probably indigenous peasants since theirs is also the name of a locality and of a barbarian tribe in the Troad. The reason there is no trace of them in the classical period may be that after the town was captured by the Persians in 494, the mountainous region of the territory was handed over to the Carians of Pedasa. Finally, some inscriptions provide information on the rural dependants of Priene and Zela. A decree issued by the Prienians in 333 grants a number of privileges to Megabyzes of Ephesus but withholds the right "to acquire landed property belonging to the Pedians" (*Syll.*[3], 282). These Pedians are also mentioned in a decree from Priene and two letters from Lysimachus dating from a little before 285, on the subject of attacks launched against the farms in the territory by Pedians in alliance with the people of Magnesia-on-the-Meander, and probably also in Alexander the Great's edict concerning his appropriation of the territory of the Pedians.[45] A decree from Zela passed in about 334–333 relates to an inquiry into public land-holdings, with the exception of those for which the Phrygian tenants paid a tribute (*Syll.*[3], 279), and in another inscription (*SGDI* 5533) there is a mention of a newly created citizen who had been given *laoi* with dwellings, as well as a *kleros* and a half, a house, a garden, and other privileges.

It thus seems that, even before the Macedonian conquest and despite the Persian interventions that long weighed upon them, the

---

45. S. M. Sherwin-White, "Ancient Archives: The Edict of Alexander to Priene, a Reappraisal," *JHS* 105 (1985): 69–89.

Greek cities of Asia Minor maintained with their barbarian neighbors relations of various kinds. Their variety depended on the reciprocal positions of the parties involved, and their capacity to expand or to resist expansion, the historical circumstances, and the relationships of power that grew out of these. At times the indigenous tribes managed to remain independent from the Greek cities, at others they found themselves forced into subjection. In the latter case, they generally appear to have preserved their own traditional political structures while, from an economic point of view, they retained the use of their own land in return for the payment of tribute. The Greeks seem to have made no attempt to assimilate them; either they did not want to or else they found it impossible to impose upon these indigenous peoples a mode of subjection more in line with those that prevailed in Greece itself. It is significant in this respect that in Rhodes most of the chattel slaves whose ethnic origin is known from the funerary inscriptions came from Asiatic regions which did not belong to Rhodes' *"peraea"* (i.e., to its possessions on the neighboring mainland).[46] So it was that a different mode of exploitation, of an essentially tributary nature, was maintained, a mode of exploitation which more closely resembled that which, in the Greek world, a victorious city imposed upon a defeated one than it resembled the kind suffered by slaves of the Athenian or Helot type.

The Laoi *of the Hellenistic Kingdoms of the East*

In his last letter addressed to King Philip of Macedon, the Athenian orator Isocrates, anxious to resolve the social crisis threatening Greece, urged Philip to invade Asia and "force the barbarians to become the Helots of the Greeks" (3.5). As it turned out, Alexander and those who succeeded him at the head of the various kingdoms born from the division of his empire made no attempt at all to extend Helotism in the strict sense of the term to the collection of territories conquered in the East, nor did they systematically endeavor to turn the natives into chattel slaves. They probably did neither for the excellent reason that another mode of production had already long been in operation there, ensuring efficient exploitation of the peasant masses by other means, even if these did present some sim-

46. An observation made by M. Rostovtzeff, *Economic and Social History of the Hellenistic World* (1941), 2: 691.

ilarities with Helotism. The Greek conquerors took over the system, more or less respecting the position of the preexisting social elites, and it continued to survive after their domination ended.[47] This is the mode of production Marxist historians call "Asiatic": the surplus was produced by indigenous communities which were theoretically free (at any rate the Greeks never referred to them as "slaves"), with relatively little social differentiation, and which lived to some extent self-sufficient lives on land recognized as their property to pass on to their heirs. The surplus was collected in the form of taxes through the intermediary of the State apparatus, to the profit of the "despot," who represented the "ruling community," and the social elite under him (usually recruited on an ethnic basis).[48]

In the documentation relating to the Seleucid empire of Asia Minor,[49] mention is sometimes made of *laoi*[50] and of *laoi basilikoi* (royal). The references occur essentially in three inscriptions concerned with land ceded by the sovereigns. The first consists of a correspondence in about 275 between Antiochus I and Meleagros, a *strategos* of the satrapy of the Hellespont, and this is followed by a letter from Meleagros to the city of Ilium, on the subject of a concession of estates made to a certain Aristodikes of Assos, amounting to a total area of over 300 hectares, in the vicinity of a place called Petra. The passage runs as follows: "As for the *laoi basilikoi* of the neighborhood in which Petra is situated, if they wish to live in Petra for reasons of security, we have ordered Aristodikes to allow them to do so." What the stipulation seems to imply is that these were the *laoi basilikoi* responsible for cultivating the royal land remaining in the

47. J. Wolski, "Les relations de Justin et de Plutarch sur les esclaves et la population dépendante dans l'empire parthe," *Iranica Antiqua* 18 (1983): 145–57.

48. See above, p. 5.

49. On the subject of the Seleucid empire, see the essential work of H. Kreissig, *Wirtschaft und Gesellschaft im Seleukidenreich* (1978), and also his numerous preparatory articles; also the following articles by P. Briant: "Remarques sur *laoi* et esclaves ruraux en Asie Mineure hellénistique," *Colloque Besançon 1971*, 193–133; "Villages et communautés villageoises d'Asie achéménide et hellénistique," *Journal of the Economic and Social History of the Orient* 18 (1975): 165–88; "Colonisation hellénistique et populations indigènes," *Klio* 60 (1978): 57–92; "Contrainte militaire, dépendance rurale et exploitation des territoires en Asie achéménide," *Colloque Camerino 1978*, 48–98; review article on H. Kreissig's book in *Klio* 62 (1980): 577–82 (articles collected in *Rois, tributs et paysans* [1982]). See also, in the *Colloques Besançon 1972* and *1973*, reflective studies by T. Alfieri and M.-A. Levi (and also the latter's work *Nè liberi nè schiavi* [1976]); M. Corsaro, "Le forme di dipendenza nella *chora* del re e in quella cittadina dell'Asia minore ellenistica," *Modes de contact et processus de transformation dans les sociétés anciennes* (1983), 523–47.

50. On this ancient Greek word, see the articles by J. Harmatta and E. C. Welskopf in *Soziale Typenbegriffe* 3 (1981): 156–62 and 163–92.

Petra region and that, living on the allotments ceded to Aristodikes, there must have been other *laoi* whose future it was not necessary to mention since the land transaction settled it automatically. The latter were no doubt subsequently known simply as *laoi* like those who are mentioned in a reference to a sale made in 254–253 by Antiochus II to the former queen Laodike: "We have sold to Laodike the village of Pannoukome, the manor (*baris*) and the land attached to the village . . . , as well as the dwellings connected with this land and the *laoi* which belonged to them, together with all their possessions and the revenue for the fifty-ninth year, for the sum of thirty talents of silver—and also the *laoi* who are natives of the village but have emigrated to other places." So the *laoi* involved in this sale were grouped in villages and family holdings, enjoyed a certain right of possession over some goods, and brought in an income for their "owner." Their condition and status do not appear to have been affected by their ceasing to belong to the royal estate and passing into the hands of a private individual. The third inscription, engraved in the temple of Artemis at Sardis, provides us with a brief description of the properties given to Mnesimachus by the king Antigonus the One-eyed at the end of the fourth century, estates that were used, around 200, as security for a loan contracted from the commissioners of the temple. These properties, situated in the vicinity of Sardis, included a number of villages and allotments as well as a few slaves (oiketai) and, above all, *laoi* who paid Mnesimachus "with tribute of silver and services," part of which was handed on to the tax authorities. In some of these cases, provision was made for the beneficiary of the concession to "assign" it to a neighboring city, an arrangement that must have involved advantages and guarantees, although we know nothing about them.

Valuable though it is, this documentation remains too sketchy—given the complexity of the problem—to avoid giving rise to many difficulties of interpretation. Thus, one wonders about the real content of these royal concessions. Did they in principle include both the land and its personnel but in practice boil down simply to its income? Still more serious is the tricky question of the diffusion of this system of exploitation. There were many indigenous "nations" in Asia Minor which either effectively eluded royal control or else had secured themselves autonomy and even exemption from the payment of tribute. We know nothing at all of their relations of production and very little more about a number of more or less Hellenized border regions except that the presence of *laoi* is attested. One example is the Caucasian kingdom of Iberia, where the *laoi* lived in rural communities, paying royal taxes and, according to Strabo (11.3.6), performing "all the services that pertain to human livelihood."[51] In some cases we find villagers acceding to the status of *paroikoi* or *katoikoi* or even voting on decrees in the same way as citizens.[52] It is difficult to conceive how such people could notwithstanding have been ceded as property or sold. And what of the rest of Hellenistic Asia? Peasant dependency, a legacy of the Persian domination or even earlier periods, certainly existed in respect to the king, the aristocracy, and particular towns and temples, and it may even have been reinforced locally, following the Greek occupation, in some mountainous or semi-deserted regions;[53] but in what forms and what proportions? Virtually our only source of information is an inscription of the late third century attesting the presence of *laoi* on a royal estate ceded to Ptolemaius, a *strategos* of Syria and Phoenicia.[54]

In about 261, when these provinces were under Egyptian control, a decree of King Ptolemy II Philadelphus (mentioned above, p. 91) also shows that *laoi*, described as "free," lived here: they could not legally be reduced to slavery except by the State (for failure to pay farm dues) although, despite royal interdictions, the Greek colonists did buy them or accept them as security so as to turn them into bondsmen. In the same period, *laoi* whose difference from those mentioned above is hard to determine are also to be found in Egypt proper, mentioned in the papyri of Zeno and, later on, in the second century, for example, also in the village of Kerkeosiris. They constituted a category of royal peasants (*basilikoi georgoi*) who, either individually or collectively, were tenant farmers on royal land (sometimes ceded as a "gift" to dignitaries such as Zeno's employer, the minister Apollonius). As members of a village community, they enjoyed a relative measure of autonomy and security, although they did not rank as notables.[55] Claude Orrieux writes: "It is tempting to see the *laoi* as peasants who benefited from the royal protection

51. O. Lordkipanidze, "La Géorgie à l'époque hellénistique," *DHA* 9 (1983): 201–2.
52. See M. Wörrle, "Antiochos I, Achaios der Aeltere und die Galater: Eine neue Inschrift in Denizli," *Chiron* 5 (1975): 59–87.
53. P. Leriche, *Colloque Besançon 1974*, 223–27.
54. Y. H. Landau, "A Greek Inscription Found near Hefzibah," *Israel Exploration Journal* 16 (1966): 54–70; T. Fischer, "Zur Seleukideninschrift von Hefzibah," *ZPE* 33 (1979): 131–38; J. M. Bertrand, "Sur l'inscription de Hefzibah," *ZPE* 46 (1982): 167–74.
55. As is believed by C. Vandersleyen, "Le mot *laos* dans la langue des papyrus grecs," *Chronique d' Egypte* 48 (1973): 339–49; O. Montevecchi expresses reservations in "Laos, Linee di una ricerca storico-linguistica," *Actes du XVᵉ Congrès International de Papyrologie* 4 (1979), 56.

afforded to villages. This is what seems to distinguish them from other, uprooted, *georgoi*, whether Egyptian or foreign, who had lost the privileges that stemmed from belonging to a village when they definitively left their own *idia* (homes)."[56]

Despite the fact that they were in a relatively better position to resist exactions, the Egyptian *laoi* thus nevertheless remained subject to the same system of exploitation as the peasant masses.[57] The system was not as a rule founded upon the direct exercise of extra-economic constraints. Zeno organized the cultivation of Apollonius' estates by concluding contracts of tenancy (involving the payment of rent in kind), labor, or management, which were debated, in principle freely, by both parties. However, these contracts were accompanied by all kinds of obligations toward the leasing party, and these rendered that freedom quite illusory. There were loans of money or of livestock, tools, and above all seed, which allowed the proprietor to influence the choice of crops; the tenant was required to swear to remain in residence at least from the time of sowing until the harvest; advances received involved the recognition of debts; the proprietor acquired rights over the person and possessions of the tenant when the latter committed himself to providing certain services and accepted clauses of *paramone* similar to those which affected certain freedmen in Greece; penalties in the form of imprisonment or even servitude could be imposed where royal land or royal allotments were involved, for then the procedure was the same as that followed for debts to the Treasury. All these various forms of labor in the countryside thus rested, more or less indirectly and insidiously, upon personal relations of dependency. This afforded a certain measure of security to the tenants so that, in hard times, they would sometimes choose to contract for a loan precisely in order to put themselves in the position of dependents. More often, however, they would be strongly opposed to such a course and express their resistance essentially by abandoning the land and taking flight (*anachoresis*). Such practices caused the system to become increasingly authoritarian. More and more promises of commitment were required from the tenant, the duration of contracts was extended, and

56. *Zénon de Caunos, "parépidèmos," et le destin grec* (1985), 213; cf. D. Crawford, *Kerkeosiris* (1971); J. Rowlandson, "Freedom and Subordination in Ancient Agriculture: The Case of the *Basilikoi Georgoi* of Ptolemaic Egypt," *Crux*, ed. P. Cartledge and F. D. Harvey (1985), 327–47.

57. J. Modrzejewski, "Régime foncier et statut social dans l'Egypte ptolémaïque," *Colloque Besançon 1974*, 163–88, and above all C. Orrieux, *Zénon de Caunos*, and C. Préaux, *L'économie royale des Lagides* (1939), and her recent work of synthesis, *Le monde hellénistique* (1978).

the practice of enforced lending was introduced, as was the principle of collective village responsibility for the payment of farm rent and land cultivation, and so on.

The Egyptian artisans, for their part, were as a general rule required to hand over part of their production as tax and sometimes also to sell a further proportion to the king at predetermined prices. In some cases it was a matter of a veritable royal monopoly. For instance, all oilworks[58]—with the exception of those of temples, where production was carefully limited—were de facto if not de jure royal property. They were leased out for exploitation and placed under the supervision of civil servants. Workers there were probably recruited under various forms of duress. As to their status, let us select a number of typical clauses from a papyrus that provides us with some information about the way this monopoly was managed in 259–258:

> They shall not allow the oil-makers appointed in each nome to migrate to another nome. Any oil-maker who goes elsewhere shall be subject to arrest by the director of the contract and the oeconomus and the controller. No one shall harbour oil-makers [from another nome]. If anyone does so knowingly or fails to bring them back when ordered, he shall forfeit for each oil-maker 3000 drachmae, and the oil-maker shall be liable to arrest. . . . If the oeconomus or his representative fails to pay the oil-makers their wages or their share in the profits from the sale, he shall forfeit to the Crown 3000 drachmae and to the oil-makers their pay, and twice the amount of any loss incurred by the contract on account of the workmen. . . . The contractors and the checking-clerk appointed by the oeconomus and controller shall have authority over all the oil-makers in the nome and over the factories and the plant and shall seal up the implements during the time when there is no work. They shall compel the oil-workers to work every day and they shall each day make into oil not less than one artaba of sesame at each mortar, and four artabae of croton and one of saffron.[59]

Meanwhile the entire population had to pay a multitude of taxes (personal, professional, or as consumers) and was liable to enforced labor (liturgies, in particular on the maintenance of dikes). Such obligations appear to have exacted a levy equivalent to that of land rents.

58. N. N. Pikous, "Situation sociale des travailleurs d'huilerie dans l'Egypte hellénistique au IIIe siècle av. n. è," *Journal of Juristic Papyrology* 16–17 (1971): 141–58.

59. A. S. Hunt and C. C. Edgar, *Select Papyri*, 2 (1934), no. 203.

In Ptolemaic Egypt, thanks to the evidence provided by papyri, we can see better than in Seleucid Asia how well the Greeks adapted to a traditional system of exploitation which, while hardly slavery, was nevertheless based on various forms of extra-economic constraint that were as effective as they were sophisticated. At this period, the system was even reinforced rather than weakened by the introduction or diffusion of some contractual practices derived from the "free" economy inspired by Greek law.

Sacred Slaves

As well as these various types of rural dependants we should mention the "sacred" slaves.[60] Sometimes they were referred to by the explicit term *hierodouloi*, but they were generally included in the very disparate category of *hieroi*. This word applied to many kinds of living and material possessions that were "sacred" because they were or had been consecrated to a deity and thus in some way or at some level belonged to it. Hence, where people were concerned, it indicated a whole range of extremely varied and subtly differentiated forms of exploitation, service, and protection that combined in various ways, at various places and times, with the secular modalities of statutory classification. Thus, the *hieroi* might be free men of fairly high rank, discharging some religious function; or freedmen more or less encumbered with obligations to the priests who had had a hand in their manumission; or, finally, veritable chattel slaves, one example being the young Ion in the sanctuary of Apollo at Delphi, who does not know whether he is "a city's votive gift or sold by someone" (Euripides, *Ion*, ll. 309–10).

So sacred slavery was not unknown in Greece. It existed not only at Delphi but, above all, at the sanctuary of Aphrodite at Corinth which, according to Strabo (7.6.20) "was so rich that it owned more than a thousand temple slaves, courtesans, whom both men and women had dedicated to the goddess." (Sacred slaves were also to be found in Italy, at Locris[61] and in the Sicilian sanctuary on Mount

60. F. Bömer, *Untersuchungen über die Religion der Sklaven in Griechenland und Rom*, 2 (1960), 149–89; P. Debord, "L'esclavage sacré: Etat de la question," *Colloque Besançon 1971*, 135–50; Debord, *Aspects sociaux et économiques de la vie religieuse dans l'Anatolie gréco-romaine* (1982), 76–100; K. Welwei, "Abhängige Landbevölkerungen auf Tempelterritorien im hellenistischen Kleinasien und Syrien," *Ancient Society* 10 (1979): 97–118. See also A. Archi, *PP* 164 (1975): 329–44, on the Hittite antecedents.

61. M. Gigante, "Nosside," *PP* 29 (1974): 22–39; *Le tavole di Locri* (1979), ed. D. Musti, passim; *contra* S. Pembroke, "Locres et Tarente: Le rôle des femmes dans la fondation de deux colonies grecques," *Annales* 25 (1970): 1240–70; E. Peruzzi, "Sulla prostituzione sacra nell'Italia antica," *Scritti in onore di G. Bonfante* (1976), 673–86.

Eryx.[62]) But most of our documentation relates to the Hellenistic East. Here, the important—even primordial—role that the temples had over a long period played in socioeconomic organization remained largely unchanged after Alexander's conquest, throughout the periods when royal power was weakening and in the regions least affected by the royal policies of urbanization. Sacred slaves were found in Egypt and in Mesopotamia,[63] and were particularly common in central Asia Minor and along its borders, where mention may be made of the State temples of Zeus Stratios at Labraunda, of Artemis at Amizon in Caria, of Anaitis at Zela, of Ma at Comana on the Black Sea and in Cappadocia, of Zeus and Selene in Caucasian Albania, and of Yahve in Jerusalem.

The temples preserved their administrative autonomy and their material infrastructures: workshops and real estate (*hiera chora*), as well as sacred prostitutes who brought the priests an income that financed the maintenance of a large temple staff. Associated with these temples we thus find a whole hierarchy of statuses ranging from "villagers," "residents," and *hieroi* of all kinds to chattel slaves, and including a host of *hierodouloi* whose condition in Asia was analogous to that of the *laoi:* that is, they benefited from certain guarantees vis-à-vis both the temporal powers (exemption from taxes and forced labor) and the priestly establishment (their persons being attached to the land). They also enjoyed a measure of economic independence since they could sometimes work for themselves, cultivating small parcels of land, and might even possess their own slaves. The best definition of their status is to be found in the inscription of Nimrud Dag in which Antiochus I of Commagene, around the mid-first century, spelled out the rights of the inhabitants of estates ceded to sanctuaries:

> Let nobody, neither king nor dynast nor priest nor magistrate, be permitted to reduce to servitude these *hierodouloi* whom I have consecrated to the gods and to my ancestors according to the will of the gods, nor their children nor their descendants, who belong for all time to this class, nor to alienate them in any other way, nor to maltreat them in any fashion, nor to constrain them to enforced labor; but let the priests take them in their charge and let kings, magistrates and all private individuals protect them.[64]

62. V. Scramozze, "Were the *Venerii* in Sicily Serfs?" *AJPhil.* 57 (1936): 326–30.

63. G. C. Sarkisian, "Von der Tempelsklaverei im hellenistischen Babylonien," *Iraq* 45 (1983): 131–35: at Uruk and at Susa.

64. Debord, "Esclavage sacré," 83; D. Musti, "Morte e culto del sovrano in ambito ellenistico," in *La mort, les morts dans les sociétés anciennes*, ed. G. Gnoli and J.-P. Vernant (1982), 189–201.

During the Hellenistic period, the tendency was for these theocratic principalities to become cities or kingdoms like any other, and the effect of this development must eventually have been to alter the status of these individuals for better or worse. But according to Strabo, at the time of Augustus it was still the *hierodouloi* who maintained the prosperity of the great Anatolian sanctuaries, for example that at Comana in Cappadocia, which was

> a considerable city; its inhabitants, however, consist mostly of the divinely inspired people and the temple servants who live in it. The inhabitants are Cataonians who, though in a general way classed as subject to the king, are in most respects subject to the priest. The priest is master of the temple and also of the temple servants (*hierodouloi*), who on my sojourn there were more than six thousand in number, men and women together. Also, considerable territory belongs to the temple, and the revenue is enjoyed by the priest. He is second in rank in Cappadocia after the king; and in general the priests belonged to the same family as the kings. [12.2–3]

In Ptolemaic Egypt,[65] it was also mainly in the sanctuaries of indigenous deities that all kinds of *hierodouloi* were to be found, working either in the sanctuaries themselves or else cultivating the attached land under the direction of priests and "sacristans" of various ranks, and in return enjoying many immunities vis-à-vis the royal power. We thus find them mentioned, even more often than in the Greek papyri, in documents written in Egyptian (whether hieratic or demotic), where they are referred to by the ambiguous name *bk,* which was applicable to any kind of dependant.

The Diffusion of Chattel Slavery in Dependent Countries

Before closing this study of the various types of dependency to be found in the Greek world, we must investigate how far and in what ways they were, from the sixth century on, affected by the diffusion of chattel slavery which appears, other things being equal, to have constituted a "superior" mode of exploitation.

Among the cities that had slavery of the Helot type, it is important in this respect to distinguish between, on the one hand, those of the

65. H. Thompson, "Two Demotic Self-Dedications," *Journal of Egyptian Archaeology* 26 (1940): 68–78; W. Otto, *Beiträge zur Hierodulie im hellenischen Aegypten, Abh. Bay. Ak. Wiss. Ph.-hist. Kl.*, N.F. 29 (1950).

colonial world which, right from the start, limited its use to the agricultural sector, and on the other those in Greece proper, which were initially without any other form of exploitation. Here there was certainly some competition from chattel slavery inside the towns, at least from the fourth century, in the recruitment of domestic servants; but in the essential sector of agricultural production, the traditional structures were much more faithfully adhered to, particularly in Sparta, right down to the Hellenistic period.

Furthermore, it has been pointed out that, where these structures were replaced, the impulse did not come from "inside," through the reduction of former dependants to the condition of chattel slaves, but on the contrary from the "outside," after they had attained liberty.[66] It would appear that in the case of the *korynephoroi* and *katonakophoroi* of Sicyon, as in that of the Megarian dependants described by Theognis, the improvement in their conditions was brought about by the sixth-century tyrants, who found themselves obliged to win the dependants' support against hostile aristocratic factions of one kind or another. The Killyrians of Syracuse are supposed to have acquired their liberty in this fashion at the beginning of the fifth century; the Mariandynians of Heraclea together with many other rural peoples of Asia Minor did so during the Hellenistic period; the Helots of Sparta did the same around the beginning of the Roman period, in circumstances about which nothing is known. In Thessaly, the process was a long-drawn-out one, lasting from the end of the fifth century to the first century A.D. (after which the word *penestai* was used to denote poor free men). The trend was, in short, in conformity with what had taken place in Athens at the time of Solon.

But it is in the Hellenistic East that the problem is posed most sharply, for there more was at stake. To resolve it once and for all, however, is no easy matter—partly because ambiguity of vocabulary sometimes makes it impossible to distinguish slaves from servants of free condition or from *laoi,* partly too because of the heterogeneity and unequal geographical distribution of our documentation. For the latter reason Egypt, so rich in papyri, once again constitutes a more rewarding field of inquiry than western, let alone central, Asia. But in both areas, it is important to distinguish clearly between the diffusion of chattel slavery in the countryside and in the towns.

---

66. C. Mossé, "Les dépendants paysans dans le monde grec à l'époque archaïque et classique," *Colloque Besançon 1974,* 85–97; Mossé, "Le problème des dépendants paysans dans le monde grec," *Colloque Nieborow 1975,* 57–64.

In Asia Minor, Greek influences had over a long period reached considerably beyond an urban framework. Despite that, however, we know virtually nothing about rural slavery before the Roman period and even less about the situation in the rest of the Seleucid empire.[67] We are much better informed on the subject of Egypt.[68] Here, especially at the beginning of the Graeco-Macedonian occupation, there appear to have been many military colonists whose possession of an allotment of land afforded them a certain ease and who at their deaths were in a position to bequeath slaves in their wills (as a rule not more than five, in exceptional cases a dozen or so). There were also numerous natives of modest condition who owned, or sometimes co-owned, one or two slaves. Altogether, however, the slaves cannot have represented more than 10 percent of the total population, and they were employed mainly on domestic tasks. It is rare to find them taking part directly in agriculture. Thus, on the large estate that Ptolemy II ceded to the *dioiketes* Apollonius, the latter's manager, Zeno, employed them chiefly as overseers, foremen, or guards. In the oilworks, brickworks, weaving workshops, and even the mines exploited for the profit of royal monopolies, slave labor was relatively uncommon.

In the Greek towns of the East, whether of ancient or more recent foundation, one would naturally expect to find a greater development of slavery during the Hellenistic period: after all, here Greeks were more numerous than in the countryside and here they must have tried to reproduce not only the political and religious but also the economic and social conditions of city life. That indeed seems to have been the case in the principal cities of the Seleucid and Pergamene kingdoms. But even here our documentation shows slaves employed in service and administrative roles rather than as artisans—even, for example, in the great workshops of Pergamum. Here, as at Seleuceia in the Eulaios (Susa), instances of manumission concern domestic slaves (mostly women). And there are no certain grounds for suggesting that the six hundred slaves of Antiochus IV and the thousand owned by his first secretary Dionysius, who paraded at Daphne near Antioch in 166, had any other occupations apart from serving the court.

67. H. Kreissig, "L'esclavage dans les villes d'Orient pendant la période hellénistique," *Colloque Besançon 1973*, 235–55; "L'esclavage à l'époque hellénistique," *Rech. int. 1975*, 99–109.
68. I. Biezunska-Malowist, *L'esclavage dans l'Egypte gréco-romaine*, 1 (1974); H. Heinen, "Für ein Corpus der auf Sklaverei bezüglichen Texte des ptolemaischen Aegypten," *Actes du XVe Congrès International de Papyrologie*, 4 (1979), 107–15; Heinen, "Zur Sklaverei in der hellenistischen Welt," *Ancient Society* 7 (1976): 127–49, and 8 (1977): 121–54.

In Alexandria, the largest and best known of all the Eastern Hellenistic towns, slaves without a doubt constituted an appreciable proportion of the population, even as early as the first half of the third century. That is attested by a number of regulations concerning them, their place in daily life as described in the idylls of Theocritus and the mimes of Herondas, and also by the information provided by the archives of Zeno about the upkeep of Apollonius' "house" in the capital: here the wide range of their special skills as cooks, janitors, coachmen, masseurs, citharists, messengers, and commercial agents is enough to prove how numerous they were. Another piece of interesting testimony on the numbers of domestic slaves in the great houses of Alexandria (or Cyrenaica?) is provided by the epigram by Theaetetus (*Palatine Anthology*, 7.444) composed in memory of the eighty-four people, free and slave alike, who perished in the fire that demolished the house belonging to Andragoras and were subsequently buried in a mass grave. The sources from the second century, essentially of a legislative nature, are much less abundant—which to many historians indicates a stagnation if not a recession in slavery. Nevertheless, slavery was still flourishing on the eve of the Roman occupation, even in families in modest circumstances. But what, once again, is difficult to determine is how far it contributed to the prosperity of artisan and commercial enterprises in Alexandria.

The explanation for the limited development of slavery in the Hellenistic East is without doubt to be found in the traditional dominance in these regions of the "Asiatic" mode of production (in all its various local forms), which the sovereigns here do not appear to have opposed. This mode of production certainly seems to have possessed great survival power, no doubt because it tied the producer particularly closely to the land, to the basic community to which he belonged, and to the power of the State. Far from being automatically eclipsed by a "superior" mode of production imported by the conquerors, it seems to have been adopted by them, just as it had been by countless earlier invaders, and to have lost little of its dominance, except perhaps in a few trading or administrative towns where slavery made some inroads in the immediate aftermath of the conquest. Even here, the Asiatic mode of production may have regained ground in the second half of the Hellenistic period, with the orientalization of the Greeks and the revival of indigenous societies.

If we wish to see to what extent chattel slavery, when it was of secondary importance as a mode of production, became contaminated from a juridical point of view by the principal mode of production,[69] then Ptolemaic Egypt once again provides our best evidence. Even in this case, however, it is difficult to form a clear idea of the situation.[70] The very most we can do is take note of particular local features which, if well established, suggest that the person of the slave was more fully recognized here than elsewhere: the slave's liability to certain capitation taxes such as the salt tax; the apparent possibility of his or her becoming more or less legally united with a free person; the acceptability, in some circumstances at any rate, of bringing direct legal proceedings against a slave without involving his master in the case; his being able sometimes to give evidence without the use of torture. But conversely, it is even less clear whether the Egyptian peasants, for their part, suffered from a certain assimilation of their status to that of the slaves: for instance, in the application of corporal punishment or in the exercise of their juridical capacities.

We are bound to conclude that the diffusion of chattel slavery was well and truly blocked, or impeded in a lasting fashion, by the preexistence of other modes of exploitation also founded upon extra-economic constraints, and that the internal influence exerted on the latter by chattel slavery, which failed to remodel them in its own image, was negligible. No historical law made its triumph inevitable in Greek Antiquity—at least not until there was some good reason to abolish the traditional forms of dependency by liberating those involved.

69. On types of slavery that existed earlier in Egypt, see E. Cruz-Uribe, "Slavery in Egypt during the Saïte and Persian Periods," *Revue Internationale des Droits de l'Antiquité*, 3d ser., 29 (1982): 46–71.

70. H. Heinen, "Sur le régime de travail dans l'Egypte ptolémaïque au IIIᵉ siècle avant J.-C. A propos d'un livre récent de N. N. Pikus," *Le monde grec: Hommages à Claire Préaux* (1975), 656–62, and "Aegyptische und griechische Traditionen der Sklaverei im ptolemaischen Aegypten," *Das ptolem. Aegypten* (1978), 227–37.

[3]

The Theory and Practice
of Slaveholding

Up to this point we have been considering slaves and other dependants chiefly in themselves, from different angles and in all the
diversity of their various conditions (right up to the threshold of
liberty). We must now study what is probably the most essential and
certainly the most difficult aspect of slavery: what was the place of
these slaves in the framework of the ideologies and social practices
that characterized the various social formations to which they belonged? I shall chiefly limit this inquiry to chattel slavery and the
communal servitude that predominated in Greece from the archaic
period onward. This also happens to be the orientation of the most
recent trends in historiography: a differentiated yet comprehensive
approach to the complex made up of free men and nonfree men.

Justificatory Theories of Slavery

Although they have left us no treatise devoted to the subject, the
Greeks were not unconcerned with the question of the justification
of slavery: they resolved it in an increasingly nuanced and complex
manner, going so far as to admit that certain individuals were unjustly enslaved, but not so far as to cast doubt upon the legitimacy of
the institution itself.[1]

1. R. Schlaifer, "Greek Theories of Slavery from Homer to Aristotle," *Harvard
Studies in Classical Philology* 47 (1936): 165–204 (=*Slavery*, 93–132); P. Milani, *La
schiavitù nel pensiero politico: Dai Greci al Basso Medio Evo* (1972); E. Klees, *Herren und
Sklaven* (=*Forsch. ant. Sklav.* 6 [1975]).

For Homer slavery stemmed quite simply from the fact of capture, being the consequence of finding oneself on the weaker side. It was the normal result of a temporary but irremediable weakness for which the gods or fate were really responsible. The victim was thus in no way predestined to be a slave through some inferiority connected with temperament, culture, or ethnic origin. In the Homeric poems the image of the foreigner is fundamentally in conformity with the Achaean heroes' image of themselves: it does not imply a servile vocation. There is consequently nothing seditious about a slave in a melancholy mood recalling his past greatness, for every man, even the son of a god or a king, always knew that he might meet such a fate. For the philosopher Heraclitus, at the end of the sixth century, it was still the hazards of war that decided the matter: "War (*polemos*) is the father of all, the king of all, and he has marked out some for gods, others for men; he has made some slaves and others free" (Fr. 53 Diels). There are echoes of such an attitude in the tragic poets of the fifth century, but before long, the dominant idea becomes that of the natural inferiority of slaves.

The first "natural" explanation for chattel slavery is attested at the very beginning of the classical period, and it relates to those who were *par excellence* subjected to it: the barbarians.

Earlier, in the days of Homer, at the end of the archaic period, this description does not appear to have any particularly derogatory sense, especially if it is true that the word was derived from the Sumerian *bar* and the Accadian *barbar,* which simply meant "foreigner." Thus, for Heraclitus, the "barbarian souls" who did not understand the language of the senses were not so much uncultivated souls as souls ignorant of a particular language. It was still relatively easy to pass from the "barbarian" world to the Greek world, provided one made an effort to adapt to its culture: some of the sixth-century Ionian philosophers, for instance, are supposed to have numbered Anatolian natives among their ancestors.

Although even at this period the non-Greek origin of most chattel slaves no doubt suggested the servile nature of barbarians, belief in the idea probably took a hold only following the Persian Wars, which gave the Greeks an acute sense of their own superiority over the Asiatic hordes ruled by the Great King. As early as 472, in *The Persians*, Aeschylus represented the battle of Salamis as a confrontation between the very principles of liberty and slavery. The Greeks, unlike the Persians, "are slaves to none nor are they subject" (l. 242). Herodotus, in his account of the wars, makes the same opposition in the words he ascribes to the Spartan ambassadors, who declare to the

Persian Hydarnes, "You know well how to be a slave, but you have never tasted of freedom" (7.135). Another lapidary formulation (one of many) can be found in Euripides' *Helen* at the end of the fifth century: "All Barbary is slave except a single man," that is to say the Great King himself (l. 276). The fact was that the barbarians lacked the Greek *logos*, which meant both language and reason and in consequence implied a particular mode of political organization, that of the city, in which alone it could flourish.

At this period, the idea of the intrinsic inferiority of the barbarian slave, while being deeply rooted in people's minds, had not yet developed into an actual theory. Not until the end of the fifth century do we find a formulated arguement, for the first time, in the Hippocratic treatise *Airs, Waters, Places*.[2] At a first level, the explanation given is political: "Where there are kings, there must be the greatest cowards; for men's souls are enslaved and refuse to run risks readily and recklessly to increase the power of somebody else" (23). But at a second level this abjection is given a climatic explanation: "The chief reason why Asiatics are less warlike and more gentle in character than Europeans is the uniformity of the seasons, which show no violent changes either towards heat or towards cold, but are equable. For there occur no mental shocks nor violent physical changes which are the more likely to steel the temper and impart to it a fierce passion than is a monotonous sameness. For it is changes of all things that rouse the temper of man and prevent its stagnation. For these reasons, I think, Asiatics are feeble" (16). This explanation is echoed in slightly different terms by Plato (*Rep.*, 4.435a–436a) and also by Aristotle:

> The nations inhabiting the cold places and those of Europe are full of spirit but somewhat deficient in intelligence and skill, so that they continue comparatively free, but lacking in political organization and capacity to rule their neighbours. The peoples of Asia on the other hand are intelligent and skillful in temperament, but lack spirit so that they are in continuous subjection and slavery. But the Greek race participates in both characters, just as it occupies the middle position geographically, for it is both spirited and intelligent: hence, it continues to be free and to have very good political institutions and to be capable of ruling all mankind if it attains constitutional unity. [*Politics*, 1327b]

In this treatise of Aristotle's, composed in about 330–320, within the framework of an analysis of the city, its constitutive parts (fam-

2. W. Backhaus, "Der Hellenen-Barbaren-Gegensatz und die hippokratische Schrift *Peri aeron, hudation, topon*," *Historia* 25 (1976): 170–85.

ilies), and its goals, we find the most fully elaborated theory of natural slavery. It strongly promotes the tendency of dominant groups to present the social order in natural terms, making it speak a physical language, and it was destined to be a key text referred to right down to modern times: "One that can foresee with his mind is naturally ruler and naturally master, and one that can do these things with his body is subject and naturally a slave' (1252b). Aristotle notes differences in aptitudes that nature has introduced in the appearances of men and women,[3] in the interests of generation, and in those of free men and slaves, in the interests of preservation: "The latter are strong for necessary service, the former erect and unserviceable for such occupations but serviceable for a life of citizenship" (1254b). Unlike the animals, which obey only impressions, the slave certainly has a share in reason, but only to the extent that he can perceive it; he does not actually possess it: "The slave has not got the deliberative part at all." So he is also distinguished from the free woman who, for her part, has it but "without full authority" and from the child who "has it, but in an undeveloped form" (1260a). The same goes for moral qualities: all these categories necessarily have a share of them, for otherwise they could not work together with a single purpose; but they have them in different forms and in different degrees, those of the slave having meaning only in relation to his master and "he needs only a small amount of virtue, in fact just enough to prevent him from failing in his tasks owing to intemperance and cowardice" (1260a).

The inferiority of slaves is thus justified, on a level that is no longer strictly ethnic, by reference to the whole complex of fundamental values that preside over the organization of human society and even, according to Plato, that of the cosmos:[4] the dualism of the slave and the free man is superposed on the dualism of body and soul, becoming and being, matter and the divine principle. Whereas the Ionian philosophers of the early sixth century imagined the universe on the model of the city, Plato instead had the idea that the world was governed by *logos,* drawing rather on the analogy of a master dominating a slave. In circumstances such as these, it seemed impossible

3. O. Gigon, "Die Sklaverei bei Aristoteles," *Entretiens Hardt,* 2 (1965), 245–83; W. W. Fortenbaugh, "Aristotle on Slaves and Women," *Articles on Aristotle,* ed. J. Barnes et al., 2 (1977), 135–39; P. Rousseau, "Remarques sur la théorie aristotélicienne de l'esclavage," *Colloque Camerino 1978,* 132–39; N. O. Smith, "Aristotle's Theory of Natural Slavery," *Phoenix* 37 (1983): 109–22.

4. G. Vlastos, "Slavery in Plato's Thought," *Philosophical Review* 50 (1941): 289–304 (=*Slavery,* 133–49, and *Platonic Studies* [1973]: 147–63); cf. L. Brisson, *Le Même et l'Autre dans la structure ontologique du "Timée" de Platon* (1974).

to eliminate slavery without destroying the harmony of the whole. It appeared an ontological necessity.

This concept of natural slavery, based initially upon the slave-barbarian equivalence, nevertheless began to be challenged, from the mid-fifth century on, by the theory of the natural unity of the human race (a unity that Plato and Aristotle themselves in fact recognized while at the same time laying strong emphasis upon its hierarchical nature). The propagators of the theory were the logician-philosophers known as the Sophists.[5] They based their argument on their political experience of the relativity of the laws passed by the latest regimes and also on the parallel thinking of the Hippocractic school of doctors. Thus, if we are to believe Plato's *Protagoras* (337c), Hippias of Elis used to tell his interlocutors: "I regard you all as kinsmen and intimates and fellow-citizens by nature, not by law." Admittedly, he was at the time addressing Greeks of the highest standing.[6] Antiphon appears to have taken a more radical line, in a fragment of his writing preserved on an Egyptian papyrus:

> We praise and revere those who are born from fathers of quality, while we take care not to praise and revere those who do not belong to a house of quality. In so doing, we turn ourselves into barbarians vis-à-vis one another; for by nature we are all in every way made in the same fashion to be either barbarians or Greeks. That is what is shown by the things which are by nature necessary to all men. All men, in similar fashion, have the possibility of enjoying them and in all this no man is marked out as a barbarian or a Greek. We all breathe the air through our mouths and nostrils, and we all eat with our hands. [*Pap. Oxy.* 11.1364]

Thus translated and interpreted, this passage (the context of which is unknown) does not explicitly state that there is a fundamental natural equality between Greeks and barbarians. The phrase "we turn ourselves into Barbarians" means rather that even with the same starting point men can evolve in opposite directions under the effects of education, a domain in which the Sophists were specialists.

In circumstances such as these, the source of slavery had, in any

5. A. M. Bayonas, "Ancient Sophistry and the institution of slavery" (in Greek), *Athèna* 68 (1965): 115–68; M. Isnardi Parente, "Equalitarismo democratico nella sofistica?" *Rivista Critica di Studi di Filologie* 30 (1975): 3–26; E. Will, *Le monde grec et l'Orient. I: Le Vᵉ siècle* (1972), 471–505.

6. G. B. Kerford, "The Concept of Equality in the Thought of the Sophistic Movement," in *Equality and Inequality of Man in Ancient Thought*, ed. I. Kajanto, *Commentationes Humanarum Litterarum* 75 (1984): 10–13.

event, to be external to those involved: a force upheld by law became the equivalent of the agents seen as responsible by Homer—fate or divine will. The question that then arose was the extent to which the slavery in accordance with the law coincided with a natural slavery: that is to say, whether there were some slaves who were such only by law, despite their natural predisposition for liberty. It was over this question of a possible mismatch between juridical status and human qualities that, at the end of the fifth century, a debate developed, a few echoes of which are already to be found in Euripides: "A slave bears only this disgrace: the name. In every other way an honest slave is equal to the free" (*Ion*, ll. 854–856); "many a slave is dishonoured by nothing but the name, while his soul may be more free than that of a non-slave" (fr. 831); "the name slave does not exclude quality. Many slaves are worth more than free men" (fr. 511).

Even Plato, under the influence of the Sophists, sometimes came around to questioning the validity of the Greek-barbarian distinction (*Politicus*, 262d) and the superiority in certain domains of the one group over the other. Aristotle, while maintaining the natural inferiority of slaves as compared to free men, nevertheless recognized that

> as a matter of fact, often the very opposite comes about: slaves have the bodies of free men and free men the souls only; since this is certainly clear, that if free men were born as distinguished in body as are the statues of the gods, everyone would say that those who were inferior deserved to be these men's slaves; and if this is true in the case of the body, there is far juster reason for this rule being laid down in the case of the soul, but beauty of soul is not so easy to see as beauty of body.
> [*Politics*, 1254b, 30–40]

So Aristotle wonders whether the power of the master is really as natural as that of the head of the family, the statesman, and the king. He is aware that some "maintain that for one man to be another man's master is contrary to nature, because it is only law that makes the one a slave and the other a free man and there is no difference between them in nature and that therefore it is unjust, for it is based on force" (1253b, 20–25). So he is obliged to acknowledge that these people "are also right in a way" and that "there is also such a thing as a slave or a man that is in slavery by law, for the law is a sort of convention under which the things conquered in war are said to belong to their conquerors" (1255a, 3–10). But does that mean that this type of slavery is purely arbitrary? To decide the question, Aristotle takes as his starting point the generally accepted postulate that the stronger is also the better. He then wonders whether this means that strength implies excellence (and is therefore enough to legitimize the result obtained) or whether, for that to be so, excellence must be added to strength. Aristotle is inclined to favor the latter proposition, that slavery cannot be imposed by the stronger party justifiably unless he is also better than the conquered man, for "otherwise we shall have the result that persons reputed of the higher nobility are slaves and the descendants of slaves if they happen to be taken prisoners of war and sold" (1255a, 25–30). Does this mean that we should envisage slavery in two forms: one absolute, reserved for barbarians, and another relative, restricted to certain Greeks? Not exactly, since nature may, in exceptional circumstances, distribute its gifts in different ways. Aristotle's judgments on the barbarians are indeed somewhat ambiguous: sometimes he assimilates them as a group to animals or plants (fr. 658); sometimes he introduces distinctions among them: the Asiatics are more slavelike than Egyptians or Carthaginians and much more so than Europeans (1285a, 21–22); 1329b, 1–5; 1272b, 24–25. But eventually Aristotle concludes—albeit not without hesitation—that, in any event, some people are certainly natural slaves for reasons that are, for the most part, perfectly clear and indisputable, whereas in some marginal cases, an element of doubt may creep in.

In the social circumstances that prevailed at the time, the problem clearly related in particular to the reduction to servitude, especially of the Helot type, of Greek peoples *en masse*. It was thus in connection with the Messenians, freed from the Spartan yoke by the Thebans in 370, that the Sophist Alcidamas declared: "The deity gave liberty to all men and nature created no-one a slave" (Ps. Aristotle, *Rhetorica ad Alexandrum*, 13.1373b, 19). It thus seems to me significant that the historians began to ponder the origins of this type of slave only after Sophist philosophical reflection on the subject got under way. This kind of questioning is absent from Herodotus and Thucydides. It appears, as we have seen (p. 96), to have started up at the end of the fifth century, with Hellanicus of Lesbos, been developed considerably during the fourth century (particularly by Ephorus and Theopompus), and continued until the end of the Hellenistic period (particularly in the work of Posidonius of Apamea).

From these Sophist sources, in conjunction with the teaching of Socrates, the "personalist" philosophers of the fourth century for their part drew the conclusion that true slavery was simply a state of mind which had nothing to do with the juridical status of individuals. This was probably the view expounded by Antisthenes in his treatise *On Liberty and Slavery*, and is also that which is suggested by the pronouncements and quips attributed to Diogenes, the founder of the school of the Cynics. Bion, one of his disciples in the early Hellenistic period, was to push the paradox to the point of declaring: "Good slaves are free, but bad men are slaves, desiring profit from things." In other words, as a fragment of Menander (fr. 857) puts it, one is a slave only if one has a servile spirit: "Be free in spirit, even if you are a slave; then you will no longer be a slave." Stoics and Epicureans were to find themselves in agreement on this point.

Nevertheless, there are no grounds for believing that an antislavery line of thought became established in ancient Greece at the end of the classical period. The facts speak for themselves: we know that even the advocaters of such doctrines themselves possessed slaves. Second, and more important, from a theoretical point of view the substitution of convention for nature as the basis of slavery, and its internalization through a shift from the juridical level to the subjective and from the social level to the personal, could not possibly lead to the institution itself being challenged. During the first centuries A.D. the Roman jurists of Stoic inspiration who declared slavery to be *contra naturam, contra jus naturale,* were equally powerless to bring such a thing about. In fact the problem had simply shifted. In the case of the Greeks, convention took over from nature as the basis of law: the effect was to make the servile condition a more relative but at the same time less controversial subject (hence the success, paradoxical at first sight, of such theories with an oligarch who despised the "people," such as Antiphon). In the case of the Romans, what was being asserted was the principle of the unity of men, not that of their equality: this made it possible, more subtly but just as irrefutably, to justify the reduction to servitude of any given individual. (To arrive at a judgment as to who was best, the Stoics distinguished between one category and another and between one individual and another whereas Plato and Aristotle distinguished on the grounds of sex, race, age, and nationality.) The ideological framework of the institution thus emerged in a more flexible but in no way weakened form from the impact of the criticisms of natural slavery introduced by the Sophists.

Slaveless Societies in Greek Political Thought

Nonetheless, a number of ideal representations of slaveless societies are to be found in Greek political thought.[7] Does their pres-

7. This section has recently been published, with few alterations, in *Klio* 63 (1981): 131–40, dedicated to Heinz Kreissig. See also J. Vogt, "Slavery in Greek Utopias," *Ancient Slavery,* 26–38.

ence justify our crediting the Greeks at least with praiseworthy aspirations where slavery was concerned? That is what tends to be suggested by historians such as Joseph Vogt or philosophers such as Karl Popper,[8] who see themselves as champions of Western humanism and accordingly endeavor to remove all taint from the reputations of their great cultural ancestors. They are advocates for the slave owners, but not for them alone: they plead the cause of all exploiter classes imbued with a sense of their own moral excellence, whose desire for universal emancipation is represented as limited only by the "objective" necessities of social life. Such arguments seem so loaded with ideological presuppositions that at this point I consider it necessary to undertake a systematic examination of the place the Greeks alloted to slavery in their imaginary states. This may enable us to determine the real reasons why slavery is occasionally absent from them.

Essentially, these states consist of plans devised to redistribute functions within the civic body, within a system that remains hierarchical and makes no provision for any overall increase in sources of revenue, for any change in their nature, or for any reduction of the society's needs.

The most ancient of these "static"[9] or "reconstructed"[10] utopias are known to us only through the cursory summaries Aristotle provides of them in his *Politics*. The first is that of Hippodamus of Miletus, a contemporary of Pericles, also known for his work as a town planner: "His system was for a city with a population of ten thousand, divided into three classes; for he made one class of artisans, one of farmers and the third the class that fought for the State in war and was the armed class. He divided the land into three parts, one sacred, one public and one private: sacred land to supply the customary offerings to the gods, common land to provide the warrior class with food and private land to be owned by the farmers" (1267b, 30). As for Phaleas of Chalcedon, a contemporary of Plato, he was concerned above all with the equality of the allotments of land held by citizens: "He thought that this would not be difficult to

8. *The Open Society and Its Enemies* (1950), in particular 44; the reason is his desire to associate the rise of individualism with that of altruism in the history of ancient Greece: "This individualism, united with altruism, has become the basis of our western civilization. It is the essential doctrine of Christianity . . . and it is the core of all ethical doctrines, which have grown from our civilization and stimulated it" (101).

9. A formula used by M. I. Finley in "Utopianism Ancient and Modern," *The Critical Spirit: Essays in Honour of Herbert Marcuse* (1967), 3–20 (=*The Use and Abuse of History* [1975], 178–92).

10. A formula used by A. Giannini, "Mito e utopia nella letteratura greca prima di Platone," *Rendiconti, Istituto Lombardo, Classe di Lettera* 101 (1967), 102.

secure at the outset for cities in the process of foundation, while in those already settled, although it would be a more irksome task, nevertheless a levelling would most easily be effected by the rich giving dowries but not receiving them and the poor receiving but not giving them" (1266b,5).

In contrast, two systematic plans for political reform devised by Plato are known to us in detail. The first is that of *The Republic*. This is supposed to be a perfect system, since it is totally modeled upon the Idea of the Good. In it, the class of the philosophers and that of the warriors are superposed upon the mass of producers. The second is that of the "second city" of *The Laws*, which is closer to the contemporary reality (particularly in Athens), in which predominance goes to an elite of citizens who draw their resources from the 5,040 allotments of land which comprise the territory. In the *Politics*, Aristotle also considers a number of constitutional projects: that of an ideal *politeia* which limits citizenship to a class of small landowners, and also other constitutions of various gradations in which citizenship is extended to such or such categories of free men who do not derive their income from the land (artisans, merchants, sailors, wage-earners). The Stoic Zeno of Kition also composed a *politeia*. All we know of it specifically, however, is that according to Plutarch (*On the Fortune of Alexander*, 1.6) its essential object was that "all the inhabitants of this world of ours should not live differentiated by their respective rules of justice into separate cities and communities but that we should consider all men to be of one community and one polity and that we should have a common life and an order common to us all, even as a herd that feeds together and shares the pasturage of a common field."

Now, slavery is something more or less explicitly postulated by all these reformers. Its existence is evident in any Aristotelian schema and also in Plato's *Laws*, where it is the subject of strict regulations that differ from the Athenian model only to the extent that they are more severe. The same goes for Phaleas, who considers that "all the artisans must be publicly owned slaves" and whom Aristotle takes to task precisely for having neglected to explain how in all this "abundance of property in the shape of what is called furniture," the wealth that "consists in slaves" could be equalized (*Politics*, 1267b, 10–15). In Plato's *Republic*, slavery is alluded to only in an extremely discreet fashion—so discreet that it has sometimes (mistakenly) been believed to be not mentioned at all.[11] The reason for the apparent

11. C. Despotopoulos, "La 'Cité parfaite' de Platon et l'esclavage," *REG* 83 (1960): 26–37; F. Joukowsky, "L'esclavage antique et les humanistes," *Actes du IXe Congrès de*

omission is that Plato is not here concerned with anything not immediately relevant to civic organization, least of all with the goods owned by the producer class—which of course includes the slaves (to be recruited only from non-Greek peoples). The problem is less easily resolved in the case of Hippodamus, but the criticisms directed against him by Aristotle appear to imply the existence of slaves here too. If not, would he not have made the point that, among the factors preventing the artisans and cultivators from taking part in the exercise of political power on an equal footing with the military, was their lack of leisure to do so? As for Zeno, most commentators[12] agree that Plutarch is probably not justified in extending the cosmopolitanism of the founder of Stoicism to include the whole of humanity. In reality, Zeno probably envisaged applying it to no more than a minority of "sages": in his social system (insofar as he imagined one, that is) slavery thus remained not only possible but necessary, for ethical reasons.

Three burlesque examples of this type of utopia are also to be found in the comic world of Aristophanes, and in these too slaves have a place. In the heavenly city of the *Birds*—the peaceful, harmonious reverse of Athens at the time of the Peloponnesian War—the hoopoe has a slave "to follow and serve" it, for the good reason that "it was once a man" (l. 75). In the *Lysistrata*, the women occupy the Acropolis and refuse to make love with their menfolk to incite them into making peace, for an oracle has prophesied that they will have their way on the day when "everything will be turned upside down by Zeus letting fly his thunderbolt up there" (ll. 772–773). All the same, they have at their disposal a female slave who is an archer of Scythian origin, and other servants too. In the *Ecclesiazusae*, which is a satire on Athenian political life in the very early fourth century, the women establish a communist regime, but the fate reserved for slaves is simply to be equally distributed among the citizens, with the male slaves continuing to cultivate the land (l. 651) while the women slaves abstain from all disloyal amorous competition with the free women: "Those servile hussies shall no longer poach upon the true-love manors of the free. No, let them herd with slaves, and lie with slaves, in servile fashion, snipped and trimmed to match" (ll. 721–724). In

---

l'Association Guillaume Budé, 2:687, n.2; *contra* G. Vlastos, "Does Slavery Exist in Plato's Republic?" *Classical Philology* 63 (1968): 291–95 (=*Platonic Studies* [1973], 140–46); J. Ferguson, "Slavery in *The Republic*," *Liverpool Classical Monthly* 2 (1977): 186.

12. See, for example, H. C. Baldry, "Zeno's Ideal State," *JHS* 79 (1959): 3–15; J. Janda, "Einige ethisch-soziale Probleme in der Philosophie des Zenon von Kition (Zur *Politeia* des Zenon)," in *Soziale Probleme im Hellenismus und im römischer Reich*, ed. P. Oliva and J. Burian (1973), 97–116.

these representations of "upside-down" cities, Aristophanes is certainly capable of imagining the destruction of private property and masculine prerogatives, but not that of the hierarchy of free men and slaves.[13]

Imaginary societies without slaves are to be found in a different kind of utopia. These are societies with an egalitarian spirit which provides for the satisfaction of the needs of all and sundry. But there are two different traditions for such utopias (with some overlap between them): in the one the satisfaction of needs stems from their limited nature, whereas in the other it stems from an abundance of resources. In the first case it is a matter of the state of nature prevailing at the origins of humanity and among primitive peoples; in the second, we are presented with a Golden Age situated either at the origins of humanity or in the Land of Cockaigne.[14]

The first of these traditions was inaugurated by Herodotus: to find a slaveless society in mankind's past, he goes back to the time when the Pelasgians, before migrating to Lemnos, were still living at the foot of Mount Hymettus. At that time "neither the Athenians nor any other dwellers in Greece had as yet servants" and men were content to send their wives and children to draw water at the Nine Wells (6.137). According to Timaeus (Athenaeus, 6.264d), in regions considered archaic, such as Phocis and Locris as late as the mid-fourth century, it was "customary in domestic matters for the younger members of the family to serve their elders" (as was still the case in Hellenistic Crete, at the communal meals). Alongside this we may also cite four lines from *The Savages* by Pherecrates, a comic poet who was a contemporary of Aristophanes: 'In those days, nobody had a slave, a Manes or a Sekis, but the women had to toil by themselves over all the housework. And what is more, they would grind the corn at early dawn, so that the village rang with the touch of the handmills" (Athenaeus, 6.263b).

Since the time of Hesiod at least, the Golden Age had been identified with the reign of Cronos when, according to Plato (*Politicus*, 271a–272b), men "had fruits in plenty from the trees and other plants, which the earth furnished them of its own accord, without help from agriculture." It seems reasonable to suppose this

13. P. Vidal-Naquet, "Esclavage et gynécocratie dans la tradition, le mythe, l'utopie," in *Recherches sur les structures sociales dans l'Antiquité classique* (1970), 63–80 (=*The Black Hunter* [1986], 205–24).

14. On these two trends, the primitivist and the antiprimitivist, see particularly A. O. Lovejoy and G. Boas, *Primitivism and Related Ideas in Antiquity* (1935), and T. Cole, *Democritus and the Sources of Greek Anthropology* (1967).

to have been a slaveless age, given that Cronos was the god who later presided over the rural festivities of the Cronia, during which masters ate with their slaves and even went so far as to wait upon them.[15]

According to Athenaeus (6.267e), an image of abundance also appeared in "the poets of Old Comedy" who, "when they tell us about life in primitive times set forth . . . lines . . . to show that in those days no use was made of slaves." The same goes for the following passage from the *Amphictyons* of Telecleides (ibid., 268b–d):

> I will, then, tell of the life of old which I provided for mortals. First, there was peace over all, like water over the hands. The earth produced no terror and no disease; on the other hand, things needful came of their own accord. Every torrent flowed with wine, barley-cakes strove with wheat-loaves for mens' lips, beseeching that they be swallowed if men loved the whitest. Fishes would come to the house and bake themselves, then serve themselves on the tables. A river of broth, whirling hot slices of meat, would flow by the couches; conduits full of piquant sauces for the meat were close at hand for the asking, so that there was plenty for moistening a mouthful and swallowing it tender. On dishes there would be honey-cakes all sprinkled with spices, and roast thrushes served up with milk-cakes were flying into the gullet. The flat-cakes jostled each other at the jaws and set up a racket, the children (*paides*) would shoot dice with slices of paunch and tidbits. Men were fat in those days and every bit mighty giants.[16]

A similar situation in the reign of Cronos was described in *The Wealthy*, by Cratinus (6.267e). In contrast to what Athenaeus himself claims, the above-mentioned texts do not specifically state that slaves did not exist. It is even possible that—if the *paides* of the *Amphictyons* are slaves rather than children—slaves are in fact present but reduced to idleness and to spending their time in play, as an indication of how inessential they are. A complete absence of slaves is specifically mentioned, however, in a passage in Crates' *Wild Animals* where, for once, the scene is set in an imaginary future:

> A: So then, no man shall own any slave, male or female, but, old though he may be, must serve himself with his own hands?
> B: Not at all, for I shall make all his utensils capable of walking.

15. F. Bömer, *Untersuchungen über die Religion der Sklaven in Griechenland und Rom*, 3 (1961), 415–23. Cf. below, p. 198.

16. Both here and for the following passage from Crates the translation is based upon those of J. C. Carrière, *Le carnaval et la politique* (1979), 264 and 256.

A: But what good, pray, will that do him?
B: Each article of furniture will come to him when he calls it. "Place yourself here, Table! You, I mean, get yourself ready! Knead, my little flour sack. Fill up, my ladle! Where's the cup? Go and wash yourself. Walk this way, my barley-cake! The pot should disgorge the beets. Fish, get up!" "But I'm not yet done on the other side!" "Well, turn yourself over, won't you? And baste yourself with oil and salt . . ." I will draw, for the benefit of my friends, warm baths from the sea, on columns, like those in the doctor's office, so that they shall flow of their own accord into every man's basin, and the water will say "Stop me!" And the ointment bottle will come immdiately, of its own accord and so will the sponge and the sandals. [Athenaeus, 6.267e–268a]

Similar themes abound from the second half of the fourth century on, in the stories of marvels which were the forerunners of the romanesque genre.

In his *Extraordinary Tales,* the historian Theopompus reports a conversation between Midas and Silenus. According to the king of Phrygia, beyond the ocean there was another world whose inhabitants were divided between two cities, the city of the Pious Ones and the city of the Belligerent Ones. The Pious Ones "lived in peace and great wealth and received their harvests from the earth without the use of ploughs and oxen, without the slightest need for labouring on the land and sowing seed," while the other group, who were born fully armed, spent their time pillaging their neighbors and as a result possessed large quantities of gold and silver (Aelian, *Variae Historiae,* 3.18). No mention of slaves here, apparently.

An account ascribed by Diodorus Siculus to a certain Iamboulos, which dates from the Hellenistic period, describes a blessed isle to the south of Arabia, the inhabitants of which "spend their time in the meadows, the land supplying them with many things for sustenance; for by reason of the fertility of the island and the mildness of the climate, food-stuffs are produced of themselves in greater quantity than is sufficient for their needs." These were consumed frugally, after a minimum of culinary preparation. They were thus in all likelihood able to manage without slaves: "They also take turns in ministering to the needs of one another, some of them fishing, others working at the crafts, others occupying themselves in other useful tasks and still others, with the exception of those who have come to old age, performing the services of the group, in a definite cycle" (Diodorus, 2.55–60), no doubt in conformity with an ideal of self-sufficiency of Cynic-Stoic inspiration.

Another Hellenistic utopia is more precisely situated in time.

Euhemerus is said to have been sent off by Cassander, the king of Macedon (316–297) on "great journeys" in the region of Arabia. His experiences are supposed to have inspired his *Sacred History,* possibly composed in Egypt around 280–270. This work is now known to us only from two passages in Diodorus Siculus. the first is concerned essentially with the history of Greek religion. In the author's view, the traditional gods were simply ancient kings who had been deified by way of popular recognition. This opinion was to remain widely known right down to the end of Antiquity, when Christian apology was to make much of it in order to discredit the gods of paganism. The second passage is devoted to a description of marvelous islands in the Indian Ocean: "One is a sacred island which has no share in any other fruit, but it produces frankincense in such abundance as to suffice for the honours paid to the gods throughout the entire inhabited world." The other island is called Panchaea and is covered with luxuriant vegetation (palms, walnut trees and vines):

> The entire body politic of the Panchaeans is divided into three castes: the first caste among them is that of the priests, to whom are assigned the artisans, the second consists of the farmers and the third is that of the soldiers, to whom are added all the herdsmen. The priests serve as the leaders in all things. . . . The farmers, who are engaged in the tilling of the soil, bring the fruits into the common store, and the man among them who is thought to have practised the best farming receives a special reward when the fruits are portioned out. . . . In the same manner, the herdsmen also turn both the sacrificial animals and all others into the treasury of the State. . . . For, speaking generally, there is not a thing except a home and a garden which a man may possess for his own, but all the products and the revenues are taken over by the priests, who portion out with justice to each man his share, and to the priests alone is given twofold.

No mention of slaves here either, only of a type of extra-economic exploitation that puts one in mind of the Eastern *laoi* and *hierodouloi.*

So the imaginary states of the Greeks certainly included societies without slaves or, to be more precise, societies that knew nothing of slavery, rather than any that had abolished it after experiencing it. Moreover, we should notice how great is the the distance that separates them from real societies.

Let us first consider those that are presented as frugal societies, where the absence of slavery is conceivable only because needs are so modest. Pierre Vidal-Naquet has convincingly shown that, in the eyes of fifth-century Athenians, such societies lay "outside history," in a precivic *time before* that predated civilization itself.[17] That is so in the case of Herodotus, for whom this absence of slavery is dated to the legendary period when the Pelasgians still lived in Attica. It is also true in the case of Pherecrates, for whom the situation is, strikingly enough, connected with a village existence (*komai*), hence with a stage prior to the synoecism of villages into cities, which marked the appearance of the existing form of political organization. It is even so to a certain extent in the case of an author at the beginning of the Hellenistic period such as Timaeus of Tauromenium,[18] given the reputation for archaism attached to the regions of central Greece which Thucydides described as "living under the old conditions," in unfortified villages.[19] "Consequently," writes Vidal-Naquet, "to maintain that there was once a time when the work was done by the women and children is to relate the slaves to those other groups which are also excluded from the Greek city, namely the women and children. It is to define a social hierarchy by means of a myth. That is not writing history."[20] In the case of the Greek cities familiar with slavery of the Helot type, the problem is not posed in quite the same terms since, from the end of the fifth century, the origin of that system was generally considered to date historically from the period of the Dorian invasions (or from the period immediately following). But here too, the existence of the institution of slavery is inseparable from the formation of civic communities.

Let us now examine the sources of the abundance (or relative abundance) that is the necessary condition for the other type of slaveless society. We notice that these sources are in no way human, but totally natural. It is nature that provides the abundance or, to be precise, another nature, an exceptionally fecund one, which in most of these cases assures man of a profusion of both services and goods. The latter offer themselves for consumption in an immediately

---

17. "Réflexions sur l'historiographie grecque de l'esclavage," *Colloque Besançon 1971*, 25–44, in particular 30 (=*The Black Hunter* [1986], 172).

18. "To a certain extent," because Timaeus, after all, does situate the appearance of chattel slavery within historical time, in the period of "Philomelus, who took possession of Delphi" and Mnason, "the friend of Aristotle." In so doing, he imitates theories formulated from the end of the fifth century onward regarding the origin of "ancient" slavery of the Helot type.

19. 1.5.3: "Even today, in many parts of Greece, life goes on under the old conditions, as in the region of the Ozolian Locrians, Aetolians, Acarnanians, and the mainland thereabouts": that is to say, people live in "villages" (1.5.1, 10.2; 2.80.8; 3.94.4, 97.1, 101.2; 4.124.4).

20. Vidal-Naquet, "Réflexions," 29.

consumable form.[21] Man makes virtually no contribution, either with his labor or with his ingenuity.

In contrast to this, we may recall a famous sentence in Aristotle's *Politics,* in which the disappearance of slavery seems to be linked with the development of machines: "If every tool could perform its own work when ordered or by seeing what to do in advance, like the statues of Daedalus in the story, or the tripods of Hephaestus which the poet [Homer, *Iliad,* 18.376] says 'enter self-moved the company divine,'—if thus shuttles wove and quills played harps of themselves, master-craftsmen would have no need of assistants and masters no need of slaves" (1253b, 35). In truth, using an example borrowed from epic, Aristotle here is simply out to illustrate the difference between animated instruments in the form of slaves and inanimate instruments (which are incapable of obeying orders and of fore-sight), in order to demonstrate their complementarity within the family unit, in the context of the "art of acquiring property": "A slave is a live article of property, and every assistant is as it were a tool that serves for several tools" (1253b, 30–35). There is no question of any technical improvement here, nor of multiplying inanimate instru-ments with a view to increasing production. Furthermore, in the following paragraphs, Aristotle goes on to note that production stems from inanimate instruments such as the shuttle "for from a shuttle we get something else besides the mere use of the shuttle" (1254a, 1–5), whereas the slave, considered as an object of property, is "an assistant in the class of instruments of action" (1254a, 5–10), a "practical" but not a "poietic" instrument from which, as Jean-Pierre Vernant writes, "one derives no more than use, and the end of which is not to make an external object separate from the act of production, but to perform an action with no goal other than that of carrying it out for its own sake."[22] Making it clear that he is dealing not with a real possibility but only a hypothetical one, Aristotle imagines the transformation of existing inanimate instruments into animated instruments that would be superior even to those already existing, because they would operate "with foresight" as well as "under or-ders." The disappearance of the slave (and also, let us note, of physical labor) thus depends on a mutation in the natural order. It is relegated to another world, not to the future of this one. Expressed in terms of the modern world, Aristotle's vision would entail deriving

21. It is hard to tell whether the *automatos bios* is a "provocative" popular theme or a discredited aristocratic one, reduced to the level of comedy: H. C. Baldry, "The Idler's Paradise in Attic Comedy," *Greece and Rome* 22 (1953): 49–60.

22. *Myth and Thought among the Greeks* (1983), 248.

the suppression of human labor from the naturalization of the machine, not from the mechanization of nature. It is therefore mistaken to hold the widely accepted view that "Aristotle alone, in the fourth century, seems to have guessed that the solution to the problem of physical labor and slavery lay in developing machinery."[23] On the contrary, in Aristotle's view there was no human solution to the problem. No more than Teleclides or Crates should he be considered the precursor of modern mechanization seen as the substitute for ancient slavery. Far from abolishing the logic of slavery the myth of automation instead reinforces it, integrating it fully into the natural order of things.

The slaveless societies present in the imaginary states of the Greeks are thus excluded from both the natural order and historical time. They are situated not on the horizon of the real world, the world of the city, but in a chronological and ontological beyond.

Nevertheless, even thus divorced from reality, does not the very idea of a slaveless society, simply by its existence, testify to a certain awareness on the part of free men of the fundamental injustice of the servile condition and of the need for its disappearance, in "the best of all possible worlds," for the good of those hitherto forced to endure it? The answer must be: certainly not if it be to the detriment of those who currently benefited from it. All the texts mentioned above show clearly that its absence without any form of substitution was virtually unthinkable. These people had no intention of sacrificing any of their leisure, income, or comforts in order to do away with slavery. Some even envisioned an improved domestic service, which would make meals immediately available to their lips.

It seems to me that, despite the silence of the texts, it is thus possible to seize upon the real reason why, instead of being more fully developed, slavery is left out of the ideal representations of societies of abundance. (Its absence from certain frugal societies, regarded as a lack, is easy to explain: as the result of the incomplete development of a particular cultural model). As well as being a necessary condition for the free man to achieve his full potential, the slave is a risk, a worry, and a responsibility for his master. He is a risk not only at the time of his capture but also in the home, where he represents a degree of at least potential danger. He is a worry if he runs away, falls sick, or dies and also from the point of view of the organization of his activities (especially if it is not possible to hire him out, to set him up on his own, or to entrust his supervision to an

23. J. Aubonnet, *Aristote, Politique,* Collection Univ. de France, 1 (1960), 17, n.4.

overseer, himself also a slave). And he is a responsibility, given that he represents an initial investment and an extra mouth to feed.

Plenty of texts emphasize the disadvantages of slavery to the master: "The mere necessity of policing their serf class is a troublesome matter" (Aristotle, *Politics*, 1269b, 7–12).[24] The art of being a master "however, is one of no particular importance or dignity: the master must know how to direct the tasks which the slave must know how to execute. Therefore all people rich enough to be able to avoid personal trouble have a steward who takes this office, while they themselves engage in politics or philosophy" (1255b, 33–40). "The slave is a necessary possession but not a pleasant one" (fragment from the comic poet Metrodorus: Kourte, fr. 58). That is why, in Xenophon's *Cyropaedia* (8.3.40–41), the Persian Pheraulus seeks to get rid of his riches:

> My only gain from having so much is that I am obliged to take care of more, distribute more to others, and have the trouble of looking after more than I used to have. For now many domestics look to me for food, many for drink and many for clothes, while some need doctors; and one comes to me with a tale about sheep attacked by wolves, or of oxen killed by falling over a precipice, or to say that some disease has broken out among the cattle. And so it looks to me . . . as if I had more trouble now through possessing much than I used to have from possessing little.

Here, slaves are seen in a negative light, as consumers, just as in Plato's *Republic*, where care is taken that the guardians should not be bothered by "the pettiest troubles, of which they would be rid . . . , the embarrassments and pains of the poor in the bringing up of their children and the procuring of money for the necessities of life for their households." According to Aristophanes' *Plutus*, a life of abundance would cut off the very source of slavery: if ever the day came when the god of wealth was in a position to reward all honest men, it would mean the end of all the labors which men perform under the constraint of Poverty (*Penia*) because they lack the necessities of life; it would mean the end of the artisans, trade, and agriculture. Is that because all these labors would be performed by servants "bought for

24. Although it occurs in a passage concerning Lacedaemonia and Crete, this remark is equally relevant to any type of slave, as can be seen from the sentence that follows: "It is clear . . . that those whose helot-system works out in this way do not discover the best mode of treating the problem." It was, indeed, the Helots who were believed to cause the most trouble, both in Plato's view (*Laws* 6. 777cd) and in Aristotle's (*Politics*, 2.1272b, 19 and 7.1330a).

money"? Not at all, since "in the first place, there would not be a single slave merchant left. . . . Naturally enough, for once rich, who would be willing to risk his life in such a profession?" (ll. 522–524).

Thus, the height of happiness for a free man is to be able to provide fully for all his needs without recourse to slaves. On this point too, the imaginary states were designed, as was political practice, to increase the liberty of the free, not to diminish the servitude of the slaves. That may seem a paradoxical and cynical conclusion. Nevertheless, it altogether tallies with the absence of any antislavery thinking in Greece (even at an implicit level), as it does with the general "law" of class societies according to which "the powers of the dominant group are experienced as a burden" by those lower in the hierarchy.[25]

Slavery as a Necessity

Not only was the legitimacy of slavery as an institution never challenged by the Athenians of the classical period (the only group that we are in a position to judge), but equally they never questioned its practical necessity. What emerges from the evidence of our documentation is that, for them, slavery was no superfluous luxury but simply the means for them to procure "necessary things" (*ta anagkaia*) and was therefore the condition of their own fulfillment. One must, of course, leave aside here the various philosophical doctrines—Cynic, Stoic, and Epicurean, among others—which, from the fourth century onward, postulated that the key to individual happiness lay in detachment, in one or another form, from material possessions (including slaves). The Greeks' view of the world was certainly in general more illusory than our own; yet their concept of society was in certain respects much less so, in that they did not attempt to disguise the practice of exploitation.

But we must be clear about the sense in which slaves were regarded as necessities, and to that end, we must, if we are not to be anachronistic, discard the assumption of productivity which nowadays is dictated by the dominant position of economic factors, for it is quite out of keeping with the ideas that prevailed in classical Athens on the normal functioning and ends of social life.

The text that examines the utility of slaves in the most systematic

25. M. Godelier, "La part idéelle du réel," *L'Homme* 18 (1976): 181 (=*L'idéel et le matériel* [1984], 211).

fashion is Aristotle's *Politics*. From the start, slaves are presented as indispensable to the constitution of the complete family, the elementary unit in the social fabric, where they are set in opposition not so much to other, free individuals who belong to it, as to the master (*despotes*) who is in charge of it. That is, they are defined in terms which are more economic than juridical, more functional than statutory, more dynamic than static, in a situation of both antagonism and complementarity (just as the ancient orators defined them in relation to the citizens). Among the items that go to make up the family property, they are regarded as animate instruments, just as the domesticated animals are. Now, according to Aristotle, unlike inanimate instruments such as the shuttle, which are ("poietic") instruments of production because they are capable of producing "something else beside the mere use of them" (1254a, 1–5) animate instruments have no utility apart from what results from their use: they belong to the "class of instruments of action" (praxis), not to that of making (poiesis). Slaves are thus positively perceived as servants, as providers of service, not as workers or, a fortiori, as producers. Neither, in fact, were the free workers, since in this society dominated by use-values, the abstract idea of labor could not, as Vernant has excellently demonstrated,[26] emerge from the diversity of existing modes of behavior nor, consequently, could it be set up as a classificatory principle in the analysis of society.

Hence the nature of the function assigned to slaves: namely, to satisfy the needs of the beneficiaries of their services, that is, their master and his family. Now these needs, inherent in any family economy, are both limited and irreducible. They do not constitute an end in themselves (as does wealth in "the art of making money," or chrematistics[27]), but are instead subordinated to the superior goal of city life, which is not simply to live, but to live "the good life." Thus, all that is expected from slaves is that they should provide their masters with whatever is indispensable, all the goods and services necessary and sufficient for their maintenance, so that their masters have the time to address themselves to all the political and cultural practices that make a citizen. This was precisely what was supposed to be prevented by an archaic law prohibiting the acquisition of slaves, imputed to the Corinthian tyrant Periander.[28]

---

26. *Myth and Thought among the Greeks*, 183–247.

27. In relation to which, significantly enough, slaves are never mentioned because they are not themselves creators of wealth.

28. O. Picard, "Périandre et l'interdiction d'acquérir des esclaves," *Aux origines de l'hellénisme: Mélanges historiques offerts à H. van Effenterre* (1984), 187–91.

The time that was "free" in the sense that it was liberated from the material constraints of existence was not defined negatively as an absence of work, a time when there was nothing to do: the derogatory term *argia* (*a* meaning "without," with the root *ergon*, meaning "work") was applied only to those who were not working when they ought to have been, either because of statutory obligation to do so or in order to avoid poverty or need. The leisure which could be procured by the "wealthy," that is, those not obliged to work for a living, was a quite different matter. It was referred to positively as "a desire for a halt" (*schole*);[29] and on that basis, work or any other form of lucrative activity was negatively defined as a lack of *schole, ascholia*. But *schole* was not devoid of all activity as was tranquility, which had been regarded as the ideal of aristrocratic life in the archaic period; nor was it a synonym for frivolity, amusement pure and simple: *paidia*. It also differed from leisure as understood by Thorstein Veblen at the end of the nineteenth century: "Time is consumed non-productively (1) from a sense of the unworthiness of productive work and (2) as an evidence of pecuniary ability to afford a life of idleness."[30] *Schole*, in contrast, created new values, for it was inseparable from the whole complex of activities to which a citizen devoted (or was supposed to devote) his time (hence the derived meaning of "study," which was eventually, somewhat paradoxically, to produce the modern term "school"!). These activities might be of all kinds, on condition that they were devoid of any basely utilitarian motive: sports, music, philosophy or, at the highest level of all, politics (the "good" kind of politics, which aimed for the well-being of the governed, not at profit for the governors), in other words all the activities that constituted the art of the "good life." There was therefore no question, at least not in Aristotle's thought, of creating a place for contemplatives within the city or even of forming citizens in their image. On the contrary, it was a matter of realizing to the full the excellence (*arete*) of those citizens, as citizens, by making it possible for them to accede to a superior and truly free mode of existence. Conversely, that is also why there was "no leisure for slaves" (Aristotle, *Politics*, 1334, 21). *Schole*, which was the final goal and to a large extent the product of the exploitation of slaves, was in this respect an indispensable element in the maintenance of social relations and, in particular, of slave relations of production.

29. E. C. Welskopf, *Probleme der Musse im alten Hellas* (1962); "Loisir et esclavage dans la Grèce antique," *Colloque Besançon 1973*, 159–78.
30. *The Theory of the Leisure Class* (1899; 1928 ed.), 43.

However, it should by no means be imagined that citizens and free men in general lived in idleness (as in the somewhat exaggerated picture of the slaveholding South painted in 1862 by the abolitionist J. E. Cairnes, in his work entitled *The Slave Power*). There was on the contrary not a sector of material production in which they were not present in one capacity or another.[31]

It is generally accepted that in the classical period the majority of citizens were landowners and most of them cultivated their own land. The same is probably true even of the fourth century, when the ravages sustained by Attica in the course of the Peloponnesian War must have resulted in an increasing role for urban activities in economic life and possibly also in a measure of concentration of landownership. Of course, that does not mean that all the *georgoi* labored unremittingly on the land: the larger landowners, of whom Ischomachus in Xenophon's *Oeconomicus* is a good example, contented themselves with paying at most a daily visit to their properties (which incidentally afforded them some excellent physical exercise) in order to organize and oversee the labor of their slaves, while yet others, such as Pericles, must have relied still more on their slave stewards (see above, p. 69). All the same, the most usual type of *georgos* was the one Aristophanes delights in portraying: the affluent peasant from the zeugite class, who was assisted in his fields by no more than a handful of domestic slaves and who felt disinclined to devote too much of his time to arguments in the assembly or to military expeditions. Right at the bottom of the hierarchy, there must have been a minority of free men who cultivated their parcels of land on their own (or with the aid of their families). Depending upon whether the *georgoi* worked their land with their own hands or simply supervised operations (*epimeleia*), they might or might not be called *autourgoi*. In fourth-century Athens, such men were probably more numerous than is suggested in the legal speeches, which are chiefly concerned with the landowning aristocracy. On the other hand, they were probably less numerous than in other regions of Greece (such as certain parts of the Peloponnese) where rural slavery was less developed. No doubt we should include in the category of *autourgoi* the small number of citizens, metics, and above all freedmen who farmed land leased from private owners, but not the

31. I here reproduce virtually unchanged a few pages from the paper "Le travail libre en Grèce ancienne," which I delivered in 1978 at the International Congress of Economic History at Edinburgh. It subsequently appeared in P. Garnsey, ed. *Non-Slave Labour in the Graeco-Roman World, Proceedings of the Cambridge Philological Society*, Suppl. 6 (1980), 7–10.

holders of property belonging to orphans and epiclerete daughters (heiresses)[32] or those of public or temple estates who, in contrast, were invariably citizens, many of them extremely affluent.

A similar hierarchy existed among the artisans, many of whom (although fewer than has sometimes been believed) were of foreign extraction. Some of them did no more than supervise, more or less closely, their workshops staffed by slaves: such were the "leaders of the people" (the "demagogues") portrayed by Aristophanes (see above, p. 72), who made a living from their trade without having to work too hard at it. But others did work hard in their shops, where they might often be sought out for a chat. Their ideal, although it was not always realized, was to acquire the assistance of a few slaves. Here again, in the absence of any statistical evidence it is impossible to form any idea of the extent of the direct contribution made by the free artisans, whether citizens or metics. And a similar problem arises in the world of commerce, which embraced a wide spectrum of merchants ranging from the small retailers (*kapeloi*) in the agora, confined to their market stalls, to the most prosperous importers (*emporoi*) and bankers, who must have delegated most of their transactions to their slave staff.

The proportion of free wage-earners (*misthotoi*) has also been the subject of various calculations which, being of a more or less modernist inspiration, are predictably widely divergent. Some scholars incline to the view that their number was roughly equal to that of the lowest census class, the thetes, with whom the free wage-earners are often closely linked, and support this theory by referring to the employment center for free wage-earners which existed in Athens: the *kolonetes agoraios,* also known as the *misthios* or *ergatikos.* Others, on the contrary, quite rightly stress that one only became a wage-earner, so to speak, by accident, finding oneself short of cash, when investment was out of the question; and that it would frequently be only on a temporary basis, performing seasonal tasks (harvesting, grape-picking, olive-collecting) or working by the day, and that most of the known examples occur during periods when the city found itself in a difficult economic position. They also point out that there is no evidence of any agricultural or artisan business staffed by wage-earning workers and that it never occurred to anybody to remedy the unemployment of free men by such means.

Then there were the women and children. While the latter were still very young, care was taken to teach them some kind of skill

32. The guardians of these orphans often leased out the properties that the latter inherited.

(*techne*), which they learned by experience—as laid down by one of Solon's famous laws. It would usually be the father who would undertake this task, or alternatively children might be apprenticed out to a third party. From earliest infancy, they were also expected to take part in the household work, as can be inferred from their sharing the role of servants with the women in the more or less utopian representations of slaveless societies. As for the women, whatever their social rank they at least held an important place in the "indoor realm" which was their natural preserve. In the first place they were, clearly, responsible for organizing life in the home in the best possible fashion. Ischomachus instructs his young wife at length on the subject (Xenophon, *Oeconomicus* 7.36–37). But she was also expected sometimes to take a hand in the work herself, in particular "to approach the loom in order to teach others what she knew better and, for her part, learn the things from them which she knew less well" for, except in Sparta, wool-work was the chief productive activity for free women. If need be, she even had to undertake tasks normally reserved for slaves (milling the grain or kneading the dough, for example). The dividing line between these domestic labors and tasks undertaken for lucrative ends is not always easy to define. But it is clear that in some cases free women destined at least part of their production for the outside market: consider the woman in Aristophanes' *Frogs* (ll. 1347–1351) who pictures herself "busy at her work, twirling in her hands a distaff full of thread, making a bobbin to take to market early next morning, to sell it," or the dozen relatives whom Aristarchus takes into his home in wartime and whom he is able to feed only by persuading them, on Socrates' advice, to set about making clothes, "the work considered the most honourable and the most suitable for a woman" (Xenophon, *Memorabilia*, 2.7–10). Sometimes a woman would assist her husband in the exercise of his craft (combing wool, for example, or gilding helmets), or she might work in the fields with him (although female labor in this domain is attested only by the existence of professional terms referring to female harvesters, gleaners, weeders, grape-pickers, and the like). Finally, necessity might compel her to take employment as a wage-earner or to open her own little workshop or rather a small business. Even in Athens, where a woman's rights to property appear to have been more limited than elsewhere, it would not appear that the law which prohibited her from "contracting for more than a medimnus of barley" (about fifty liters) really constituted a serious obstacle that made her reliant at every turn upon the good offices of her lord and master (*kyrios*).

Although we know enough to prevent us from representing the

Athenians of the classical period as citizen-landowners, we do not possess any quantitative evidence that would allow us to gauge their overall role in production in relation to that of the slaves, nor have we any means of estimating the numbers involved in the various categories of workers we have distinguished. And what is true for classical Athens is, a fortiori, also true of most Greek cities, whatever the period, where our only means of assessing the diffusion of free labor is on the basis—fragile enough (as we have seen)—of suppositions concerning the converse diffusion of slave labor. Only for a very few cities is the problem somewhat more circumscribed by the prohibition affecting free men, or to be more precise, all citizens with full rights, which forbade them to work as artisans or in trade: the best example is Sparta, or rather Sparta during the classical period, which exploited the myth of Lycurgus to impose such prohibitions.[33] But even in this case we know nothing about the extent to which the Equals took part in the agricultural work that, in principle, was regarded as being particularly prestigious. All that we know is that the constraints of their public life (warfare, sports, communal meals, and, to a lesser degree, politics) must barely have left them the time to control the exploitation of their *kleroi* from a distance.

Considered theoretically indispensable to the fulfillment of free men, servile labor thus does appear to have played a determining role in it in the places where we can form the clearest picture, that is, in classical Athens and even more, but in a different way, in Sparta. That is not to suggest that its disappearance would have compromised the physical survival of citizens, but it would have compromised the sociocultural situation they were creating or endeavoring to create. In this sense (and I can hardly see that any other is justifiable to a historian) it is therefore undeniable that chattel slavery in classical Athens and communal servitude of one type or another elsewhere did constitute the "basis" of Greek society or—to put it another way—the necessary element for it to affirm its identity. (Of course such a judgment requires considerable qualification when it comes to the archaic period, when chattel slavery was still relatively undeveloped. We must also bear in mind the exceptions represented by peripheral regions such as the Eastern Hellenistic kingdoms, where the dominant mode of production was based upon other forms of dependent labor.) In other words, the problem con-

33. P. A. Cartledge, "Did Spartan Citizens Ever Practise a Manual *Techne?*" *Liverpool Classical Monthly* 1 (1976): 115–19. Any criticisms addressed to the Spartans on this point would relate solely to the fashion in which they used their *schole*, entirely with a view to warfare.

sists in determining not so much whether slaves did most of the work but rather the role that they played in the socioeconomic process.

The Servile Condition

It is usually with the more or less avowed intention of minimizing, if not denying the "slave" nature of the Greek societies that some scholars underline all the elements which, on a practical level, in the day-to-day reality of social and personal relations, helped to diversify the servile population and eventually to integrate its better, or at least luckier, members into the world of the free. This position is certainly based upon a number of acknowledged facts,[34] but, in my view, it distorts the lessons to be drawn from the situation.

It is clear that the social condition of Athenian slaves varied considerably depending on their origins, their juridical status, and above all their position in the work process.

Those employed in the mines—principally to hew out the ore and carry it along the insalubrious and narrow underground passages— were regarded as the most unfortunate. For there is every reason to believe that, in this domain, working conditions in classical Greece differed hardly at all from those Diodorus described for Ptolemaic Egypt (3.13): "No leniency or respite of any kind is given to any man who is sick, or maimed, or aged, or in the case of a woman for her weakness, but all without exception are compelled by blows to persevere in their labours, until through ill-treatment they die in the midst of their tortures. Consequently, the poor unfortunates believe, because their punishment is so excessively severe, that the future will always be more terrible than the present and they therefore look forward to death as more to be desired than life." In the evening, the Laurium slaves were all assembled in wretched hamlets which were cursorily fortified (against possible escape attempts more than enemy attacks). The lot of those subjected to other forms of forced labor, such as milling grain, can hardly have been more desirable.

Slightly better was the position of most of the artisans grouped in

---

34. I should, perhaps, note that I am fully in agreement with, for example, the following remark made by A. J. Gourevitch in *Les catégories de la culture médiévale* (1982), 263: "It was not purely self-interest that associated the feudal lord with his land and the serfs who cultivated it; it was a complex mixture of relations of exploitation, political power, dependency, tradition, customs, emotions, protection, and respect."

workshops and that of the agricultural workers, especially those who had some special qualification. One such, in all probability would have been the painter by the name of Lydos, a native of Myrina, whose signature appears on an Attic vase of 530–520.[35]

A similar hierarchy was to be found in, for example, the world of prostitution, whose members were essentially drawn from the servile population. Its levels ranged from the generally available *pornai* who "worked" in the slums of Piraeus to the high-grade courtesans who were more sophisticated and cultivated than most free women (one example being Neaera, who acquired her freedom thanks to the generosity of her official lovers and even managed to infiltrate Athenian "high society"); and it included *hetairai* of every kind, such as the musicians and dancers whom the citizens would occasionally hire to enliven their banquets and drinking parties.

At the top of the ladder were the public slaves—such as the Pittalakos whom Aeschines, in his *Against Timarchus* (54–55), depicts as a wealthy connoisseur of cock fights and a bit debauched—and the slaves who lived and worked in an independent fashion in return for a fee (in particular those employed in banking).

The mass of domestic slaves found themselves in an intermediate, but somewhat contradictory situation. To the extent that they were better integrated into family life than the rest, they were more likely to enjoy a minimum of comfort and security or even to win the affection and favor of their master or mistress.[36] One particular case in point were the nurses, to whom many funerary stelae bear touching dedications. There were also the playmates of the master's children and the pedagogues, indulgent toward the escapades of youth; and, of course, the concubines, more or less tolerated by the legitimate wife, and the fruits of their lovemaking. Then there were the pretty youths who attracted the first amorous passions of the master's sons;[37] and also the trusted housekeepers and stewards. However, it is equally clear that these domestic slaves, who found themselves in a position of maximum dependence in every respect, were also the ones most likely to suffer on the rebound from any difficulties encountered by their master and from his bad temper.

35. F. Canciani, "Lydos, der Sklave," *Antike Kunst.* 21 (1978): 17–22. It is not simply a matter of the famous Lydos; other contemporary vase painters also bore slave names: Brygos, Sikelos, Sikanos, Skythos.

36. See J. Vogt, "Human Relations in Ancient Slavery," *Ancient Slavery*, 103–201; for the funerary epigrams of slaves, see H. Raffeiner, *Sklaven und Freigelassene: Eine soziologische Studie auf der Grundlage des griechischen Grabepigramms, Comm. Aenip.* 23 (1977).

37. See K. J. Dover, *Greek Homosexuality* (1978).

Thus Aristotle remarks: "We come into collision most with those of our servants whom we employ most often for ordinary attendance" (*Politics*, 1263a, 19–21). The position of these slaves was all the more wretched given that they were not necessarily the ones whom it was in their master's interest to treat carefully in order to derive the greatest profit from them. Hence the decidedly double image, easy to whitewash or to blacken, which we find so often in the comedies of Aristophanes: slaves who are at the same time confidants and scapegoats.

These differences in social status in the servile world appear to have been easily detectable, particularly from the clothing worn (the symbolic function of which, in this kind of society, has by now surely been adequately demonstrated). This was the method adopted by Ischomachus, in Xenophon's *Oeconomicus* (13.10), to encourage the zeal of his rural slaves: "The clothes that I must provide for my work-people, and the shoes, are not all alike. Some are better than others, some worse, in order that I may reward the better servant with the superior articles, and give the inferior to the less deserving."

That in appearance and in their whole way of life slaves, in Athens more than elsewhere, were liable to be confused with citizens is something one writer went so far as to remark. This was the anonymous author of *The Constitution of the Athenians,* which was probably written in about 430 by an extremely perspicacious detractor of the democratic regime often referred to as "the Old Oligarch":[38]

As for the slaves and the metics, in Athens they enjoy considerable license. It is forbidden to strike them here, and a slave will not make way as you pass. I will tell you the reason for this local peculiarity. If it were customary for the free man to strike a slave, metic, or freedman, he would very often mistake an Athenian for one of these, and strike him. The Athenian people is not distinguishable by its clothing from the slaves and metics, and its outward appearance is no better. If surprise is also felt at the sight of Athenians allowing their slaves to lead a comfortable life and at the fact that some of them have an easy existence, it is also quite possible to show that even here they act sensibly. In a country which is a sea power, in order to have money it is necessary to become the slaves of the slaves (so that they will earn money and pay their dues) and to let them live freely. And where there are wealthy slaves, there is no point in my slave being afraid of you (it is in Lacedaemonia, on the other hand, that my slave *will* be afraid of you), for if your slave is afraid of me there is a good chance that he will give me his money in order to

38. See C. Leduc, *La constitution d'Athènes attribuée à Xénophon* (1976).

save his skin. So that is why we have allowed our slaves to speak freely to free men. [1.10–12]

These remarks, coming from a resolute opponent of Athenian democracy, should certainly not be taken too literally. To some extent they purvey a favorable idea of the servile condition simply in order the better to emphasize the degradation of the "people"—and moreover we have no way of establishing any comparison with what was going on elsewhere. Nevertheless, they testify to the degree of socioeconomic differentiation reached in Athens within the servile class as early as the beginning of the Peloponnesian War.

It is a tendency that must have become accentuated subsequently—if only because more slaves were given the opportunity of working on their own, outside their master's household, in return for the payment of a fee (above, p. 71).

In my opinion, however, the increasing heterogeneity of the forms and degrees of servile exploitation does not authorize us to conclude that either the principle of slavery or the statutory hierarchy, the very basis of the social edifice, was weakening.

The Treatment of Athenian Slaves

Nor is such a conclusion warranted by a study of the individual behavior of masters toward their slaves. The best way of forming a clear picture of the situation is not to pose the problem, as is usually done, in terms of "humanity." If one adopts that point of view one can reach no better than a partial or, at best, an ambiguous conclusion, given that it will be based upon a multiplicity of individual cases ranging from cruelty to affection and including pure indifference. It could have been otherwise only if passions had become exacerbated and polarized as the result of a conflict between the partisans and the adversaries of slavery. But generally speaking, such conflicts did not arise. So the problem is not so much to discover whether slaves (or, at another level, women) were well or badly treated. It is more a matter of understanding how a slave was regarded, as a cultural product. One can then see—and this is the essential point—that he was always considered in the light of his master's interests (avowed interests, moreover, which it was not felt necessary to disguise in order to conceal the mechanics of exploitation, as happens in capitalist societies). Alternatively (and it boils down to the same thing) he was seen as the Stoics saw him, that is, from the point of view of the interests of the slave *qua* slave.

In classical Athens consequently, the rule of behavior toward slaves was fundamentally the same as that which applied for domesticated animals which, according to Xenophon (*Oeconomicus*, 12.6), "learn obedience in two ways: by being punished when they disobey and by being rewarded when they are eager to serve you. . . . In dealing with slaves, the training thought suitable for wild animals is also a very effective way of teaching obedience." It was up to the master to learn how to mete out the appropriate material rewards and corporal punishments, encouragement and censure, in such a way as to obtain the best possible results.

Seen from this point of view, it was a matter of opinion whether a master should take into account the slaves' reasoning capacities and establish friendly relations with them. According to Plato, to treat them as free men was to "spoil" them: "An address to a slave should be mostly a simple command; there should be no jesting with slaves, either male or female, for by a course of excessively foolish indulgence in their treatment of their slaves, masters often make life harder both for themselves and for their slaves, as subject to rule" (*Laws*, 6.777d–778a). He assures the reader (6.757a) that "slaves will never be friends with masters." In contrast, in the opinion of Aristotle, who is here opposing Plato's ideas: "those persons are mistaken who deprive the slave of reasoning and tell us to use command only; for admonition is more properly employed with slaves than with children" (*Politics*, 1260b, 5–7). In his view, the slave is, as we have seen (p. 122), quite capable of understanding reasons when they are given to him. The Aristotelian author of the *Nicomachean Ethics* wonders whether one can go so far as to conceive of friendship with them. His own answer is yes and no: no insofar as they are slaves, yes to the extent that they are men "capable of participating in law and contract" (8.11.6–7), particularly within the framework of a household.

All these questions, which multiply from the fourth century onward,[39] about the best way of behaving toward slaves, seem to me to be a response to two essential preoccupations that sometimes prove difficult to reconcile.

The first was a desire to found the domination of the masters not only on the use of violence, but also on the consent of those dominated: to replace enforced obedience with spontaneous obedience and thus to reduce the sources of tension within the social organism. It was in this spirit that, during the Hellenistic period, the Stoics

39. See in particular E. Grace, "What Is a Slave? . . ." *Vestnik Drevnei Istorii* (1970), no.1:49–67; Klees, *Herren und Sklaven*.

advocated kinder behavior toward slaves, although they never brought into question the discretionary authority of the masters.

The second preoccupation was, in contrast, to reinforce the social hierarchy by connecting every type of action with a statutory coefficient and thus to avoid the possibility that, in a comparable situation, the behavior of a free man and that of a slave could assume an equal significance. In medicine, a similar situation obtained. It is true that some texts, such as the Hippocratic oath (early fourth century) and the collection of cases mentioned in the treatises of the *Epidemics* (late fifth–mid-fourth centuries) suggest that slaves were tended by free doctors. There are others, however, in particular Plato's *Republic* and above all the *Laws* (4.720), which make a clear distinction between two types of medicine: one a patient process based on persuasion, which is practiced by doctors possessed of knowledge; the other, expeditious and authoritarian, which is administered by assistants, either free men or slaves, who act as doctors on the basis of practical experience. The former was generally reserved for the free, the latter for slaves. And given that the distinction established by Plato does not appear to be merely theoretical, it does seem likely that, as modern humanists who believe in the effective unity of these two types of medicine would have it,[40] slaves were usually treated by the doctor's assistants, the doctor himself attending their bedside in person only in exceptional cases, at the express request of the slave's master.

We should consequently beware of forming a mistaken impression of the "good" treatment meted out to slaves. It is usually easy enough to see that in the last analysis it never appears to be dictated by any consideration of the so-to-speak personal interests of its beneficiaries. By way of examples, first let us examine two passages, of tricky interpretation, taken from the Pseudo-Aristotle's *Oeconomica*. In one we are told that slaves "should have work and punishment, but no food is tyrannical (*biaion*) and destroys their efficiency" (1.5.3); in the other, that "it is just (*dikaion*) and beneficial (*sumpheron*) to offer slaves their freedom, as a prize" (1.5.6). Before openly addressing himself to the master's interests might the author, in both instances, perhaps be taking into account the interests of the slave? In truth he is doing nothing of the kind. In the first case, it is simply a question of averting from the social body as a whole the defilement

40. F. Kudlien, *Die Sklaven in der griechischen Medizin der klassischen und hellenistischen Zeit, Forsch. ant. Sklav.* 2 (1968); *contra* R. Joly, "Esclaves et médecins dans la Grèce antique," *Sudhoffs Archiv* 53 (1969): 1–14.

provoked by any act of violence against a human being (for the same reason one could not kill a slave without good cause and without the due formalities). In the second, it is a matter of not going against what it is *normal* to do in particular conditions in order to obtain a given result.[41] So these recommendations are not based upon an autonomous system of transcendental moral values; they are not really ethical in nature, but normative. They are designed simply to bring the treatment of slaves into harmony with the superior interests of the master-slave combination and the civic body (and those interests are, of course, the interests of free men).[42]

Perhaps, though, one might invoke the touching flight of rhetoric which Demosthenes addresses to the barbarians in his *Against Meidias* (21.49–50): 'There are in Greece men so mild and humane in disposition that though they have often been wronged by you and though they have inherited a natural hostility towards you, yet they permit no insult to be offered even to men whom they have bought for a price and keep as their slaves. Nay, they have publicly established this law forbidding such insult, and they have already punished many of the transgressors with death." But no: the humanity which is here made much of is "simply" *philanthropia*, that is, a kind of commiseration which can develop only on the periphery of justice, within the framework of liberty not encompassed by law.[43]

In Xenophon's *Cyropaedia*, Cyrus the Elder is prompted by quite different motives when he ensures that his servants are well fed on his hunting expeditions:

Whenever they were to drive the animals down into the plains for the horsemen, he allowed those of the lower classes, but none of the free men, to take food with them on the hunt; and whenever there was an expedition to make he would lead the serving men to water, just as he did the beasts of burden. And again, when it was time for luncheon he would wait for them until they could get something to eat, so that they should not get so ravenously hungry. And so this class also called him "father", just as the nobles did, for he provided for them well so that they might spend all their lives as slaves, without a protest. (8.1.43–44).

41. Klees, *Herren und Sklaven*, 128–29; cf. E. Will, "Un nouvel essai d'interprétation de l'*Athenaion Politeia* pseudo-xénophontique," *REG* 91 (1978): 80, n.5: "There are plenty of examples where *dike, dikaios, dikaiōs* simply express the *normal* nature of a situation created by well-defined conditions. . . . 'Justice' here is simply a matter of balance: a manifestation."

42. Even if some Stoics, such as Poseidonius, went so far as to justify slaveholding relations as being in the interest of the slaves; but of course they interpreted slaves as inferiors and had no view to promoting their emancipation.

43. J. de Romilly, *La douceur dans la pensée grecque* (1979), 51.

Here we have an extreme case, in which slaves are treated better than free men in order to underline the distance between them. The fact is that the scales of values of the two groups are completely different, as Aristophanes amusingly emphasizes in a passage of the *Plutus* (ll. 190–191) in which, while the master dreams of "love, ... of music, ... of honour, ... of manliness, ... of ambition, ... and of command," his slave speaks only of "loaves, ... of sweets, ... of cheesecakes, ... of dried figs, ... of barley-meal, ... and of pea soup." In contrast to this laxity, which is tolerated or even encouraged in slaves, the free man's control over others presupposes control over himself (*enkrateia*), the very leit motif of Greek morality on account of its power to master the passions, which might otherwise dominate him.[44]

This is also the explanation for the sexual relations between masters and slaves. As Michel Foucault has rightly observed,[45] in the fundamental relationship that here links the active subject who does the penetrating with the passive object who is penetrated, the place of the slave is definitely and irremediably marked out: on the same side as that of the free woman. But in the case of the slave there are none of those elements that confer a relative prestige on the free woman and thus give rise to certain ethical problems where sexual life is concerned. The fact that a slave, whether female or male, could serve as a normal object of pleasure for his or her master within the *oikos* or for the general community of free men, after their banqueting, in houses specializing in this field, really poses no problem, as is repeatedly borne out by the evidence. But a situation involving a reversal of the natural roles, in which the slave becomes the active lover of a free woman or man, is difficult to envisage (in cases involving a free woman) and heavily sanctioned (in cases involving a free man). That is attested by, for example, an ancient Athenian law which ruled that "a slave shall not be the lover (*erastes*) of a free boy or follow after him, or else he shall receive fifty blows of the public lash" (Aeschines, *Against Timarchus*, 139) and also by laws in the same spirit which banned slaves from the gymnasium.[46] Furthermore, on the rare occasions when mention is made of a married man more or less avoiding sexual relations with his slaves (in Plato's *Laws*, Isocrates' *Nicocles*, and the Pseudo-Aristotle's *Oeconomica*), his "temperance" is, obviously enough, in no

44. R. Just, "Freedom, Slavery and the Female Psyche," *Crux*, ed. P. A. Cartledge and F. D. Harvey (1985), 169–88.
45. *The History of Sexuality*, 2: *The Use of Pleasure* (1985), 215–16.
46. M. Golden, "Slavery and Homosexuality at Athens," *Phoenix* 38 (1984): 308–24.

way motivated by consideration for others any more than it is prompted by any mutual commitment inherent in the marital relationship; instead "it is the result of a political regulation that is imposed by fiat in the case of the Platonic laws, or—in the case of Isocrates or Aristotle—by the husband himself through a sort of self-limitation of his power",[47] because desires and pleasures would otherwise become embodied in domestic servants over whom he needed to retain his authority. Situated at the opposite pole from this willed and positive liberty is the license that characterizes lovemaking in the servile world, only mentioned in our texts when it is a matter of either encouraging or restricting it in accordance with the interests of the slave's master.

The Treatment of Helots

In Sparta, the treatment meted out to the Helots by the Equals was reputed in Antiquity, and still is today, to have been "harsher" than that of the Athenian slaves. But here too, what is interesting is not so much the degree of its inhumanity (which it is easy to deny on the basis of numerous edifying anecdotes) as the principles, compounded of scorn and violence, upon which it was based. What is different in the case of Sparta is that the treatment of the Helots was regulated by institutional measures and ritual practices that were more highly elaborated than those elsewhere.

Some of these measures were solemnly designed to hold the Helots up as objects of derision: for instance forcing them to "undertake the most ignominious and degrading work"; making them "wear dog-skin caps and be wrapped in a leather jerkin" (Myron of Priene in Athenaeus, 14.657d); getting them "to drink too much strong wine" and then introducing them "into their public messes . . . to show the young men what a thing drunkenness was"; making them "sing songs and dance dances that were low and ridiculous and . . . let the nobler kind alone" (i.e., be reserved for free men) (Plutarch, *Lycurgus,* 27.8.10).

It was in the same spirit that the Helots were subjected to various officially approved forms of direct violence. According to Myron, for example, "every year they shall receive a stated number of blows even when they are blameless, so that they may never forget that they are slaves. In addition to this, if any of them presented any

47. Foucault, *Use of Pleasure,* 167.

appearance of vigour exceeding that of a slave, they laid upon them the death penalty, and upon their owners punishment for failure to prevent them growing fat." Of the ritual Spartan slayings of Helots, the most renowned was the *crypteia* which Plutarch (*Lycurgus,* 28.3– 5) describes as follows: "The magristrates from time to time sent out into the country at large the most discreet of the young warriors, equipped only with daggers and such supplies as were necessary. In the day time they scattered into obscure and out of the way places, where they hid themselves and lay quiet; but in the night they came down into the highways and killed every Helot whom they caught. Often too, they actually traversed the fields where the Helots were working and slew the sturdiest and best of them." This institution is extremely complex and has been interpreted in various ways. It is understood on the one hand in the light of the rites of passage from adolescence to adulthood, as observed by modern anthropologists in African societies.[48] Seen in this perspective, it constitutes, in the education of the young Spartans (or at any rate some of them), a phase of segregation and living in the wild, before their integration into the civic community. But why were these nocturnal hunters assigned Helots as their prey? Was this a policing measure designed to intimidate the Helot population by doing away with a number of them (preferably the most dangerous), or was it, rather, a symbolic action seldom carried out, the effect of which would be periodically to reaffirm the Equals' powers over life and death and, as Jean Ducat puts it, "at regular intervals to reactivate a 'scorn' strong enough to maintain the social hierarchy in all its integrity"?[49]

In any event, these precautions appear to have been sanctioned by legislation and social practice much more clearly in Sparta than in Athens. Why is that? Was it because the Spartans were less suscepti- ble to "humane" feelings than the Athenians? Or was it, rather, because, dealing with two different types of slaves, the two groups had perforce to underline the difference between themselves and their slaves with different degrees of emphasis? We shall discover that the latter explanation is the correct one when we consider the

48. See H. Jeanmaire's famous *Couroi et Courètes* (1939) and his article devoted to the Spartiate *crypteia* in *REG* 26 (1913): 121–50; A. Brelich, *Paides e Parthenoi* (1969); and two stimulating articles by P. Vidal-Naquet, "Le chasseur noir et l'origine de l'éphébie attique," *Annales* 23 (1968): 947–64; and "Les jeunes, le cru, l'enfant grec et le cuit," in *Faire de l'histoire*, ed. J. Le Goff and P. Nora, 3 (1974), 137–68 (=*The Black Hunter* [1986], 106–59).

49. "Le mépris des Hilotes," *Annales* 29 (1974): 1451–64 (in particular 1462); P. Oliva, "Die Helotenverachtung," *Acta Univ. Carolinae, Philol.* 2 (1976), 159–65.

evidence from a comparative study of the politico-military role of serfs of the Helot type and slaves of the Athenian type.

Slaves in Political Life

In theory, the political role of the Greek slaves was bound to be nonexistent because they were in no sense part of the civic body.

Their exclusion was reflected generally by various legal prohibitions. They were forbidden not only to attend the peoples' assemblies but likewise to frequent gymnasia and *palestrai*, to court young citizens and even, in Athens, to bear the names of tyrannicides, such as Harmonius or Aristogiton—quite apart from the fact that, as we shall see presently, in normal circumstances they were excluded from the army. In this context slaves, by very reason of the political and social neutrality conferred upon them by their depersonalization, could rightfully play no more than an instrumental role, performing various service tasks: for instance, the public slaves constituted an embryonic bureaucracy.

However, the gap between slave and citizen took a somewhat different form depending on whether the slave in question was of the Athenian or the Helot type. The former was always seen as a barbarian, an absolute foreigner whom it would be absurd to envisage ever acceding to a political existence (that is to say, to life in the city, the *polis*); the Helot, on the other hand, remained a member of an autochthonous community reduced to servitude by conquest but not on that account dissolved; he thus still had a residual claim to autonomy. When affranchised, slaves of the Athenian type were still held at just as much of a distance from citizenship, whereas slaves of the Helot type would, if abroad, recover all their political rights vis-à-vis their former masters; otherwise, if they remained on their home ground, they would be granted an intermediary status that to a certain extent integrated them into the dominant community. (In Sparta, for example, affranchised Helots, while obviously not acceding to the rank of Equals, nevertheless became entitled to the name of Lacedaemonians, on the same footing as the *perioikoi*). According to Ernst Lévy, that is the reason Sparta was considered an oligarchy whereas Athens was not, despite the fact that the ratio of citizens to the rest of the population was barely greater in Athens than in Sparta: "The reason why nobody ever claims Athens to have been an oligarchy, on the basis of the number of Athenian slaves, is that, unlike the Helots or the *perioikoi,* the slaves were never considered as possible citizen-material."[50]

The ancient Greek idea of a "City of Slaves" (*Doulopolis*) affords us a way of grasping both the principle of their political nonexistence and also the qualifications that apply depending on which category of slaves is involved. In general, the idea was regarded as quite absurd, unthinkable, because it was a contradiction in terms. Aristotle tells us why in his *Politics:* it is that the city "is formed not for the sake of life only, but rather for the good life" (1280a, 31–33). "Surely it is quite out of the question that it should be proper to give the name of state to a community that is by nature a slave, for a state is self-sufficient, but that which is a slave is not self-sufficient" (1291a, 8). That is how a character in the *Anchises* of Anaxandrides (a poet of Middle Comedy) can exclaim: "My good fellow, there is no such thing as a city for slaves!" (2.137.4 Kock). Nevertheless, some writers did imagine such a thing. But where did they situate it? Either in barbarian territory (Egypt, Libya, Caria, Syria, Arabia) or in Crete. (Sosicrates, the author who chose Crete, is also known to have been interested in the whole variety of forms of dependency that existed on that island.) Never were these cities located in an area of Greece in which chattel slavery predominated. Pierre Vidal-Naquet consequently concludes: "It would thus appear that when the Greeks wanted to define a 'Slave City,' their only alternative was to situate it either right outside the Greek world (in a barbarian country) or else in a country where a 'slave' was not exactly a slave," where the gap between slave and citizen seemed less impossible to cross than in a city such as Athens.[51]

In this respect it is most illuminating to follow Vidal-Naquet and compare the question of servile power with that of gynecocracy, or female power. Athough they in a sense represented a constituant element of the city, women, like slaves, nevertheless found themselves totally excluded from its government. For Aristotle indeed, female power and slave power represented two linked forms of subversion characteristic of extreme democracy and the tyranny that follows in its wake: "Dominance of women in the homes, in order that they may carry abroad reports against the men, and lack of discipline among the slaves, for the same reason; for slaves and women do not plot against tyrants and also, if they prosper under tyrannies, must feel well-disposed to them, and to democracies as

50. "Cité et citoyen dans la *Politique* d'Aristote," *Ktema* 5 (1980): 228–39.
51. "Esclavage et gynécocratie," 67.

well" (*Politics*, 1313b, 33–38; cf. 1319b, 27–30). However, the only historical example that he provides is taken, precisely, from warrior states such as Sparta: in his view, Sparta is under threat from both the Helots and the women, who live there "dissolutely, in respect of every sort of dissoluteness and luxuriously" (*Politics*, 1269b, 22–23).

Legendary tradition recorded three examples of the establishment in Greece of regimes both servile and female. In Argos, which found itself depleted of citizens following its defeat at the hands of the Spartans at the end of the sixth or the beginning of the fifth century, the women with the help of slaves (probably the local Gymnetes), whom they married, assumed responsibility for the survival of the city until the sons of the slain citizens reached adulthood. It was an episode that apparently acquired great notoriety beyond the frontiers of Argos, if it is true that the tetralogy Aeschylus devoted to the subject of the Danaids in 463 was designed to give poetic expression to the legal conflicts and serious social and psychological difficulties which faced Argos at that time. He is supposed to have evoked the dilemma of forced marriage and the resistence of women to the cruel destiny that faced them, and also to have commemorated the self-sacrifice of those who, like Hypermnestra, accepted husbands whom they loathed out of a sense of patriotism and a natural desire to produce children. In Locris, when the citizens were detained far from home by the Messenian War, their wives are supposed to have consoled themselves in the arms of their slaves (who were probably of the Helot type, as we saw above: p. 101) and subsequently to have founded the Italian colony of Epizephyrian Locris in collaboration with them. Polybius (12.5.6) tells us that that is the reason why "at Locris, all ancestral nobility is derived from women, not from men." Another tradition held that the Lacedaemonian social outcasts known as the *Parthenoi*, who founded Tarentum, were the bastards born during the First Messenian War from the unions of Spartan women with their Helots. It thus seems significant that it was only in cities with a system of servitude of the Helot type that the slaves were sometimes given the chance, in times of crisis, to come together with the citizens' wives and thereby become associated with the life of the community.[52] In some of these cities such

52. The association of servile and female power has been denied in these three cases by R. van Compernolle in two articles: "Le mythe de la gynécocratie-doulocratie argienne," *Le monde grec: Hommages à Claire Préaux* (1975), 355–64; and "Le tradizioni sulla fondazione e sulla storia arcaica di Locri Epizefiri e la propaganda politica alla fine del V e IV secolo av. Cr.," *ASNP*, n.s., 6 (1976): 329–400. D. Musti ("Sviluppo e crisi di un'oligarchia greca: Locri tra il VII e il IV sec.," *Studi Storici* 18 [1977]: 59–85) has pointed out that the "servile" origins of the Locrians did not prevent them from

alliances were more or less recognized, as the Gortyn code makes clear, whereas in others, where chattel slavery flourished, they would have been possible only at the cost of a total subversion of the social and political order. In his *Ecclesiazusae*, Aristophanes is quite capable of stretching fantasy to the point where the women decide to set up a communist regime, but not so far as to envisage sexual promiscuity with their slaves—or, for that matter, economic emancipation for the latter. Here, the civic promotion of women in the upside-down utopian world is disassociated from that of the slaves, whereas in the examples mentioned above, the two were intimately linked both in political thought and in legendary tradition.

We know of other historical examples of such collusion between women and slaves, in cases where the collusion is forced, not spontaneous, and its imposition is generally imputed to tyrants.

The two for which we have the most evidence took place in countries with systems of serfdom of the Helot type. One concerns Clearchus of Heraclea who in 364 slaughtered or exiled the aristocrats and, according to Justin, replaced them with their slaves (*servi*)—that is, most historians believe, with Mariandynians: "He forced their wives and daughters, on pain of death, to marry their own slaves, in order to attach the latter to himself even more, at the same time as setting them up once and for all against their masters. But for the women, such dismal marriages were a misfortune harder to bear than death itself. So many of them committed suicide before their marriages, as many did during the marriage, after having killed their new husbands, thus avoiding such fateful misfortunes through the noble virtue of their honour" (*Epitome Historiarum Philippicarum*, 16.5.2–4). The second example features Nabis,[53] the tyrant of Sparta who, according to Polybius, after expelling some of the citizens at the end of the third century, "freed the slaves" (by which we should understand some of the Helots) and "married them to their masters' wives and daughters" (16.13.1). According to Livy, he also promoted them to citizenship, after allotting them plots of land. When the system set up by Nabis was dismantled in 188, "in the case of those who had been made citizens of Sparta, [Philopoemen] removed them all into Achaea, with the exception of three thousand

---

opting for a long time for a political regime of a distinctly aristocratic nature. See also L. Gallo, "Colonizzazione, demografia e strutture di parentela," *Modes de contact et processus de transformation dans les sociétés anciennes* (1983), 721–28.

53. B. Shimron, "Nabis of Sparta and the Helots," *CPhil.* 61 (1966): 1–7; G. Texier, "Nabis et les Hilotes," *DHA* 1 (1974): 189–205, and *Nabis* (1975); D. Mendels, "Polybius, Nabis and Equality," *Athenaeum* 67 (1979): 311–33.

who would not obey him and were unwilling to go away from Sparta. These he sold into slavery" (Plutarch, *Life of Philopoemen*, 16.4).

In other cases, the nature of the slaves involved is left indeterminate (although it seems likely that some may have been of the Athenian type). In the colonial city of Cumae, in southern Italy, the tyrant Aristodemus in 505–503 allowed them to enter into union with the wives and daughters of their former masters, whom they had just massacred (Dionysius of Halicarnassus, *Antiquitates Romanae*, 7.6–11). In Sicily, in 405, the elder Dionysius married slaves to the wives of the aristocrats who had been banished from Syracuse (Diodorus, 14.7 and 66) and, at an unspecified date and place, also to the "daughters, wives and sisters of their masters" whom he had just exterminated (Aeneas Tacticus, 40, 2–3). In Achaea, soon after 332–331, the tyrant Chairon, installed at Pellene by Alexander the Great, after banishing the "best" of the citizens, "bestowed upon their slaves the property of their masters, and forced the masters' wives into wedlock with the slaves" (Athenaeus 11.509b, in a passage probably inspired by Demochares, the Athenian orator of the late fourth century). In Chalcedon, which in 315 "suffered a great dearth of men" following a bloody defeat at the hands of Zipoites, the king of Bithynia, "most of the women were obliged to cohabit with freedmen and metics" (Plutarch, *Moralia*, 402E). In 201, during the siege of Chios, the king of Macedon, Philip V, is supposed to have promulgated a decree aimed at the defenders which the "virtuous" Plutarch describes as "barbarous and insolent," urging "the slaves to defect to him, their reward to be freedom and marriage with their owners, meaning thereby that he was intending to unite them with the wives of their masters" (*Mora.*, 245B.C.).

Extrapolating from the fact that some of these examples must have involved chattel slaves and that we know of plenty of others in which it was colonists, conquerors, and mercenaries who gained access to the houses of citizens in this fashion, one might feel tempted to account for the frequency of the appeals made to serfs of the Helot type not so much on the basis of their particular status as in terms of the particular cities where they lived.[54] Warlike cities such as Sparta, which could muster only a minority of citizen-sol-

54. D. Asheri, "Tyrannie et mariage forcé," *Annales* 32 (1977): 21–48. There has probably been a tendency to underestimate the elementary satisfaction derived by the dominated, at every period, from possessing the women of their masters. Thus, at Romans (E. Le Roy Ladurie, *Carnival in Romans* [1979], 254), "the 'rebels'' plan, the judge [Antoine Ginérin] declared, . . . had been to . . . marry the wives of the said notables whom they had killed."

diers and were liable to find themselves, at the first setback, suffering from a "deficiency of men" (*oligandria*), were therefore more often than other cities forced to proceed to "complement" their civic body (*anaplerosis*) by more or less imposing such institutional marriages upon the women who, in the absence of the masters, symbolized the continuity of the traditional *polis*. However pertinent the above observation may be, I nevertheless do not believe that we should underestimate the particular aptitude for political life which, in times of crisis, dependants of the Helot type were recognized to possess.

Identical conclusions are prompted by the cases in which, without going so far as to impose such forced marriages, one faction or another in a civil war sought to rally to its side a large slave labor force by granting it at least liberty. It was a practice that Plato also attributed to tyrannical regimes when "the *demos*, trying to escape the smoke of submission to the free would have plunged into the fire of enslavement to slaves, and in exchange for that excessive and unseasonable liberty, has clothed itself in the garb of the most cruel and bitter servile servitude" (*Republic*, 8.569bc).

In Sparta, this was the principal threat brandished by all those who, either out of a desire to regenerate the city's military power or simply through personal ambition, attempted to tamper with the established order. It was probably not a course contemplated by the king of Sparta, Cleomenes, when after being exiled he attempted in about 490 to return to power, launching his attack from Arcadia.[55] However, the regent Pausanias' collusion with the Helots following the Second Persian War is, for its part, clearly attested by Thucydides: "He was promising them freedom and citizenship if they would join him in a revolt and help him accomplish his whole plan" (1.132). His appeal was apparently not heeded, possibly through lack of time (for Pausanias was shortly afterward convicted of Medism and put to death). Rather better known is the plot hatched in 398 by a "lesser Spartiate" by the name of Cinadon,[56] who was convinced "that he knew the secret of all the Helots, freedmen, lesser Spartiates and *perioikoi;* for whenever among these classes any mention was made of Spartiates, noone was able to conceal the fact that he would be glad to eat them raw" (Xenophon, *Hellenica*, 3.3.6). This plot too, however, was so rapidly defused that what the reaction of the Helots would

55. J. Wolski ("Les Ilotes et la question de Pausanias, régent de Sparte," *Colloque Bressanone 1976*, 7–19) thinks that Pausanias aimed to use the Helots in this fashion simply to reestablish the naval power of Sparta.

have been and exactly how he would have promoted his various allies never became known. From that time on the crisis of the Spartan society went from bad to worse, with all the wealth becoming concentrated in the hands of a minority (composed mostly of women) and the number of citizens continuing to dwindle (to the point where, around the mid-third century, they numbered no more than a few hundred). It was this situation that the reformer kings Agis IV and Cleomenes III tried to rectify during the third quarter of that century. The former managed only to proclaim the abolition of debts before he was deposed,[57] but the latter, before suffering the same fate, had enough time to introduce a new division of land allotments and to free an elite of six thousand Helots in return for a ransom, for each, of five hundred drachmas.[58]

Xenophon ascribes a similar attempt to Critias, the future Athenian oligarch, who in 406 was "in Thessaly, along with Prometheus, arming the serfs against their masters." He must also have promised them the rights of citizenship if we are to believe the reproaches his opponent Theramenes addressed to him two years later: "For my part, Critias, I have always been at war with the men who do not think there could be a good democracy until the slaves and those who would sell the state for lack of a shilling should share in the government" (*Hellenica,* 2.3.36 and 48).

In the city of Corcyra, in a clash between democrats and aristocrats in which one party favored Athens, the other Sparta, each side attempted to win the support of the slaves during the Peloponnesian War. According to Thucydides (3.73 and 74), in 427 "both parties sent messages round into the fields, calling upon the slaves and offering them freedom; and a majority of the slaves made common cause with the people, while the other party gained the support of eight hundred mercenaries from the mainland. After a day's interval another battle occurred, and the people won, as they had the advantage in the strength of their position as well as in numbers."[59] Then in 410, according to Diodorus (13.48.7), six hundred Messenian mercenaries led by the Athenian Conon, "setting out unexpectedly with the partisans of the people's party, at the time of the full market,

---

56. See E. David, "The Conspiracy of Cinadon," *Athenaeum* 67 (1979): 239–59.

57. A. Fuks, "The Spartan Citizen-Body in the Mid-Third Century B.C. and Its Enlargement Proposed by Agis IV," *Athenaeum* 40 (1962): 244ff.; more generally, B. Shimron, *Late Sparta: The Spartan Revolution, 243–146 B.C.* (1972).

58. T. W. Africa, "Cleomenes III and the Helots," *California Studies in Classical Antiquity* 1 (1968): 1–11; I. Didu, "Cleomene III e la liberazione degli iloti," *Annali della Facoltà di Lettere e Filosofia della Università di Cagliari,* n.s., 1 (1976–77): 5–39.

59. A. Fuks, "Thucydides and the Stasis in Corcyra," *AJPhil.* 92 (1971): 48ff.

against the supporters of the Lacedaemonians, arrested some of them, slew others and drove more than a thousand from the state; they also set the slaves free and gave citizenship to the foreigners living among them, as a precaution against the great number and influence of the exiles." We note that in 427 it is specifically stated that the slaves were recruited in the countryside. This leads us to wonder (albeit no answer is possible) whether this colony of Corinth perhaps made use of rural dependants similar to the Killyrians of Syracuse (another Corinthian colony), who in 485 had in similar fashion been brought into alliance with the "people" in opposition to the large landowners (*gamoroi*).

But it is not possible to consider such a hypothesis in all cases: for example, in Samos where, after the collapse of the tyranny toward the end of the sixth century, it had proved necessary to strengthen the civic body by selling political equality (*isopoliteia*) to the slaves at the price of five staters. That is why Aristophanes was later to make a mockery of this "extremely well educated" (*polugrammatos*) people partly composed of branded slaves. Sicyon is a similar case; there in about 370–360 the tyrant Euphron "made slaves not only free men but even citizens" (Xenophon, *Hellenica,* 7.3.8).[60] Another is Cassandreia in Macedonia where, between 280 and 276, Apollodorus made himself tyrant with the assistance of Galatian mercenaries and the support of "the servants and workers in the workshops whom he had incited to revolt" (Polyaenus, 6.7.2), although it is not known whether, at the same time, he also liberated them.

That is a more or less exhaustive list of the cases in which slaves, in one way or another, became directly associated with political life in Greek cities. We should note that it seems relatively limited considering all the political disturbances and civil wars that we know to have taken place.[61] These were obviously quite exceptional measures, and furthermore they appear to have been imposed not on their own account by reason of their sociopolitical content and under pressure from those who stood to gain, but simply as tactical expedients in line with the fundamental interests of a small proportion of citizens.[62] As

60. D. Whitehead, "Euphron, Tyrant of Sikyon: An Unnoticed Problem in Xenophon, *Hell.,* VII,3,8," *Liverpool Classical Monthly* 5 (1980): 175–78; P. A. Cartledge, "Euphron and the *Douloi* Again," ibid., 209–11.

61. See A. Fuks, "Social Revolution in Greece in the Hellenistic Age," *PP* 111 (1966): 437–48; "Patterns and Types of Social-Economic Revolution in Greece from the Fourth to the Second Century B.C.," *Ancient Society* 5 (1974): 51–81.

62. The same can be said of the few freedmen who wielded tyrannical power in the name of or following their former masters (Meandrius at Samos around 520, Micythus at Rhegium around 470, and above all Aristotle's friend the eunuch Hermias, at

is stated in the pact of 338 which united the Greeks with the king of Macedon, in all these instances it was a case of liberating the slaves "with a view to revolution"; the decision was taken in order to reverse a particular power relationship just as much for practical reasons as on grounds of principle.[63] It was only in such circumstances and with such objectives that it was even thinkable to turn to the slaves, or at least to some of them—those considered the "best" by reason of their conditions of labor or existence—and it was a course that apparently, was regarded as more acceptable if those involved were serfs of the Helot type.

The Military Role of Slaves

In military,[64] as in political life, slaves (alongside a minority of free men of lowly origins) normally played a purely instrumental role: as army orderlies called *hyperetai* (assistants), *hypaspistai* (shield bearers), *akolouthoi* (followers), *skeuophoroi* and *hoplophoroi* (weapon carriers), *hippokomai* (grooms), or, more generally, *thereapontes* or simply *paides*. They represented a necessary element in the classical and Hellenistic armies.[65] In Xenophon's *Cyropaedia*, which is largely based on the facts of Greek life, we also find the king of the Persians noting that "all those who take the field must have someone to take care of the tent and to have food prepared for the soldiers when they come in" (4.2.34). More generally, these servants relieved the fighting men, both individually and collectively, of the normal chores of military life and thus assumed the same social functions in their behalf as they did in civilian life. Are these the figures that we find represented, as early as the archaic period, on the sides of Attic vases? Some scholars think that the Scythian archers or those dressed in the Scythian manner who lend their support to hoplites on the field of battle were

Atarnaea and Assos in the Troad); see L. A. El'nickii, "The role of slaves and freedmen in certain forms of government in Greece in the fifth–fourth centuries" (in Russian), *Vestnik Drevnei Istorii* (1972), no.4:100–106.

63. C. Mossé, "Le rôle des esclaves dans les troubles politiques du monde grec à la fin de l'époque classique," *Cahiers d'Histoire* 6 (1961): 351–60.

64. I am here using material from two of my articles: "Les esclaves grecs en temps de guerre," *Colloque Besançon 1970*, 29–62; and "Quelques travaux récents sur les esclaves grecs en temps de guerre," *Colloque Besançon 1972*, 15–28. I also bear in mind more recent studies by K.-W. Welwei, *Unfreie im antiken Kriegsdienst*, 1: *Athen und Sparta* (1974), and 2: *Die kleineren und mittleren griechischen Staaten und die hellenistischen Reiche* (1977) (=*Forsch. ant. Sklav.*, 5 and 8).

65. H. Heinen, "Zum militärischen Hilfspersonal in *P.Med.* inv. 69.65," *Egypt and the Hellenistic World* (1983), 120–42.

indeed normally slaves. But in reality they are more likely to have been Scythian mercenaries or citizens possessing bows, believed to have been integrated into the army between roughly 530 and 490. Elsewhere, alongside the hoplites reporting to the battlefield on horseback, we find similarly mounted grooms whose task it was to hold their master's horse at the ready until such time as a retreat or a pursuit was ordered. There is, however, no evidence that they were slaves rather than free men. Thus, in this domain too, slaves appear to have been less numerous in the archaic period than subsequently when, despite the restrictions advocated by certain military leaders, they did sometimes come to swell the ranks of the armies to a dangerous degree.

In his *Cyropaedia* (7.5.79), Xenophon writes: "The science and practice of war we need not share at all with those whom we wish to put in the position of workmen or tributaries to us, but we must maintain our superiority in these accomplishments, as we recognize in these the means to liberty and happiness that the gods have given to men. And just as we have taken their arms away from them, so surely we must never be without our own, for we know that the nearer to their arms men constantly are, the more completely at their command is their every wish" (cf. 8.1.43). Here the motivation for the exclusion of slaves from military life is forthrightly explained; however, there were exceptions, imposed by particular circumstances but nevertheless revealing a certain pattern of behavior dictated as much by the juridical status of the slaves involved as by the military arm to which they might be assigned.

On board the warships as in the armies, whether slaves were present is not the issue. There can be no doubt that they were, given that the elite of the crew (pilots, steersmen, and marine infantrymen) could not do without their personal servants. That fact is tacitly assumed by Thucydides (7.73.5) when he tells us that the crew of the Athenian *Paralos* (a ship detailed to perform religious and diplomatic missions) was composed entirely of citizens. And in all probability those servants sometimes also did service as oarsmen. Thus, from our point of view, the presence of slaves in the Greek navies would be significant only if we were sure that they were taken aboard specifically as oarsmen; or, to put it another way, only if it is manifestly clear that they are present in greater strength than is warranted simply for the personal service of the crew, for only then would their military function unquestionably be more important than their social one.

On at least one occasion the Athenians did call upon this mobilizable force: in 406, when despite the depletion of their forces they launched the expedition of one hundred and ten ships that was to defeat the Spartan coalition at Arginusae. According to Xenophon's *Hellenica* (1.6.24), they took on board "all who were of military age, whether slave or free. . . . Even the knights went aboard in considerable numbers" (the knights being the elite of the civic body, who were normally not required to serve in the galleys). What became of these slaves when they returned home to Athens? A number of passages in Aristophanes' *Frogs,* which was performed at the Lenaea of 405, suggest that they derived special renown from the exercise (ll. 33–34, 290–291) and were not only freed but furthermore granted the status of Plataeans (ll. 693–694), that is, they were assimilated to those traditional allies who, after the capture of their town by the Peloponnesians in 427, were welcomed by the Athenians and treated as privileged foreigners. It might, however, rather be the case that,[66] after the victory of Arginusae, the Athenians went back on their promises made to the fighting slaves, or perhaps Aristophanes' allusions are really connected with the naval battle of Salamis (480).

However that may be, it is by no means certain that Athenian slaves did in fact take part in the famous battle of Salamis. Herodotus and Aristotle, in particular, have nothing to say about it. Nevertheless, in recent years several historians have argued that in all likelihood they did, and on the strength of that likelihood they have sought evidence in the famous "decree of Themistocles" discovered at Troezen in 1959.[67] These historians calculate that the Athenian civic body could not on its own have mustered the forty thousand crewmen needed to man the two hundred triremes on that occasion and that it must consequently have been necessary to supplement the citizens not only with foreigners but also with slaves, in a movement of mobilization which called upon "all men of an age to bear arms." They claim that for this reason, in his decree, Themistocles took the precaution of dividing the main body of his citizen and metic forces into two hundred groups (*taxeis*), each of one hundred men, whose strength was to be doubled in one way or another when the time for embarkation arrived, by supplementary contingents of citizens, foreigners, and slaves. Even if one thus interprets this passage in the decree of Themistocles, given that the authenticity of this text is extremely doubtful, it does not really provide grounds to

66. F. Sartori, "Riflessi di vita politica ateniese nelle *Rane* di Aristofane," in *Scritti in onore di C. Vassalini* (1974), 426–27.

67. For an extremely full bibliography on this subject see J. Robert and L. Robert, *Bulletin Epigraphique,* which appears annually in the *REG.*

argue that oarsmen-slaves were present on the Athenian ships in the straits of Salamis.

To Xenophon's text of the *Hellenica,* which we took as our starting point, scholars often add a famous epigraphical item of evidence of a quite fragmentary nature (*IG* 2², 1951) which lists the various members of some of the triremes' crews. Each mentions, in descending order of importance, the names of two trierarchs, ten marine infantrymen, six navigation officers, two or three bowmen, and finally an indeterminate number of oarsmen (probably between 150 and 200), divided into three groups (citizens, foreigners, and slaves). In the four lists partially preserved, the slaves (referred to as *therapontes*) appear to account for 20–40 percent of the galley oarsmen, while the citizens vary between 30 and 40 percent, as do the foreigners. On the average, almost half the slaves in each trireme were owned by the citizens who made up the officer staff of the ship. Most of these officers were attended by one slave (or, very occasionally, by two or three), while a few appear to have had none (although it is possible that, in their cases, a relative or friend put one at their disposal for the duration of the expedition). The distribution of these slaves among the ship's officers suggests that they were detailed to domestic tasks; however, they may have taken their places at the oars. Unfortunately we have no means of knowing in what circumstances the Athenians resorted to the slaves for this purpose or for what reasons they decided to commemorate the fact in an inscription which, to date, is unique of its kind. All we know for certain is that these circumstances must necessarily be dated to later than 411, when double trierarchies were introduced, and that this memorial must, for paleographic reasons, be situated roughly between 410 and 390. The rest is matter for speculation. For a long time, this inscription was regarded as a list of those who died in the battle of Arginusae. But, it has been objected, it would be very strange if all hands in the crews of the triremes disappeared without exception, and it is stranger still to find in these lists the names of Athenians who seem still to have been alive and kicking at the beginning of the fourth century! Rather than a funerary memorial, the monument is much more likely to have been an honorific one designed to record the names of the crew members who took part in a particularly glorious naval success. Some believe this to have been a small expedition mounted against Eretria in 411; others, the successful withdrawal to Cyprus or even Athens itself of eight ships that escaped from the defeat at Aigospotami in 404. This last hypothesis is all the more justifiable given that the presence of slaves in the Athenian fleet two years after the costly victory of Arginusae appears to be mentioned by Justin (*Epitome Historiarum Philippicarum*, 5.6.5) and that in any case there would be nothing particularly surprising about it.

If the Athenians found themselves obliged to call upon slaves to fight at sea, if not in 480 at any rate in 406 and 404, one wonders whether they were not also forced to do so in 415–413, at the time of the Sicilian expedition, which put an exceptional strain on their resources. During the siege of Syracuse, the Athenian hoplites certainly had at their disposal orderlies (*therapontes* or *akolouthoi*) whom Thucydides describes as indispensable to the successful functioning of the fleet. All these measures were certainly dictated to a certain extent by the practical necessities of the particular moment,[68] as is shown by the fact that in the fourth century we hear virtually nothing more of them—except, that is, in connection with the *choris oikountes* which, we are told in Demosthenes' *Philippic* I (4.36), the Athenians in about 351 set aboard triremes, in the company of the metics or citizens, and also the few slaves who went to sea in 323–322 during the Lamian War. More than ever before, it seems, the poorest citizens, who belonged to the category of the thetes, monopolized this privilege, for which they were paid a wage. The situation was such that, in about 356, Isocrates in his speech *On the Peace* exclaimed: "In those days, when they manned their triremes, they put on board crews of foreigners and slaves but sent out citizens to fight under heavy arms. Now however we use mercenaries as heavy-armed troops but compel citizens to row the ships." His claims regarding the mid-fifth century are clearly exaggerated, but there must have been some truth in what he says about the mid-fourth century for it to have had any credibility at the time.

That is all we know so far as Athens is concerned; it does not amount to much, considering the size of the fleet the city maintained for almost two centuries. But that does not mean that a similar situation obtained in the rest of the Greek world. There, the impression given by the admittedly sparse documentation is that slaves were used as oarsmen on a more regular basis.

Thucydides (1.55.1) tells us that after their victory over a Cor-

---

68. B. Jordan's thesis (in *The Athenian Navy in the Classical Period* [1975], 260–67), that the Athenians normally used slaves as oarsmen in the galleys, has been refuted several times: by me in 1972 (above, n.64), by E. Ruschenbusch ("Zur Besatzung athenischen Trieren," *Historia* 28 [1979]: 106–10), and also by J. S. Morrison ("*Hyperesia* in Naval Contexts in the Fifth and Fourth Centuries B.C.," *JHS* 104 [1984]: 48–59).

cyraean fleet comprised of one hundred and ten vessels, the Cor-
inthians upon their return, "of their Corcyraean prisoners . . . sold
eight hundred who were slaves but two hundred and fifty they kept
in custody and treated them with much consideration, their motive
being that when they returned to Corcyra, they might win it over to
their side; and it so happened that most of these were among the
most influential men of the city." It is surprising that these prisoners,
who must have been taken from the seventy Corcyraean vessels put
out of action in the battle, should include three times as many slaves
as free men. That proportion may be partly the result of pure
chance, but it may also be explained by the situation Corcyra faced
both internally and externally, finding itself forced to resort to
extreme measures in order to resist Corinthian aggression.

But there were also slaves serving in the navies of Athens' enemies
at the beginning of the Peloponnesian War: so much is made clear by
a passage in Thucydides (2.103.1) in which we learn that when
Phormion returned to Athens in 428, following an expedition along
the Peloponnesian coast, he brought back "the prisoners of free
birth whom they had taken in the sea-fights. These were exchanged
man for man." He had presumably sold off the slaves on the way
home. Some texts from the fourth century also suggest that the
crews of the Lacedaemonian ships were largely composed of Helots,
so that when the Athenians became Sparta's allies in 397, they found
that the only sailors under their command were "their slaves and
their men of the least account" (Xenophon, *Hellenica*, 7.1.13).

A few other cases are known at the end of the fifth century (in
Chios in 412, in Syracuse and Thurii in 411) and also in the fourth
century, when it is mostly tyrants who are involved, including Dionysius the Elder of Syracuse and the Thessalian Jason of Pherae,
who, for his part, boasted of the mass of Penestae at his disposal. And
Aristotle (*Politics*, 1327b, 12–16) tells us that these were the type of
dependants most suitable for recruitment: "If there exists a mass of
perioikoi and tillers of the soil, there is bound to be no lack of sailors
too. If fact we see this state of things existing even now in some
places, for instance in the city of Heraclea; the Heracleotes man a
large fleet of triremes, although they possess a city of but moderate
size as compared with others."

It would thus appear to be established that the use of slaves as
oarsmen was more common or, if you like, less exceptional in the rest
of the Greek world than it was in Athens. That would explain how it
is that in Aristotle's *Politics* (1291b, 20–25), the role played by citizens
in manning the triremes is presented as a peculiarly Athenian custom: "[The class] occupied with the sea . . . is divided into the classes

concerned with naval warfare, with trade, with ferrying passengers and with fishing (for each of these classes is extremely numerous in various places, for instance fishermen at Tarentum and Byzantium, navy men at Athens, the mercantile class at Aegina and Chios, and the ferryman-class at Tenedos)."

In the army, the enlistment of slaves is attested rather more frequently than in the navy—not that the latter ranked higher in the scale of civic values, for it did not. The attested presence of slaves serving on land is explained by two practical reasons: (1) we are on the whole better informed about military operations on land than those at sea; and (2) in the last resort a city's destiny was generally played out on land, often in a siege, which might well make it necessary to take extreme measures in the interests of public safety.

Roughly half of our documentation concerns the Lacedaemonians. In the Second Messenian War, around 675, the poet Tyrtaeus composed a number of elegies to raise the morale of his compatriots after a defeat and, according to Pausanias (4.16.6), "he filled their ranks from the Helots to replace the slain." At the battle of Plataea against the Persians in 479, five thousand Spartan hoplites took part who, according to Herodotus (9.28–29) were protected by "a guard of thirty-five thousand light-armed Helots, seven appointed for each man," quite apart from the further 34,500 light-armed infantrymen who flanked the other Greek hoplites. Although they do not appear to have played a particularly important role in the battle, these Helots, whom Herodotus describes as "fighting men" (*machimoi*), nevertheless lost some of their number on the field of battle, and these were laid to rest in their own burial mound.

The Spartans must have resorted to similar methods right from the start of the Peloponnesian War since, according to Thucydides (4.80.2–4), they announced

that all Helots who claimed to have rendered the Lacedaemonians the best service in war should be set apart, ostensibly to be set free. They were, in fact, merely testing them, thinking that those who claimed, each for himself, the first right to be set free would be precisely the men of high spirit who would be the most likely to attack their masters. About two thousand of them were selected and these put crowns upon their heads and made the rounds of the temples, as though they were already free, but the Spartans not long afterwards made away with them and nobody ever knew in what way each had perished.

Similarly in 424, the Lacedaemonians were only too glad to seize the pretext of an expedition to the Chalcidice to "have an excuse for sending out some of the Helots in order to forestall their attempting a revolt at the present juncture when Pylos was in the possession of the enemy [the Athenians] . . . so they gladly sent with Brasidas seven hundred Helots as hoplites." We later learn that in 421 the Lacedaemonians decided that those Helots who fought under Brasidas in Thrace "should be free men . . . and dwell wherever they preferred; and not long afterwards they settled them with the Neodamodes at Lepreum on the borders of Laconia, for they were by this time at variance with the Eleans" (5.34.1). (This text is the first to mention the existence of the Neodamodes.) In 413, as their contribution to the defense of Syracuse "the Lacedaemonians . . . picked out the best of the Helots and the Neodamodes, of both together about six hundred hoplites" (7.19.3; 58.3).

Even stronger were the reasons for adopting the same procedure in 370–369, when the town of Sparta itself was under direct threat of a Theban invasion.

> It was determined by the authorities to make proclamation to the Helots that if any wished to take up arms and be assigned to a place in the ranks, they should be given a promise that all should be free who took part in the war. And it was said that at first more than six thousand enrolled themselves, so that they in their turn occasioned fear when they were marshalled together and were thought to be all too numerous. But when the mercenaries from Orchomenus remained true and the Lacedaemonians received aid from the Phliasians, Corinthians, Epidaurians, Pellenians and likewise some of the other states, then the Spartiates were less fearful of those who had been enrolled. [Xenophon, *Hellenica*, 6.5.28–29).

Although many of these Helots appear to have deserted, a thousand at least were rewarded for their loyalty by being granted their freedom (Plutarch, *Agesilaus*, 32.12). When, at the end of the third century and the beginning of the second, Cleomenes III and Nabis took steps to integrate former Helots into the civic body, in all likelihood the latter, or some of them at least, were enrolled in the army; however, that is not directly attested.[69]

In the rest of the Greek world, particularly wherever chattel slavery existed, recourse to the slaves' services in time of war seems to have been less regular. It was not even considered unless the very survival of the city was at stake and the decisive engagement was

---

69. It is not known whether the two thousand soldiers "armed in the Macedonian fashion" by Cleomenes III on the eve of the battle of Sellasia (Plutarch, *Cleomenes*, 23. 1) were some of the recently freed six thousand Helots; see M. Daubies, "Les combattants laconiens de Sellasie: Périèques ou Hilotes?" in *Le monde grec: Hommages à Claire Préaux* (1975), 383–92.

generally believed to be at hand, to be fought out either in open country or, more often, on the very walls of the town itself.

The threat represented by the barbarians landing at Marathon accounts for the Athenians taking such a decision in 490. It was a decision which, once the danger was past, was felt to be so little to their credit that the writers of the classical period were at pains not to mention it. It is only through Pausanias (1.32.3) that we learn, almost accidentally, that on the burial tumulus at Marathon there were erected slabs "giving the names of the killed according to their tribes; and there is another grave for the Boeotian Plataeans and for the slaves; for slaves fought then for the first time by the side of their masters." For them to do so, it had been necessary for the people to vote in favor of a decree proposed by Miltiades, which first granted them their liberty (Pausanias, 7.15.7).

The following two centuries provide us with very few examples to mention. There is an inscription from Chios, consisting of a list of slaves grouped into units known as "decades," whom the city apparently freed toward the end of the Peloponnesian War in order to make soldiers (or perhaps sailors) of them.[70] There are also instances of slaves being freed in the early Hellenistic period in the course of a number of sieges: the siege of Thebes by Alexander in 335, that of Cyzicus by Arrhidaeus in 319, that of Megalopolis by Polyperchon in 318, that of Rhodes by Demetrius Poliorcetes in 305–304, and that of Syracuse by the Carthaginians in 310 (in order to form the expeditionary force sent to Africa under the command of Agathocles). As for the Athenians, they always ended up deciding against renewing the decision they had taken at the time of the First Persian War. In the *Athenian Constitution* (40.2), Aristotle praises Archinus for having acted as a good citizen "in his indicting as unconstitutional the decree of Thrasybulus admitting to citizenship all those who had come back together from Piraeus, some of whom were clearly slaves." We should note in this connection that it does not seem to have been Thrasybulus' deliberate intention in 404 to grant citizens' rights to slaves. Rather, slaves had slipped into the ranks of the foreigners who were to be given citizenship. In any event, the decree was annulled. The situation following the battle of Chaeronea in 337 seems more clear-cut: here, on the proposal of Aristogeiton, the Athenians abrogated Hyperides' decree granting citizens' rights to metics and freedom to such servants as were willing to fight in the event of the war continuing.

During the rest of the Hellenistic period, it was usually the Roman

70. L. Robert, *Etudes épigraphiques et philologiques* (1938), 118–26.

threat that prompted such extreme measures. Thus, in 214, the Syracusans invited "slaves . . . to wear the cap of freedom" (Livy, 24.32.9); in 146, the Achaean *strategos* Diaeus issued written orders to the towns of his confederation instructing them "to set free twelve thousand of such of their home-born and home-bred slaves as were in the prime of life, and after arming them to send them to Corinth," having, if necessary, made up the numbers of the contingent by supplying "the deficiency from their other slaves" (Polybius, 38. 15.3–5). Finally, at the beginning of the first century, in 86 and again in 65, the king of Pontus, Mithridates Eupator, at war with the Greek cities of Asia which had entered into alliance with the Romans, offered liberty to their slaves and enrolled some of them in his armies—forcing some of his adversaries to take a similar course (the Ephesians, for example, who, once free from the overlordship of the kingdom of the Pontus, in 85 granted freedom and the status of domiciled foreigners to those of their public slaves who had fought to liberate the city; and also the people of Aphrodisias in Caria, who in 88 decided to come to the aid of a Roman proconsul, together with their *paroikoi* and their slaves.[71]

Along with these examples, passages from Philo of Byzantium's *Syntaxis mechanica,* written during the second half of the third century,[72] afford us a precise and nuanced view of the situation. At the start of the siege operations of which the author writes, slaves were not included in the fighting forces. Indeed it was in order to dissuade the citizens from arming their servants that Philo advised the assailants to promise liberty to those of the slaves who would work actively for the town's downfall. But the fact that, when the enemy breached the walls, the male slaves were not present to protect the children, female servants, women, and young girls by striking at the enemy from the rooftops certainly shows that, when the crisis came, they were fighting alongside the free men (whether or not they had been formally enrolled in the army). We may compare this information with that provided, just before the middle of the fourth century, by Aeneas Tacticus. He certainly believed it preferable not to bring the rural slaves in to swell the numbers in the besieged town; but at the same time he did not advise evacuating the urban slaves nor did he advocate any particular measures regarding them. What is certain is

71. J. Reynolds, *Aphrodisias and Rome* (1982), no.3.
72. Y. Garlan, "Le livre 'V' de la *Syntaxe mécanique* de Philon de Byzance, texte, traduction et commentaire," in *Recherches de poliorcétique grecque* (1974), 279ff.; "Cités, armées et stratégie à l'époque hellénistique d'après l'oeuvre de Philon de Byzance," *Historia* 22 (1973): 16–33.

that, during the last phase of street fighting, slaves were sometimes to be found throwing themselves spontaneously into the conflict. In 431, for example, when the Plataeans ejected a Theban commando force from their town, they did so with the aid of "the women and slaves on the house-tops, uttering screams and yells while pelting them with stones and tiles" (Thucydides, 2.4.2).

Sometimes such loyalty could be turned to active use by making military orderlies of the slaves. Certainly many of them were capable of sacrificing their own lives in order to rescue their wounded masters from the field. In Athens, it would appear that from the early fifth century onward, they were officially rewarded with "a public funeral" and having "their names inscribed on a slab" (Pausanias, 1.29.7); and a *therapon* is indeed included in a list of war dead set up in 464 (*SEG*, 24.67). When military orderlies demonstrated such good will they tended to be regarded as trustworthy. According to Polyaenus (*Stratagems*, 3.9.52), it was thus that the Athenian *strategos* Iphicrates was able to take the enemy by surprise and defeat them, by disguising his military orderlies as soldiers and his soldiers as orderlies. The orderlies would, in any case, probably have managed to acquire a few weapons of their own in the course of their activities, and these they would use chiefly to defend the camp.

These various examples of military collaboration between slaves and free men chiefly indicate that it usually took place in critical circumstances, when the citizens had no recourse other than to request or accept the help of the slaves, in a situation that, in the short term, might moreover well lead to a deterioration in the slaves' own lot. For (with the possible exception of the Helots), slaves could expect no advantages from a defeat: at the best a change of master, but that would often entail the brutal rupturing of the relations of kinship or friendship which already existed within the servile class. Equally, they might be slaughtered by a victor overcome with a desire for vengeance so strong that it overrode his economic interests. Under direct threat from the enemy, a solidarity based upon practicalities thus often came to unite the slaves with their masters.

So far, my conclusions have been very much in line with those which K.-W. Welwei produced some years ago, after studying the subject in depth.[73] But now our positions diverge. For this disciple of Joseph Vogt, the idea that "necessity dictates" is enough to account for every aspect of reality: it is all a matter of circumstance. One can see where his determined emphasis upon the circumstantial nature

73. See n.64 above.

of the appeal made to the slaves in times of war is designed to lead; however praiseworthy in itself, its purpose is to block reflection at this level, to reject in advance any structural interpretation of the behavior underlying the circumstantial phenomena, as if historical circumstance were connected with nothing outside itself, reflecting nothing of the structures that inform it. In this instance, the end result is to suggest that, exceptional though it was, the military role of the slaves was perfectly "natural." In this way, Welwei minimizes the gap between their status and that of free men since it cannot have amounted to much, after all, if the simple weight of circumstances was enough to sweep it away. Paying no attention to the particular type of slavery involved or the nature of the military functions assumed by the slaves, he implies that, in the presence of danger, the unity of the human race somehow reconstitutes itself spontaneously, uninhibitedly, without qualification and without prejudice. We are back with the old positivist and historicist tradition which, under cover of paying all due respect to the facts, in effect consists in dislocating them, isolating them into separate compartments in order the better to preclude any ideological interpretation of them. The next step is to reintroduce ideology by means of ideas presented as self-evident truths that emanate naturally from common sense. K.-W. Welwei's work is a typical product of the Mainz school in this respect.

It seems to me, on the contrary, that behind these circumstantial phenomena, it is possible to detect a number of constant patterns of behavior and tendencies by posing the following questions.

In which arm did the slaves usually serve? Apparently in the navy, in the classical period at least. That seems a perfectly normal alloca-tion, not simply because large numbers of men were needed here but also because, throughout Antiquity, the prestige of oarsmen was lower than that of infantrymen. When slaves took part in fighting on land, they usually did so as light-armed infantrymen or else per-formed the functions of orderlies. Very rarely would they serve as hoplites, since service in the heavy infantry was in theory reserved for the social elite.

What types of slaves were usually called upon? In my view, there can be no doubt that it was those who belonged to peoples collec-tively reduced to servitude, such as the Penestai and above all the Helots—that is, the very ones who, as we shall presently see, also most clearly manifested their desire for emancipation. The paradox is easily explained when we take into account their own ancient traditions and their persistent attempts, contained and repressed with difficulty, to regain their liberty as a people. Among the chattel slaves, on the other hand, those called upon were apparently in the main those who, by virtue of their origins, functions, or type of life, were most likely to have an interest in preserving the safety of the city and citizens: sometimes the public slaves, more generally domestic servants and, on one occasion at least, specifically slaves born-in-the-house or those brought-up-in-the-family.

What benefits did the slaves derive from their participation in the defense of the community? When our texts mention the granting of a collective reward, it is almost invariably liberty. Citizenship is given only by "social reformers" such as Dionysius the Elder, whose objectives were not solely military or, in exceptional circumstances, by the Rhodians as a reward to the slaves who had displayed the greatest courage. In Sparta, and possibly also in other cities with a system of communal servitude, it is not known whether this reward was normally envisaged for oarsmen; probably not. It was sometimes granted to those who served in the land army, if the Lacedaemonians felt so inclined and had made promises to this effect when the slaves were enlisted. But it was a measure that was apparently always taken *afterward*, when the military operations were over. In the rest of the Greek world, the procedure appears to have varied depending on whether the slaves were called upon to serve at sea or on land: the former were always granted their freedom *after*, the latter usually *before* seeing action. Why such a distinction? No doubt partly for reasons of efficiency. Service on land demanded a greater sense of responsibility. But that explanation does not account for the case of Sparta. We must therefore seek another, possibly one of an ideological nature: for a slave to be considered suitable for military service on land, it was necessary first to raise his status, for otherwise the ideological gap between his status and the function he was expected to perform was too great; whereas that was not the case for the oarsman slave, whose function was less honorable, or for the Helot, whose status was higher.

Can we detect any pattern of development in the practice of the enlistment of slaves? Owing to the quantitative and qualitative un-evenness of our documentation, there is on this point such a risk of being misled that it is tempting simply to reply in the negative. Nevertheless, it is not inconceivable that during the Hellenistic period new "rules of the game" may have come into play: rules for a game which was less regular, that is, less codified, than in the classical period and also more complex. Now, the threat of foreign imperialism, by transposing the problem onto a political level, favored an increasing awareness of the opposition between masters and slaves, while at the same time it strengthened their de facto solidarity.

In conclusion to our remarks on this point, let us try to gauge the precise implications of the proposal that Xenophon makes in his *Ways and Means* (4.41–42). He suggests the possibility of at some point putting to military use the mass of public slaves which, according to him, the State would be well advised to acquire in order to exploit the Laurium mines more successfully: "If any fear that this scheme would prove worthless in the event of war breaking out, they should observe that, with this system at work, war becomes far more formidable to the aggressors than to the city. For what instrument is more serviceable for war than men? We should have enough of them to supply crews to many ships of the State; and many men available for service in the ranks as infantrymen could press the enemy hard, if they were treated with consideration." So far as I know, Xenophon is the only Greek author who coolly envisages a systematic use of slaves in times of war. On this point, as on many others, he thus manifests a certain intellectual audacity in this work—though less than may at first sight appear. These are public slaves, and the only wars in which they are to take part are those of a defensive nature, in which the purpose is to repulse an enemy invasion. Their being used as oarsmen in the navy is envisaged before the possibility of enlisting them in the army to fight on land. Finally, the author is careful not to disregard completely all the difficulties that could arise from putting such plans into practice. He declares prudently that the war would be rendered "far more formidable to the aggressors than to the city" and recognizes that, if good military use is to made of these slaves, it will be necessary to "treat them with consideration."

Slave Revolts

We have noted both how slaves were sometimes brought into revolts against the authorities in power, to promote the interests of a particular faction of citizens, and also how the State authorities would call on them to fight against some enemy power. In neither situation was it possible for the slaves themselves to take autonomous action; in both, the most they could hope to gain was some improvement in their personal condition. But were there not also occasions when they did manifest their own aspirations and initiative in the form of more or less spontaneous, latent or open hostility toward their masters? The question of the "class consciousness" of the slaves is a particularly thorny one that certainly requires to be answered with caution, for it is necessary to pay the greatest attention to the degree of their alienation, the historical circumstances, and also all that recent inquiries have taught us in general about the primitive forms that social consciousness may assume.

In the classical period, serfs of the Helot type, in particular the Helots themselves and, first and foremost among them, the Messenian Helots, were reputed to be particularly disruptive. They it was whom Plato (*Laws*, 6.777cd) and Aristotle (*Politics*, 1264a, 34–36; 1269a, 36–39; 1272b, 18–19) had in mind when they insistently recommended that, in the interests of security, servile stock should not be constituted from an ethnicly and culturally homogeneous people. And a fragment from Critias, dating from the end of the fifth century, states: "Out of distrust of the Helots, the Spartiate, when at home, removes the handle of the latter's shield. As he cannot do so when out in the countryside (for here emergencies often arise), he himself goes nowhere without his spear so that, in the event of a revolt, he is certain to be stronger than the Helot, who only carries a shield. The Spartiates have also put bolts on their doors in the belief that these will afford them protection against Helot attacks" (Diels, 88, fr. 377; cf. Xenophon, *Constitution of the Lacedaemonians*, 12.4). Similarly, Thucydides, writing of the disturbances during the Peloponnesian War, remarks: "In fact, most of their measures have always been adopted by the Lacedaemonians with a view to guarding against the Helots" (4.80.3). It is a point of view echoed and developed by certain modern historians, who regard this as the fundamental explanation for the measures taken during the archaic period which were designed to turn Sparta into a kind of entrenched camp, in which symbolic war was ritually declared upon the Helots annually, at the "beginning of the hunt" in which the *cryptes* tracked them down. There were, as we shall see, fairly good grounds for such an obsession.

If we are to believe Plato's account, the reason the Spartans "arrived too late by one single day for the battle which took place at Marathon" in 490 was that they had been "hindered by the war they were then waging against Messenia and possibly by other obstacles" (*Laws*, 3.698e). According to Herodotus, on the other hand, it was for religious reasons: because they could not set out "when the moon was not full" (6.106), that is, before the expiration of the sacred truce which lasted throughout the month of Carneios. Of the two explanations, the second is perhaps the more probable.[74] The first could well be simply the late fruit of a campaign of pro-Laconian propaganda

---

74. *Contra* Cartledge, "Did Spartan Citizens," 153–54.

determined to whitewash the Spartans for their absence from Marathon by providing reasons even more compelling than their religious scruples, and to blacken the Messenians, who had only recently won their independence. It is an account all the more likely to be false given that these operations were supposed to have taken place under the reign of a king, Leotychides II, who happened to bear the same name as the ruler in 675, at the time of the Second Messenian War.

Much better attested is the revolt known as the "Third Messenian War," which broke out in about 464, timed to take advantage of an earthquake and possibly also sparked off by the discontent provoked by the massacre of Helots who had taken refuge as suppliants in the temple of Poseidon on Cape Tenarum. The rebels were probably mostly natives of Messenia (as Thucydides states) rather than of Laconia (as Diodorus and Plutarch claim). They managed to rally to them a number of *perioikoi* towns and even marched on Sparta itself but were then forced to withdraw to Mount Ithome. To put them down, the Spartans appealed for help to the Plataeans, the Aeginetans, the Mantineans and, above all, the Athenians. Four thousand Athenian hoplites, led by Cimon, then laid siege to Mount Ithome, but they were not successful and were eventually sent home for fear that they would side with the enemy camp. The situation dragged on and on. According to Thucydides it did so for ten years, that is, until about 455–454, after the battle of Tanagra (457). Now, it does not seem conceivable that the Spartans would have risked committing themselves to such a battle without having first resolved the problem of the Helots. That is why some modern historians have suggested various corrections to Thucydides' text, to make him say that the war lasted for only four, five, or six years, while others accept the text but suggest that the war must have started in about 469–468.[75] The defenders of Mount Ithome eventually obtained a safe-conduct to leave the Peloponnese. They were taken in by the Athenians, who installed them at Naupactus in western Locris.

The struggle for freedom flared up again, however, during the Peloponnesian War, in the neighborhood of the frontier fortifications controlled by the Athenians. It started in the Pylos region, in about 425:

The Messenians at Naupactus, regarding this territory as their fatherland—for Pylos belongs to the country that was once Messenia—sent

75. See M. Buonocoro, "Ricerche sulla terza guerra messanica," *Ottava miscellanea greca e romana 1982*, 57–123.

thither such of their number as were best fitted for the task and proceeded to ravage the Laconian territory, and they did a great deal of damage since they were men of the same speech as the inhabitants. As for the Lacedaemonians, they had never before experienced predatory warfare of this kind and therefore when the Helots began to desert and there was reason to fear that the revolutionary movement might gain still further headway in their territory, they were uneasy. [Thucydides, 4.41.2–3].

Their position had deteriorated further still by 424, with the Athenian occupation of the island of Cythera, and this was a crucial reason for the conclusion of the armistice of 423: "Their territory was ravaged from Pylos and Cythera; the Helots were deserting and always there was apprehension that those who remained, relying on those beyond the border, might revolt in the present state of affairs, just as they had done before" (5.14.3) Hence the (unilateral) clause contained in the treaty of alliance between the Lacedaemonians and the Athenians in 422–421: "If there shall be an insurrection of slaves, the Athenians shall aid the Lacedaemonians with all their might, to the utmost of their power" (5.23.3). In 413 the Spartans once again found themselves in a similar if rather less dramatic situation when the Athenians, "landing on the coast of Laconia opposite Cythera where the sanctuary of Apollo is . . . , ravaged portions of the land and fortified a place shaped like an isthmus in order that the Helots of the Lacedaemonians might desert thither and that, at the same time, marauders might make it, as they had made Pylos, a base for their operations" (7.26.2). The only times when such a situation seems to have arisen subsequently are when the Thebans invaded Laconia in 370[76]—but it was then probably less critical, despite the fact that Xenophon claims that "all the Helots" defected (*Hellenica*, 7.2.2)—and, in an even more sporadic fashion, at the beginning of the second century, at the time of the Roman war against Nabis, the tyrant of Sparta (Livy, 34.27.9).

In his *Politics* (1269d, 36–1269b, 7), Aristotle also notes:

the serf class in Thessaly repeatedly rose against its masters, and so did the Helots at Sparta, where they are like an enemy constantly sitting in wait for the disasters of the Spartiates. Nothing of the kind has hitherto occurred in Crete, the reason perhaps being that the neighbouring cities, even when at war with one another, in no instance ally themselves with the rebels because, as they also themselves possess a serf

---

76. E. David, "Revolutionary Agitation in Sparta after Leuctra," *Athenaeum* 68 (1980): 299–308.

class, this would not be to their interest; whereas the Laconians were entirely surrounded by hostile neighbours, Argives, Messenians and Arcadians. For with the Thessalians too, the serf risings originally began because they were still at war with their neighbours, the Achaeans, Perrhaebi and Magnesians.

Serfs of the Helot type thus do appear to be moved by a latent animosity toward their masters, but they express it only from time to time and here or there, when the chaotic conditions produced by natural cataclysms or military operations seem to offer then some chance of success.

Even that much cannot be said of the chattel slaves. They appear to have started or organized very few revolts.[77]

The first of these, known to us through a late compiler, Polyaenus (*Stratagems*, 1.43.1), took place in about 415–413 during the Athenian Sicilian expedition:

When the slaves rebelled at Syracuse and a strong force of them assembled, Hermocrates sent as ambassador to their leader, Sosistratus, one of his hipparchs by the name of Daimachus, who was related to Sosistratus and was his friend, to tell him from the *strategoi* that, out of consideration for his resolution, they would grant liberty to them all, would arm them all as hoplites, and would pay them the regulation wage. They invited Sosistratus himself to share their magistracy and to come at once to confer with them, the magistrates, on the matter of the hoplites. Sosistratus, trusting in the friendship of Daimachus, sought them out accompanied by twenty slaves who held positions of command. They were arrested and clapped in irons. Hermocrates then attacked with six hundred hoplites and, having captured the slaves, promised them that they would not be punished if each one returned to his master. They allowed themselves to be persuaded and returned home, all except for three hundred of them, who took refuge with the Athenians.

It is not possible to establish the authenticity of this event, which is not mentioned by Thucydides. And in any case assessing its importance and significance is difficult, for many points remain unclear. In particular, what was the social origin of the slaves' leader, Sosistratus? Was he a slave himself? (If he was, this would indeed be a veritable slave revolt taking place, significantly enough, in a time of war.) Or was he, rather, a citizen of high rank who aspired to the tyranny or favored the Athenians and felt no compunction about

77. J. Vogt, "The Structure of Ancient Slave Wars," *Ancient Slavery*, 39–92.

stirring up the slaves in his support? The fact that he was related to and friendly with one of the hipparchs would suggest the latter hypothesis to be more likely.

The only revolt of chattel slaves, the course, organization, and aims of which are relatively well known to us (although it was probably only of secondary importance in itself) took place on the island of Chios, probably during the first half of the third century.[78]

Our source is the *Voyage along the Coast of Asia* by Nymphodorus of Syracuse, written toward the end of the same century (cf. Athenaeus, 6.265d–266e). His account runs as follows:

The slaves of the Chians ran away from them, and gathering in great numbers, started for the mountains . . . inflicting injury on the country houses of their masters. A little before our time, a certain slave, as Chians themselves tell the story, ran away and made his abode in the mountains. Being a brave man and successful in warfare, he led the fugitive slaves as a king leads an army. The Chians often sent expeditions to attack him, but were quite unable to effect anything. When Drimacus, (for that was the fugitive's name) saw that they were throwing their lives away without result, he said to them: "Chians and masters, the trouble you are in because of your slaves will never stop. Why should it, when it happens according to an oracle once given by the god? If, however, you will make a treaty with me and let us alone in peace and quiet, I will initiate many blessings for you." So the Chians made a treaty and an armistice with him for a certain period, and he devised measures, weights and a special seal. Showing the seal to the Chians, he said: "Whatever I take from you I will take according to these measures and weights and after taking what I require, I will seal up your storehouses with this seal and leave them unharmed. Those of your slaves who run away I will examine to find out the reason, and if in my judgement they have run away because they have suffered something irreparable, I will keep them with me, but if they can urge no justification I will send them back to their masters." The other slaves therefore, seeing that the Chians willingly accepted this condition, were much less inclined to run away, because they dreaded the trial before him; while the runaways in his band feared him far more than their own masters and did everything that he required, obeying him as

78. I. A. Sisova, "Slavery in Chios" (in Russian), *Escl. périph.*, 149–92; A. Fuks, "Slave War and Slave Troubles in Chios in the Third Century," *Athenaeum* 56 (1968): 102–11; J. Vogt, "Zum Experiment des Drimakos: Sklavenhaltung und Raüberstand," *Saeculum* 24 (1973): 213–19. For a comparison, see E. D. Genovese, *From Rebellion to Revolution* (1979); S. B. Schwartz, "Brésil: Le royaume noir des Mocambos," *L'Histoire* 41 (1982): 38–48; and above all P. Cartledge, "Rebels and Sambos in Classical Greece: A Comparative View," in *Crux*, ed. Cartledge and F. D. Harvey (1985), 16–46.

they would a military officer. For he not only punished the disobedient, but he would also allow none to plunder a field or commit any other act of injury whatever without his consent. On festival days he would sally forth and take from the fields wine and unblemished victims, except what was voluntarily given him by the masters; and if he discovered that anyone was plotting against him or laying an ambush for him, he took vengeance on him. Now, the State had proclaimed that it would give a large reward to the man who took him alive or brought in his head, and finally, when this Drimacus had grown old, he summoned his favourite boy to a certain place and said: "I have loved you more than anyone else in the world. You are my favourite, my son, everything that I have. But I have lived long enough, whereas you are young and in the flower of life. What then remains? You must become a good and noble man. Since now the Chian State offers a large sum to the man who kills me and promises him freedom, you must cut off my head and carry it to Chios. Then you shall receive the money from the State and live in wealth." The lad remonstrated but was finally persuaded; and, cutting off the head of Drimacus, he received from the Chians the reward that had been proclaimed and, after burying the body of the runaway, he removed to his own country. And once more the Chians suffered injuries at the hands of their slaves, and when they were plundered they remembered the probity of the dead runaway and founded a shrine in his country, giving it the name of the Kindly Hero. In his honour, to this very day, fugitive slaves render the first-fruits of everything they purloin. They also say that he appears to many Chians in their sleep and warns them of plots among their slaves; and those persons to whom he appears go to the place where his shrine is and make offerings to him.

This then, Athenaeus concludes, is the story told by Nymphodorus. The account is so spirited that I have ventured to cite it in full before commenting upon it.

It contains many details that are perfectly convincing historically. From a chronological point of view, Drimacus could well have been a contemporary of the first Hellenistic kings. There is nothing surprising about the fact that the story is set in Chios (see pp. 37 and 186) or about many of the practices to which it refers: the consultation of oracles, the fixing of units in weights and measures, the existence of royal seals, the homosexual relationship between the older man and the youth, the offering of tithes levied on all kinds of revenue (in particular, booty), the belief in omens conveyed through dreams, and so on. These are the practices of free men, to be sure, but it is quite natural that the slaves should take them over in their own "kingdom." The setting of the play and the relations between the actors can thus not be faulted. But what about the plot?

It has frequently been given a more or less skeptical reception. It has been called a "moral novel imagined for the express purpose of inspiring the master with a greater sense of justice and the slave with more patience" (Fustel de Coulanges) and "a fantastical story" concocted at the end of the second century B.C. under the influence of the great servile revolts in Sicily (I. A. Sisova). Meanwhile other scholars have separated it into two independent legends, that of the leader of fugitive slaves and that of the Benevolent Hero. Why? Clearly because of the alternation of hostility and connivance in the relations between Drimacus and the Chian masters—an alternation found unacceptable because it seems contrary to "logic." But that is a contradiction immediately resolved by a comparison with the relations that existed in America between the independent communities of "Maroon" slaves on the one hand and the colonists on the other, before the development of the abolitionist movement—that is, so long as these servile revolts, of which Eugene Genovese has produced a recent analysis, "had a restorationist or isolationist, rather than a revolutionary, content" (p. xiv). In this context there exist plenty of treaties, particularly in Jamaica and Surinam, which grant "the maroons, freedom and autonomy in return for a pledge of allegiance to the colonial regime, including the duty to return new runaways and to defend the public order—that is, to suppress slave rebellions" (p. 51). In the ancient world, we may cite, as another parallel, the as-it-were counter-states founded by Cilician and Cretan pirates in the second half of the second century: although their ranks included a number of fugitive slaves, the slaves they took prisoner do not appear to have benefited from any special treatment.

There are only two other purely servile revolts to cite.[79] The first broke out at the news of the successes of the Sicilian slaves against the Roman legions in 135–134.[80] According to Diodorus (34.2.19), it involved "more than a thousand slaves in Attica, and . . . yet others in Delos and many other places; but thanks to the speed with which forces were brought up and to the severity of their punitive measures, the magistrates of the communities at once disposed of the rebels and brought to their senses any who were wavering on the verge of revolt." Given the numbers of slaves in Italy and Sicily who were of Greek origin at this time and the role that they frequently

79. S. Lauffer, *Die Bergwerkssklaven von Laureion*, 2d ed. (1979), 227–51.

80. For the bibliography, see W. Hoben, *Terminologische Studien zu den Sklavener-hebungen der römischen Republik* (1978), in particular 116ff.; M. Thompson (*The New Silver Coinage of Athens* 1 [1961], 486 and 636, n.1), dates the insurrection at Delos to 129 for numismatic reasons.

played as messengers, it is not at all improbable that news of the Sicilian events should rapidly have reached the Aegean. But that does not mean that we should see this as a veritable "slave International," organizing coordinated action throughout the Mediterranean region. It is difficult to gauge the scope of these uprisings. According to Jean Hatzfeld, it was this particular revolt that seems "to have prompted an *entente* between the different groups that made up the population of Delos. Apparently, when the danger was past, this organization became permanent and it was this 'combination' of Athenians, Italians, and foreigners which, under the presidency of an Athenian *epimelete,* replaced the previous Athenian cleruchy, the disappearance of which is indicated by the absence, after 130, of any decrees from the Delian *ecclesia.*"[81] The second of these two uprisings is known to us from a passage of Athenaeus (6.272e–f) which runs as follows: "Most of these Athenian slaves, counted in myriads, worked in the mines as prisoners. Poseidonius, the philosopher [early first century] says that they revolted, murdered the superintendents of the mines, seized the hill of Sunium and for a long time plundered Attica. This was the period when in Sicily also the second uprising of slaves occurred (104–100). There were many of these uprisings and more than a million slaves were killed." Apart from the figures suggested and allowing for Poseidonius' taste for synchronisms (he was the author of a universal history),[82] this text appears no less acceptable than the one quoted earlier. These do seem to be two authentic servile revolts, but they were, precisely, uprisings which seem to have led nowhere and which apparently provoked no feelings of solidarity in the slaves in the surrounding vicinity, despite the repercussions produced by the events in Sicily.

Greek resistance to the Roman invaders sometimes led to popular revolts in which slaves found themselves more or less involved, but never as the driving force.

One of these took place in the kingdom of Macedon, which had been dismantled after the defeat of Perseus in 168. It was brought about by the appearance, around the middle of the second century, of a pretender to the throne by the name of Andriscus, who passed himself off as Philip, the son of Perseus and the sister of the Seleucid king Demetrius I.[83] When his "nephew" went to seek the latter's aid,

81. *Les trafiquants italiens dans l'Orient hellénistique* (1919), 310.

82. Z. W. Rubinsohn, "Some Remarks on the Causes and Repercussions of the So-called 'Second Slave Revolt' in Sicily," *Athenaeum* 70 (1982): 436–51.

83. Cf. P. A. MacKay, "Studies in the History of Republican Macedonia, 168–148 B.C." (diss., Univ. of Calif., Berkeley, 1964), 66–106; M. Gwyn Morgan, "Metellus Macedonicus and the Province Macedonia," *Historia* 18 (1969): 412–46.

Demetrius handed him over to Rome, with which power it was clearly in his interest to be on friendly terms. But the pseudo-Philip managed to escape from Italy and eventually, in 149, to gain control of Macedon, where he set about minting coins bearing his name. A Roman legion, hurriedly dispatched, was crushed, and Thessaly fell into the hands of the usurper, who could also call upon considerable support in Thrace. Now the Roman Senate began to take the matter seriously and sent out two legions which, supported by the navy of Attalus II of Pergamum, defeated Andriscus in the vicinity of Pydna during the summer of 148. Andriscus took refuge in Thrace, failed in an attempt to regain power, and was then delivered over to the Romans by a Thracian king. Some modern historians have suggested that the slaves of Macedon supported Andriscus' cause and that his enterprise may consequently in some respects be regarded as a slave revolt.[84] But the evidence available to support such a view is far from conclusive. It consists of the following documentation: according to Florus (1.30 following Livy), "Andriscus was a man of the lowest extraction . . . , whether free or a slave is not known, but certainly a mercenary"; according to Diodorus (32.9a), after his first victory over the Romans, he "put many wealthy persons to death, after first throwing out false and slanderous charges against them, and murdered not a few even of his friends" and he was reputed by the Romans to be a "brigand" (*latro*). The very most that can be inferred from these texts is that the attachment of part of the Macedonian aristocracy to the Roman order must have lent a social nuance to a revolt that was basically national.

It is certain, on the other hand, that about fifteen years later slaves were involved in another similar type of revolt, the circumstances of which, however, are difficult to determine.

At the beginning of 133 Attalus III died. He had been the ruler of the kingdom of Pergamum which, thanks to Roman encouragement, had expanded greatly in the western part of Asia Minor during the second century.[85] Being childless, he bequeathed his

84. For example, N. F. Murygina, "Der Widerstand der thrakischen Stämme gegen die römische Aggression unter der Andriskosaufstand," *Biblioteca Classica Orientalis* 6 (1961): 204–7 (summary of an article that appeared in Russian in *Vestnik Drevnei Istorii* [1957], no.2:69–84).

85. From a bibliography that, as regards sources, is vast, I mention only V. Vavrinek, *La révolte d'Aristonicos* (1957) and "On the Structure of Slave Revolts: The Revolt of Aristonikos," *Soziale Probleme im Hellenismus und im römischer Reich* (1973), 201–12; J. C. Dumont, "A propos d'Aristonicos," *Eirene* 5 (1966): 189–96; F. Carrata Thomes, *La rivolta di Aristonico e le origini della provincia romana d'Asia* (1968); J. Hopp, *Untersuchungen zur Geschichte der letzten Attaliden* (1977), 121–47; F. Collins, "The Revolt of Aristonicus" (diss., Univ. Virginia, 1978); Collins, "The Macedonians and the Revolt of Aristonicus," *Ancient World* 3 (1980): 83–87; and Collins, "Eutropios and the

personal possessions and royal lands to his Roman protectors, probably not so much out of caprice or resentment against his subjects as
on account of the political and social disorders that threatened his
country. At this news, Tiberius Gracchus, who had just won acceptance for his law on the division of land, immediately proposed to the
comitia that this royal fortune should be distributed among the beneficiaries of his agrarian law. However, it proved impossible to settle
the future of the kingdom of Pergamum until after Tiberius Gracchus' assassination, at the end of 133 or in 132. A senatorial commis-
sion, with a mandate from the *senatus-consultum* then set out for Asia
with the purpose of organizing the new province. By the time it
arrived, however, the country had already been put to fire and the
sword. As soon as the throne was vacated, or perhaps even earlier, a
bastard half-brother of Attalus III, by the name of Aristonicus, born
from a union between Eumenes II and a concubine of his, the
daughter of a citharist, had proclaimed himself king and proceeded
to adopt the name Eumenes III. Coins minted in his name in the
towns in the Mysian hinterland (Thyateria, Apollonis, and Stratonicaea in Caicus) from the second year of his reign onward have
been identified.[86] The Greek cities of northwestern Anatolia, both
those that were independent and those belonging to the Attalid
kingdom, immediately split into two camps. A minority aligned
themselves with Aristonicus, the representative of monarchical
power, while most, motivated by fear as much as by self-interest,
espoused the cause of Rome. The latter group included Pergamum,
the capital, which along with many other of the kingdom's cities had
been declared "free" by the will of Attalus III. Initially, Aristonicus
pulled off some spectacular successes. Thanks to the Pergamene
fleet, which he had seized at Leukai, and with the aid of Mysian and
Thracian contingents, he subdued a number of neighboring regions
stretching from Caria to Thracian Chersonese, although certain
fortified towns such as Pergamum itself put up a stubborn resistance
to him. At first the Roman ambassadors could do little more than stir
up the kings of the Pontus, Cappadocia, Bithynia, and Paphlagonia
and several cities (Ephesus, Byzantium and Cyzicus) against the

---

Dynastic Name Eumenes of the Pergamene Pretender Aristonicus," *Ancient World* 4
(1981): 39–43.
    86. Identified by E. S. G. Robinson, "Cistophori in the Name of King Eumenes,"
Numismatic Chronicle 14 (1954): 1–8. It is doubtful whether other coins stamped with
BA/ΕΓ/AP belong to the first year of Aristonicus' reign; see J. P. Adams, "Aristonikos
and the Cistophoroi," *Historia* 29 (1980): 302–14, and the informative review of J.
Hopp's book by E. Badian in *Journal of Roman Studies* 70 (1980): 200–203.

"imposter." Then, in 131, the consul Publius Licinius Crassus Mucianus arrived with some troops. But he was a poor general, overly preoccupied with seizing booty, and was soon defeated and killed. The Ephesians had meanwhile won a naval victory off Kyme, however. Aristonicus was now forced to withdraw to the interior, where he repelled an invasion by Ariarathes V of Cappadocia before being besieged at Stratonicaea in Caicus by the new consul, Marcus Perpenna, in the following year. He was captured and sent to Rome, where he died in prison, no doubt after having taken part in the triumph of the consul Manlius Aquilius who, between 129 and 127, had been responsible for the definitive pacification of Mysia and Caria. The Romans then either rewarded or punished the cities in the area, depending on the attitudes they had adopted toward them. The salvation of Pergamum was commemorated by the institution of the festival of the *Soteria* while other cities, such as Phocaea, were razed to the ground.

On the basis of the rare texts that allow us to glimpse the social origin and ideology of the partisans of Aristonicus, some historians have deduced that this conflict was, essentially, a slave war comparable to those which were taking place in Sicily during the same period. It is a theory that has aroused some strong reactions in recent years. Some even go so far as to regard the conflict as strictly political, simply as an instance of "national" resistance against Roman imperialism.

The first sources of information to be considered, before coming to any conclusions, are provided by two texts. The first comes from Strabo (14.1.38), according to whom Aristonicus, having withdrawn inland, "quickly assembled a large number of resourceless people, and also of slaves, invited with a promise of freedom." The second is a passage in Diodorus which states that "the slaves, because of their owners' maltreatment of them, joined him in his mad venture and involved many cities in great misfortunes" (34–35.2.26). Should we supplement, or even replace, these two social categories with the rural dependants known as *laoi*? It is a plausible hypothesis, supported mainly by the fact that the principal centers of resistance were situated in the interior regions of Mysia and Caria, which were less urbanized than the seaboard. In any event, these two texts would not justify a claim that right from the start Aristonicus' forces were mainly drawn from the "resourceless poor" and the "slaves" since, according to Strabo, the latter groups were "mobilized" only during the second phase of the revolt. Furthermore, an inscription from Pergamum (*OGIS*, 338) proves that in this city certain public and royal slaves, along with 'the descendants of freedmen, were also promoted in 133 to the rank of resident foreigners (*paroikoi*) while some citizens of high rank, in contrast, took the side of the insurgents. Consequently, Aristonicus must initially have depended on a proportion of the civic and military elite of Pergamum and was only later reduced to calling also on the slaves and the poor. There was nothing particularly revolutionary about his behavior for, as we have seen, it was a course of action to which plenty of other leaders in the Greek world, not least those of Pergamum itself, had resorted as soon as the military situation became critical. Nevertheless, that does not necessarily mean that his behavior was without social significance or social impact of any kind, for we also know that some of those who acted in this way, such as the fourth-century tyrants and Hellenistic kings, felt no compunction about changing the social basis of their power at the same time. It is quite possible that Aristonicus entered upon a similar project, thereby rallying the most deprived elements of society spontaneously to his cause.

The rest of the evidence available to us is of an ideological character. Strabo's text goes on to tell us that Aristonicus dubbed the poor and the slaves who gathered round him "Heliopolitans," inhabitants of the "City of the Sun." Now, that was the name of the ideal slaveless city imagined by Iamboulos at the beginning of the Hellenistic period (see above, p. 132). The name alluded to the virtues of justice and liberty traditionally connected, especially in the East, with the sun. It might be deduced that these supporters of Aristonicus themselves entertained such aspirations. But it seems unlikely that they would have had any thought of copying the theoretical model proposed by this Jules Verne of Marxism or that they held doctrinaire attitudes aiming to establish a new type of society. They were probably simply seeking to integrate themselves in the existing society of free men, within the customary framework proposed by a king who, like many others before him, was assuming the role of a city-founder.

Modern historians who like to think that greater ambitions lay behind this dream of city-founding further support their hypothesis by appealing to the fact that the Stoic Blossius of Cumae, exiled from Rome after having to a certain extent inspired the agrarian reforms of Tiberius Gracchus there, took refuge with Aristonicus. Might he not have won him over to some "revolutionary theory" of a more or less utopian nature and thus affected the ideological coloring of his movement? In fact, however, there is nothing to prove that this philosopher was particularly concerned about the lot of the slaves. If he was, why did he not rather take refuge in Sicily, with the slave king

Eunous? If he chose Aristonicus, it was probably in the hope, entertained by many a Greek philosopher (particularly Stoics), of helping a monarch (and an anti-Roman one to boot) to set up an enlightened form of power, on the basis of *his* advice.

To complete clearing this ground littered with mistaken interpretations, I must say a few words about the revolt of Saumacus.

Just before the end of the second century (probably in about 108–107), Pairisades (V?), the king of the Cimmerian Bosphorus (a kingdom that included both the Greek cities and the Scythian tribes in the neighborhood of the straits of Kertch), doubting his ability to resist the incursions of the Scythians who remained independent, handed his kingdom over to the king of the Pontus, Mithridates Eupator. An inscription discovered in the Chersoness (*Syll.*[3] 709) sheds some light on the circumstances of his abdication. It takes the form of a decree promulgated by the Chersonesites in honor of Diophantus, one of Mithridates' generals, and it says of him:

> Having moved into the territory of the Bosphorus, he also put affairs in order for King Mithridates Eupator. But the Scythians belonging to Saumacus' party, having risen in revolt and killed the king of the Bosphorus, who had brought up Saumacus, organized ambushes against Diaphantus. The latter escaped by setting sail on the ship which our fellow-citizens had sent him. . . . Having punished the authors of the revolt and seized Saumacus, the assassin of King Pairisades, he sent him to the royal residence and restored the authority of King Mithridates Eupator.

S. A. Zebelev has situated the uprising of the Scythians in a context of class struggles in the Bosphorus region.[87] He suggests that while the Greek and Hellenized subjects of Pairisades welcomed his abdication in favor of Mithridates, the exploited Scythian population took advantage of the situation to rise against the dominant class. Zebelev believes that the insurgents belonged to the rural population of the Bosphorus, which was composed of slaves. From what social background did Saumacus himself come? The decree states that he killed Pairisades "who had brought him up." Zebelev's thesis rests essentially upon the interpretation of the verb *ektrephein,* which he associates with the term *threptos,* meaning "the slave born and brought up in the master's house." The suggestion thus is that Saumacus was a slave brought up in the palace. The term *neoterizein,* which is used to

---

87. "L'abdication de Païrisadès et la révolution scythe dans le royaume du Bosaphore," *REG* 49 (1936): 17–37.

refer to the uprising, is furthermore supposed to indicate that this was "a revolutionary movement, not simply a slave rebellion." Seven silver coins showing a head surrounded by rays reminiscent of the sun (*Helios*) and the name of the king Saum(acos) are said to show that, after the assassination of Pairisades and the flight of Diophantus, Saumacus ruled as king of the Bosphorus, albeit only briefly, and introduced a program of social justice there. In his conclusion, Zebelev situates "the uprising of the Scythian serfs" in "the long chain of slave revolts that broke out during the last third of the second century and sometimes assumed extremely threatening proportions." He also claims that in this respect this revolt in the Bosphorus has unique features:

> The insurgent serfs there formed a homogeneous mass of Scythians, which was not the case where the slaves in other regions of the ancient world were concerned. Saumacus was not a utopian: the kingdom he set out to found was already provided with a prototype by the Scythian kingdom of Skilurus and Palacus. In effect causing the throne of the Bosphorus to be vacant for a time, the abdication of Pairisades in favor of Mithridates seemed favorable for the creation of a new Scythian kingdom.

Zebelev's article attracted considerable attention and provoked some vigorous controversies. But today his conclusions are not considered convincing.[88] It has been shown that the verb *ektrephein* usually applied to free men, not to slaves, and that if Saumacus had been a slave, the Chersonesites would in all liklihood have said so more clearly. So Saumacus was a free man, probably a Scythian prince "adopted" by Pairisades for some political reason. It may also be found surprising that, if this was a slave revolt, only its leaders were punished. There is furthermore nothing to prove even that Saumacus was supported by the lowest social strata or that he favored a "revolutionary" program: for it is by no means certain that the seven coins stamped with the head haloed by rays, mentioned above, should be attributed to him, given that the fourth letter of the incomplete inscription that they bear might just as well be an L as an M and that the place where they were discovered would indicate rather that they are coins from Colchis. Besides, even if they are attributable to Saumacus, the sun motif could be regarded quite

88. Summary of the debate in Z. W. Rubinsohn, "Saumakos: Ancient History, Modern Politics," *Historia* 29 (1980): 50–70; D. B. Selov, in H. Heinen, *Die Geschichte des Altertums im Spiegel der sowjetischen Forschung* (1980), 401.

simply as an affirmation of the charismatic nature of royalty. We must therefore resign ourselves to not knowing the social content of Saumacus' revolt. All that we know is that it was not simply a slave revolt (which is not necessarily to say that no slaves took part in it).

All in all, it does appear that chattel slaves seldom, except possibly in the last third of the second century, attempted to mount collective revolts against their masters and, in any event, that in the classical period they did so much less frequently than serfs of the Helot type. The reasons for this difference are no doubt similar to those mentioned earlier to account for the respective degrees of the two groups' participation in political and military activities. The chattel slaves, by reason of their origins and status, found themselves, as it were, depersonalized and in consequence lacked the aspirations for liberty and the obsession with unity which rendered serfs of the Helot type capable of opposing their oppressors with some chance of success, as one people against another. The difference in the behavior of the two groups has often been emphatically underlined. No doubt too emphatically,[89] for a number of reasons: (1) the Helot revolts were by no means continuous. Nearly all of them occurred during a relatively limited period in Spartan history, and they appear to have involved not so much the Laconian as the Messenian Helots, who had been reduced to servitude much more recently and whose "national" consciousness was much stronger. (2) The ancient historians were writing political history. They therefore had every reason to pay more attention to revolts of the Helot type, which were regarded as an ethnic phenomenon. (3) Conversely, the possession of chattel slaves was not without its own attendant problems.

From Resistance to Acceptance

It must be recognized that in their masters' eyes the Athenian slaves represented a serious threat, apparently just as great as that which hung over cities such as Sparta. According to Xenophon (*Hiero*, 4.3), the citizens in effect owed their security entirely to their solidarity, to the fact that they guarded "one another without pay from their slaves and from evildoers, to the end that none of the citizens might perish by a violent death." According to Plato, (*Re-*

89. A correct observation of D. Musti, "Per una ricerca sul valore di scambio nel modo di produzione schiavistico," *Analisi marxista*, 171. The "Helot danger" should not be totally dismissed, as it is by A. Roobaert, in *Ktema* 2 (1977): 141–55.

public, 9.578e–579a) this was particularly true of those who owned large numbers of slaves and who owed their survival to the fact that the entire city was there to come to their aid, if need be:

> But now suppose some god should catch up a man who has fifty or more slaves and waft him and his wife and children away from the city and set him down with his other possessions and his slaves in a solitude where no free man could come to his rescue, what and how great would be his fear, do you suppose, lest he and his wife and children be destroyed by the slaves? . . . Would he not forthwith find it necessary to fawn upon some of the slaves and make them many promises and emancipate them, though nothing would be further from his wish? And so he would turn out to be the flatterer of his own servants.

According to a legal speech in Lysias, slaves "were by nature very badly disposed towards their masters." For Aristotle (*Politics,* 1334a), the reason military training is so necessary for citizens is in particular "to hold despotic power over those who deserve to be slaves." And there are plenty of texts that spell out the precautions to be taken when choosing slaves: those of strong character and in general a psychological disposition comparable to that of free men should be avoided: "There is no greater scourge than a slave with more reasoning ability than is good for him, no acquisition more fatal or more useless to a household" (Euripides, fr. 45, Nauck). Whatever is likely to set them against one another should be fostered; and so on. Furthermore, even when it is not a matter of serfs of the Helot type, one should "avoid the practice of purchasing many slaves of the same nationality [for the home], as men avoid doing in towns" (Pseudo-Aristotle, *Oeconomica,* 1.5.6). Meanwhile, a master cannot count too strongly on those members of the slave group who do support him, if it is true that, as Euripides states (fr. 51, Nauk), "slaves who are fond of their masters provoke violent hostility among their fellows."

But the situation probably differed from that which we have noted in Sparta. The Athenian masters of slaves no doubt went more in fear of individual actions by their slaves than of those on the part of the slave community aimed against the community of free men as a whole. It is not as if very many appear to have suffered the fate a certain Demetrius, son of Pankrates, is recorded as having suffered at Amizon in Caria in the second century. His epitaph has quite recently been published: "Mourned by all, I Demetrius, overcome by sweet slumber and draughts of the nectar of Bromios at a banquet, slaughtered at the hands of a slave and consumed in a great fire together with the house, descended to Hades while my father, brothers, and old mother gathered up my bones and ashes to their bosoms. But as for the one who committed such actions, my fellow citizens crucified him alive, leaving him as prey for the beasts and birds."[90] More to be feared were acts of malevolence such as theft, plundering in the fields, or pilfering in the wine cellar, all activities at which the slaves of comedy excel and against which Xenophon, in his *Oeconomicus,* puts the master on his guard even where his steward is concerned: "He must be honest and not touch his master's property. For if the man who handles the crops dares to make away with them and doesn't leave enough to give a good profit on the undertaking, what good can come of farming under his management?" (14.2)— sensible observations that do credit to the "economic theories" of the author. Alternatively, at least where slaves not working on their own account were concerned, it might, rather, be a matter of laziness or negligence bordering on sabotage. This would explain why, for example, in the Pseudo-Aristotle's *Oeconomica* (1.5.1), good will on the part of ("conscientious") slaves, stimulated if necessary by promises of freedom (1.5.6), is one of the most highly prized qualities to be hoped for in them. Manifestations of hostility, the frequency and scope of which are difficult to gauge, are still today assessed in remarkably divergent ways. It seems to me that their endemic existence in most societies based on extra-economic constraints is so clearly attested[91] that, in the case of the ancient Greek world, we must beware of underestimating their importance. At the same time, however, we should underline their natural and spontaneous character and not go so far as to regard them as a conscious form of struggle aiming to weaken, if not destroy, the system.

A similar situation obtains with regard to flight,[92] which was the most direct if not the most certain way for slaves to recover their liberty. Except for those who were well integrated in their master's family or those who enjoyed a relative autonomy, escape must have represented a constant temptation. Hence the frequent expressions of praise[93] for the slave who was *paramonimos,* "disposed to stay," as opposed to the one who was *drapetes* (a fugitive) and likewise the clauses in Babylonian sale contracts which guarantee the buyer against the escape of his slave within a period of one hundred days.

90. J. Robert and L. Robert, *Fouilles d'Amizon en Carie,* 1 (1983), 259–63, n.65.
91. See, for example, the justified remarks of M. Foucault, *Discipline and Punish* (1977), in particular Part 2, chapter 1.
92. There is to date no work of synthesis on runaway slaves in the Greek world.
93. Klees, *Herren und Sklaven,* 89, n.174.

Clearly, slaves took to flight for a variety of reasons: most, no doubt, because of the harsh treatment they received; others for fear of what was in store for them at the hands of a new master; yet others to avoid punishment when they had done something wrong. Rather than take a chance on their own, they would usually make a break for it in twos and threes: that, at least, is what is suggested by the Egyptian papyri, most of which are provided by Zeno's correspondence and which allude to a number of concrete cases.

The moment chosen for such escape attempts varied. It would often be during a voyage or, better still, a period of crisis and insecurity—hence the large number of examples in times of war. With a territory under threat from an enemy army or pirates, escape attempts by chattel slaves, normally endemic anyway, could escalate into a veritable mass movement.

Such was (as we have seen, p. 66) the case in Attica during the Peloponnesian War, when over twenty thousand took flight after the occupation of Decelea by the Peloponnesians in 413; and a similar situation occurred on the island of Chios between 412 and 406, following the installation of an Athenian garrison at Delphinion, three hours march away to the north of the city, for "the slaves of Chios, who were numerous—and indeed the most numerous in any single city except that of the Lacedaemonians—and at the same time, on account of their multitude were punished more severely for every misdeed, now that the Athenian army seemed, with the advantage of a fortified position, to be firmly established, immediately began to desert to them in large numbers" (Thucydides, 8.40.2). After this, the phenomenon seems to have again reached serious proportions only during the Hellenistic period, above all in its final phases, at the time of the Roman conquest and an increase in piracy. Most of the peace treaties containing clauses relating to settling the fates of fugitive slaves date from this period.

Some of these fugitives were certainly military orderlies, for whom the temptation to desert their masters and put themselves out of their reach was particularly strong when they sensed the wind of defeat blowing through their camp. In contrast to the massive escapes of "civilian" slaves, these individual defections were common in every period and in every Greek army. That is proved by the widespread practice of giving supposedly defector-slaves the task of relaying false intelligence to the enemy and also by an anecdote from the Pseudo-Aristotle's *Oeconomica*, which describes the oldest known insurance system organized and guaranteed by the State. Antimenes of Rhodes, a contemporary of Alexander the Great, "invited the owners of any slaves in the camp to register them at whatever value they desired, undertaking at the same time to pay him eight drachmae a year. If the slave ran away the owner was to recover the registered value. Many slaves were thus registered, and a large sum of money was paid [in premiums]. And when a slave ran away, Antimenes instructed the governor [of the province] where the camp lay either to recover the man or to pay his master his value" (2.2.34b).

Unlike a Helot, a chattel slave who escaped and reached the enemy camp or a foreign land did not recover his freedom automatically.

In time of war the conquered were expected to return such fugitives when the hostilities were over, as is apparent from the peace treaties mentioned earlier. At the very best, such slaves might benefit from an amnesty—probably granting them the favor of escaping punishment on their return. As for the victors, they regarded them as welcome booty, like any other property taken from the enemy. Thus the slaves who, according to the author of the *Hellenica Oxyrhynchia* (17.4) were "bought cheaply" by the Thebans at the time of the Lacedaemonian occupation of Decelea (413–404) must for the most part have been fugitives from Attica. The granting of freedom could be considered only for individual cases, as a reward for outstanding services. At the end of the third century, Philo of Byzantium in his *Syntaxis mechanica,* for example recommends that any slave who has informed the besiegers of the battle positions of the defenders or who has stirred up some sedition in the town should be promised his freedom; and he also recommends that, in similar circumstances, mercenaries should be offered promotion and metic hoplites a crown (5.4.12–13). Philo is well aware that such proclamations "are generally deeply disturbing to the minds of the enemy, dissuading them from arming metics and servants and forcing them to provide the latter with normal rations. In this way there will be fewer fighting men and they will consume more food and it will not be long before there is sedition in the town" (5.4.14–15). We should note that there is no question of encouraging any defection, let alone any massive revolt on the part of the slaves, by granting them unconditional liberty. The fact is that such a ploy would have contravened the tacitly recognized and generally respected code of the "laws" of warfare. On the rare occasions when individuals as suspect as the tyrant Aristodemus of Cumae and Dionysius of Syracuse, or kings such as Philip V of Macedon and Mithridates of the Pontus resorted to such methods, they invariably provoked shock and indignation. Thus, according to Plutarch (above, p. 159), following the call to desert issued by Philip V on the occasion of the siege of Chios in 201, "the women, suddenly possessed of a fierce and savage spirit, in company with their slaves, who were themselves equally indignant and supported the women by their presence, hastened to mount the walls, both bringing stones and missiles and exhorting and importuning the fighting men until finally, by their vigorous defence and the wounds inflicted on the enemy by their missiles, they repulsed Philip. And not a single slave deserted to him."

A limited number of possibilities were open to fugitive slaves. They could take to the hills, like Drimacus and his companions, and launch guerrilla attacks against their masters (a course seldom followed, according to Xenophon, *Cyropaedia*, 4.2.21); they could live incognito in some populous location; they could more or less legally take advantage of the right of asylum in some sanctuary;[94] or they could join some band of pirates or mercenaries.[95] Otherwise, if he was to escape from slave law, a fugitive had no alternative but to try to get back to his native land, with the less chance of success the farther away it happened to be, for in order to reach it, he would have to slip through the mesh of an extremely fine net. He would have to elude the pursuit of his master or his master's agents, avoid denunciation (highly rewarded) and also seizure by any individual acting to his own advantage or with a view to restoring the slave to his master, and avoid falling victim to the measures laid down in extradition treaties specifically drawn up for such purposes between neighboring cities. One example of such a treaty is that concluded between the Anatolian cities of Miletus and Heraclea of Latmos at the beginning of the second century:

> With regard to servants who, having fled from Miletus to Heraclea or from Heraclea to Miletus, are handed over to the mountain guards of either city as from the year following Menandros' assumption of the crown, those who are responsible in Miletus must report the individuals to the *prytaneis* and superintendent magistrates, in each case within ten days from the time when the slave was handed over. These officials must send a letter explaining the circumstances in detail to the *prostatai*

94. F. van Woess, *Das Asylvesen Aegyptens in der Ptolemäerzeit* (1923), and F. Dunand, "Droit d'asile et refuge dans les temples en Egypte lagide," *Hommages à S. Sauneron*, 2 (1979), 77–97, in particular 91–93. On the measures taken to limit this practice, see C. Habicht, *Mitteilungen des deutschen archäologischen Instituts, Athenische Abteilung* 72 (1957): 226–30, focusing on a Samian decree of the third quarter of the third century.

95. See, for example, M. Capozza, "Il Brigentaggio nelle fonti della prima rivolta servile siciliana," *Atti Ist. Veneto* 133 (1974–75): 27–40.

of Heraclea. Those who hold the posts of mountain guards in Heraclea must inform the *prostatai* within a similar period and the latter must similarly send a letter to the *prytaneis* of Miletus and the superintendent magistrates. The masters of the slaves of each city will be allowed to take them away, provided they pay the mountain guards ten of the old Rhodian drachmas by way of a recovery fee and, in addition, one obole per day for their keep, and this must be done within four months from the date of the letter addressed to the magistrates: otherwise the slaves will become the property of the mountain guards. [*Syll.*³ 633, 1.87–89][96]

If they were returned to their masters' homes, they could expect a beating and chains and in many cases also to be branded or tattooed on the forehead with a word or symbol which made their degradation publicly known.[97]

However a slave might express his defiance, a whole battery of repressive measures were thus available to his master, and these must have had a powerful deterrent effect. Thus, scholars have detected an apparent decrease in escape attempts in Egypt at the end of the Ptolemaic period, following an improvement in the efficiency of census operations and of the organization of State employed posses to hunt down runaway slaves.[98] But no system of repression and exploitation can depend upon violence and terror alone. The success of such methods presupposes a measure of resignation and consent[99] on the part of those subjected to them, a degree of accommodation, to use a fashionable expression, or to be more precise, a "natural" acceptance of a power that, in the words of Pierre Bourdieu, "exerts itself without having to be exerted" because it stems from a "bewitched" perception of the relation of forces, which "transfigures them into relations of legitimate domination, authority or prestige."[100] On this point, I must beg to differ from those

96. Cf. M. Wörrle, *Chiron* 9 (1979): 97–103.
97. E. Solimonik, "The marking of livestock and slaves in Antiquity" (in Russian), *Gesellschaft und Recht im gr.-röm. Alt.*, 2 (1969), 219–23; U. Fantasia, "Asikton chorion," *ASNP*, n.s., 6 (1976): 1165–75; K. Zimmermann, "Tatowierte Thrakerinnen auf griechischen Vasen bildern," *Jahrbuch* 95 (1980): 163–77.
98. Biezunska-Malowist, *L'esclavage dans l'Egypte gréco-romaine*, 132.
99. M. Godelier, "Infrastructures, sociétés, histoire," *Dialectiques* 21 (1977): 51: "Here it can be seen that there is no consent without violence, even if the latter remains on the horizon. But it would be equally mistaken to imagine that a period of domination and oppression which rested upon nothing but violence and terror or upon the total consent of all members of society could endure. Those were extreme cases in the evolution of history, ones that were no more than ephemeral and transitory."
100. "Capital symbolique et classes sociales," *L'Arc* 72 (1978): 17 and 18.

Western historians who, paradoxically taking over some of the aberrations of the Marxism of around 1935, today in their turn delude themselves with a comforting vision of activist and spontaneous "struggles on the part of the slaves."[101]

For such struggles to have been qualitatively superior to those sustained in modern times by a working class which, for revolutionary purposes, has managed to elaborate its own theory, its own organizations, and to a certain extent its own culture, the slaves would, at the very least, have had to elaborate an embryonic counterideology strong enough to provide them with a *raison d'être* other than that assigned to them by the dominant ideology, and to manifest that counterideology in various ways in social life. But that does not appear to have happened either in Athens or in Sparta.

In the case of Athens, let us ignore a whole collection of edifying anecdotes or statements that may be regarded as suspect since they come from the slaves' masters,[102] and instead turn for evidence to religious life. Although this has been the subject of an extremely thorough study[103] and traditionally constitutes an area in which the oppressed are prone to express their self-awareness, there are hardly any signs of original thought or practice on the part of the slaves in this domain. Not, at any rate, on the part of the slaves *qua* slaves. As foreigners from one or another "barbarian" region, they are naturally to be found in religious contexts, but always in association with free men, among the devotees of many exotic deities such as the Thracian Bendis or Atargatis, the Syrian goddess, who were more accommodating to foreigners than the great *polis* deities. Furthermore, the place of the slaves, as slaves, in religious life was simply that assigned to them by their masters. In the public cults they were no more than spectators (although rare exceptions were made in the case of public slaves of Greek origin, who were allowed to become

101. For example, P. Dockes, *La libération médiévale* (1979).

102. I note only the following passage of Polybius (12.6a), because I have seldom seen it quoted: "It is foolish to suppose, as he hints, that it was improbable that the slaves of those who had been the allies of the Lacedaemonians should adopt the friendly feelings of their masters for the friends of those masters. Men, indeed, who have once been slaves, when they meet with unexpected good fortune, attempt to affect and reproduce not only the likings but the friendships and relations of their masters, taking more pains to do so than those actually connected by blood, and hope to wipe out their former inferiority and disrepute by this very effort to appear rather as descendants than as freedmen of their late masters."

103. F. Bömer, *Untersuchungen über die Religion der Sklaven in Griechenland und Rom*, *Abh. Ak. Wiss. Mainz*, 4 (1957–63). These conclusions are confirmed by, for example, M.-F. Baslez, *Recherches sur les conditions de pénétration et de diffusion des religions orientales à Délos* (1977), 168–75.

initiates of the Mysteries of Eleusis). They held a subordinate position in family ceremonies and certain fertility rites that underpinned the popular orgies of the Dionysia and the Anthesteria (especially during the second day, known as the day of the Pots (*chous*), in honor of Dionysus). Only on rare occasions do slaves appear as protagonists in various carnavelesque ceremonies of social inversion. These went by different names in various cities. In Athens, they were held at the end of June, on the occasion of the *Cronia* in which, according to Philochorus (Macrobius, *Saturnalia*, 1.10.22), "the fathers of families ate the grain and fruits already harvested, mingling without ceremony with their slaves." At Cydon, in Crete, it was in honor of the *Clarotai* that "certain festivals are regularly held . . . during which no free persons enter the city, but the slaves are masters of everything and have the power to flog the free men" (Ephorus, in Athenaeus, 6.263f). Also in Crete, there was a festival of the *Hermaea* in the course of which "while the slaves are feasting, their masters assist in menial duties" (Carystius, in Athenaeus, 14.639b) and similarly, at Troezen "a festival is held lasting many days, on one of which the slaves play at knucklebones in company with the citizens, and the masters entertain the slaves at a feast" (Athenaeus, 14.639c). Among the Thessalians, it was during the festival of the *Peloria*, the origin of which, significantly enough, was supposed to go back to the Pelasgian period, that "they set up gaily furnished tables and carry out the festivities so generously that all foreigners, even, are welcomed to the feast, prisoners are set free, and slaves, reclining on couches with the utmost liberty, are entertained while their masters wait on them" (Baton of Sinope, in Athenaeus 14.640a). But it is well known that, as Emmanuel Le Roy Ladurie writes, such rites of inversion "emanating from a dominant association or Herrschaft had the appropriate function—conservative, integrating, reinforcing the hierarchy—of creating a momentary inversion on feast days, the better to maintain order in the long run, in everyday society outside Carnival. Such inversion was ultimately counterrevolutionary."[104]

Similar observations have been made in relation to Sparta by Jean Ducat, who in particular cites the passage from Plutarch (*Lycurgus*, 28.10) in which the Helots taken prisoner by the Thebans between 371 and 362 were ordered "to sing the songs of Terpander, Alcman and Spendon the Spartan, but they declined to do so, on the plea that their masters did not allow it."[105] Fear proves too strong even when

104. *Carnival in Romans*, 302.
105. *Aspects de l'hilotisme*, 24.

there is no occasion for it, because it has already engendered an imitative type of behavior. Conversely, the possibilities for the betterment of the slaves' position offered by such festivals did not damage the system either, for these were taken up only in accordance with procedures fixed by the masters, and they always retained control of the situation.

There is nothing more effective, whatever the circumstances, than violence thus internalized, assimilated, made to seem natural, incorporated and accepted as a part of the order of things, as is shown by a famous anecdote told by Herodotus. It relates to offspring born, during a protracted period of absence on the part of the Scythian warriors, from the unions between their wives and their slaves. Upon their return, they met with a determined resistance from these bastards so long as they fought them as though they were free men. But when someone had the idea of abandoning spears and bows and instead confronting them with whips, the situation was quite changed: "As long as they saw us armed, they thought themselves to be our peers and the sons of our peers; let them see us with whips and no weapons of war, and they will perceive that they are our slaves; and taking this to heart, they will not abide our attack." It was a clever strategy for "the slaves, amazed by what they saw, had no more thought of fighting, but fled" (4.4).

Conclusion

Without presuming to pronounce on the whole complex of theoretical questions that historians and anthropologists are today posing in relation to precapitalist societies, I nevertheless think it would be hypocritical to bring this study to a close without attempting to set out and justify my answers to the questions that most directly concern it: (1) Can Greek Antiquity be described as a "slave society"? (2) Did the Greek slaves constitute a social class? In actual fact, the two virtually boil down to one, namely, the question of the validity of the Marxist approach to the subject and, in a much wider sense, that of the extent to which such an approach would be justified, in one way or another, in taking over the entire historical field. There is much at stake here, and there can be no question of deciding the answers a priori, at the outset of one's research—if, that is, one aims to escape from the infernal cycle of mechanical professions of faith, attacks on personal motivation, and all the other types of condemnation which have in the past all too frequently poisoned the debate.

The answer to the first question depends first of all on the meaning one gives the term "slaves": the narrow sense of chattel slaves of the classical Athenian type (more or less as the word has traditionally been used in the West), or a wider meaning encompassing all types of legally defined personal dependency to which the Greeks sometimes referred as *douleia*. It was only in view of the theoretical extrapolations to which each of these solutions so easily lends itself that I eventually, but not without hesitation, decided to adopt the first. To opt for the second, even taking care to stress the differences among these various types of slavery, would have been to revert to the implication that Greek Antiquity basically produced only one type of exploitation founded upon extra-economic constraint. Indeed, why not say the whole of Antiquity (the East included)—albeit taking care to distinguish among different forms ("primitive," "patriarchal," "generalized," and so on)? That is a conclusion which seems to me both to misunderstand Marx's thought and also dangerously to distort the historical facts. Precapitalist societies, where exploitation generally proceeds through the direct application of extra-economic constraints to economic life by various institutional means, are characterized precisely by the diversity that results from the modes of appropriating the surplus to the profit of minority groups. These modes include not only slavery and serfdom but various others too, an analysis of which Marx himself undertook on the basis of the empirical data at his disposal, but of course never completed. That is why, wishing to avoid the error, pernicious both from a political and from a historical point of view, of confusing things that should be kept distinct, I have in general used terms that underline the specificity of the modes of exploitation which I considered irreducible to slavery in the strict sense of the term: in particular, tribute-paying servitude of the Helot type and debt-bondage, both of which seem to me to be deeply affected, in different ways, by the context of the community in which they apply.

It is important to be clear about the different senses in which a society may be described as a slave society: (1) if it incorporated slaves within it; (2) if it was "based" upon them from a socioeconomic point of view, that is, if it essentially derived from their exploitation the material conditions of its existence (I am, naturally, in complete agreement with Maurice Godelier's view that by this "we should understand not only the material means which make it possible for individuals to subsist physically but also whatever allows them to exist socially (and at the same time permits the reproduction of the social relations that make for such an existence");[1] (3) if it held a majority belief in the legitimacy of slavery. If we reject the anecdotal approach and also a moral or psychological one, we must recognize that it is from the second of these three points of view that the problem is most meaningful for a historian.

It was thus only in certain places and at certain times that the Greek world produced truly slave societies: in Athens, certainly, and probably in many other cities during the classical and Hellenistic

1. *La production des Grands Hommes* (1982), 225.

periods, when the effect was felt "from cellar to attic," to borrow the title of a work by Michel Vovelle (*De la cave au grenier*): at every level, from the cosmic to the personal and including the political, a dominant mode of thought was imposed, in which autonomy was set in opposition to dependency, and the position of the commander to that of those commanded.

It goes without saying, however, that even in these special cases the slave mode of production existed only within the framework of a particular social conditioning, in other words as an *ancient slave* mode of production, bearing the mark of the historical conditions in which it developed and coexisting with secondary modes of production. All of which means that it by no means always predominated over other relations of dependency or in the economic system as a whole. Its occasionally acquiring such a predominant position was the result not of an internal process of maturation or of an autonomous development of the phenomenon of exploitation, but of a combination of more or less independent forces affecting various sectors of social life.

Such are the—certainly restrictive—terms in which I would define Greek "slavery." I would nevertheless take the precaution of making it quite clear that in my view those restrictions do not bear upon the diffusion of the phenomenon of exploitation as such, that is, that they in no way minimize the role played elsewhere by various other modes of dependency which, in a similar and no less effective fashion, ensured that the direct producers would be despoiled.[2] I would freely acknowledge that, at a certain level of generality, it is quite possible to describe Greek society as a whole as "slave," to the extent that of all the modes of dependency to be found within it, slavery was the one that introduced the greatest degree of complexity into the social organism, made possible the highest degree of cultural development, and constituted the archetypal form of non-free labor.[3]

The second general question that cannot be avoided in connection with Greek slaves (and other dependants) has to do with what they represented as a group. To put it more precisely (and since these

2. This remark I aim at all those who, by introducing qualifications, nuances, and distinctions and by emphasizing the flexibility of the social fabric, whittle away the phenomenon of exploitation or turn ancient societies into "open" societies that prefigure capitalist societies.

3. I. Hahn, "Die Anfänge der antiken Gesellschaftsformation in Griechenland und das Problem der sogenannten asiatischen Produktionweise," *Jahrbuch für Wirtschaftsgeschichte* 2 (1971):29–47.

days, one normally locates one's position, in this context, in relation to Marxism): to what extent did they constitute a social class?

According to Marxist dogmatism of the period between 1930 and 1950, it was taken for granted that the slaves of Antiquity could not conceivably have contravened the famous, if misunderstood, pronouncements of the *Communist Manifesto*. During the 1960s, many historians, reacting against that view, responded to the question either in a forthrightly negative fashion or else with qualified answers of various kinds. They all agreed that there can be no such thing as a social class, in the strict sense of the term, until the individual, "liberated" from the complex of rights and duties afforded him by his natural membership in a community, reaches the point where he is regarded by capital as nothing but a simple force of production and is therefore essentially defined socially only in terms of his place in the production process, from an economic point of view. But when it came to providing a positive definition for the type of classification which existed in precapitalist societies, such as the Greek ones, positions diverged. For some, all that mattered was the politico-juridical organization of the societies into "orders" (or "estates," since these groups were not always solidly, if at all, structured).[4] Others, who considered that legal frameworks were extensively undermined even as early as Antiquity, under pressure from various economic forces (essentially of an artisan or commercial nature), deemed it also desirable to conduct an analysis from the point of view of classes.[5] In their opinion, the interconnections between orders and classes may be understood by studying the overlaps between these two hitherto isolated categories. Last, but not least, there is M. I. Finley's attempt to apprehend the complexity of the lived experience directly, by making use of the "admirably vague" concept of "status." This term encompasses the full range of

4. This, for example, is the principal tendency noticeable in *Recherches sur les structures sociales dans l'Antiquité classique* (1970), in general conformity with the theses defended in France by R. Mousnier. See his *Les hiérarchies sociales de 1450 à nos jours* (1969); "Le concept de classe sociale et l'histoire," *Revue d'Histoire Economique et Sociale* 48 (1970): 449–95; and other works.

5. This way of looking at things is typical of many historians from socialist countries: see, for example, K. Zelin, "Principles for the morphological classification of forms of dependency" (in Russian), *Vestnik Drevnei Istorii* (1967), no.2:7–30 (in French as "Principes de classification morphologique des formes de dépendance," *Rech. int., 1975*, 45–77); V. I. Kuziscin, "The concept of socioeconomic formation and the periodization of the history of slave society" (in Russian), *Vestnik Drevnei Istorii* (1974), no.3:69–87; M. A. Dandamayev, "Social Stratification in Babylonia," *Acta Antiqua* 22 (1974): 433–44; E. C. Welskopf, "Soziale Gruppen und Typenbegriffe Klasse, Stand, Schicht, Privatman, Individualität, Hellenen und Barbaren, Polis und Territorialstaat," *Hell. Poleis*, in particular 2155–59. Cf. also G. E. M. de Ste. Croix, "Karl Marx and the History of Classical Antiquity," *Arethusa* 8 (1975): 7–41.

the known facts in varying proportions, in particular their psychological aspects, and thus achieves a general representation of the social body as a spectrum of degrees.[6]

Nonetheless, none of these solutions appears entirely satisfactory to me; the first because, having excluded economic factors from the genesis of the various orders, it is no longer in a position to integrate those factors with the ways the orders function and develop; the second because, having taken the social situation apart, it tries to reconstruct it by introducing purely economic criteria which, as they stand, are quite alien to it; and the third, despite its descriptive value, because it dispenses the ancient historian from pondering the relative importance of the various elements that enter into the definition of "status" and their modes of articulation, as if this nonhierarchical schema of a synthetic system of gradation (of the type favored by American sociology)[7] possessed a timeless and universal validity.

In any event, the point I would fasten upon in this debate (the scope of which far exceeds that of the present study) is that the dividing lines between ancient societies, as they are institutionally established and psychologically perceived, deserve to be taken seriously. On the other hand, it is not enough to define them in a mainly negative fashion, simply in opposition to the types of classification characteristic of capitalist societies. At the risk of being accused of empiricism or even of idealism, one must also seek, however difficult the task, to understand why it was that, in ancient Greece, for example, social classification was founded upon orders and statuses. Here I believe that Godelier's inquiries, based on a rich collection of anthropological documentation, may prove useful to us.[8] By extending the results of his ethnological inquiries to classical Antiquity, he has been able to show that if kinship relations here, jurido-political ones there, played a dominant role at every level of social life, the reason was that these relations, which are today relegated to the level of superstructure, then operated as relations of production. They assumed from within the society an economic function essential to the reproduction of the various groups and, on that account, belonged to the infrastructures. Or, conversely, to borrow the terms used by Karl Polanyi,[9] it was because economics

6. See particularly *The Ancient Economy*, 35–61.

7. Cf. S. Ossowski, *Class Structure in the Social Consciousness* (1957; in English 1963).

8. Particularly his introduction to the Editions sociales collection *Sur les sociétés précapitalistes: Textes choisis de Marx, Engels, Lénine* (1970), and also his collections of articles entitled *Horizon: Trajets marxistes en anthropologie* (1973), and *L'idéel et le matériel* (1984).

9. See essentially K. Polanyi and C. Arensberg, *Trade and Markets in the Early Empires* (1957). Cf. S. C. Humphreys, "History, Economics and Anthropology: The

found itself "embedded" in social relations. This came about because, given the state of development of the productive forces (human as well as material), if these were to be efficiently put to work, society had to be structured in ways that would, at least to some extent, maintain community solidarities. In such cases, one can truly say that ("in the last analysis") it is for economic reasons that the dominant social relations are of a noneconomic kind. Many texts from Marx could (were it necessary) be cited in support of this interpretation.

The human groups that emerge are therefore not "classes" in the strict, economic sense of the term—and in this respect too, in opposition to what is often believed, we find ourselves unequivocally in agreement with Marx himself who, in the context of ancient or medieval societies, speaks frequently of either *Stände* or *Klassen* without either assimilating or absolutely opposing them.[10] As Godelier observes, for Marx

> in Antiquity, there were no classes *hidden behind* the orders or *contained* within them or which gradually emerged from them. By using the word "classes" to refer to the orders, Marx wished to present them in a different guise from that in which they were seen in the context of the dominant ideology of these societies and in the works of the historians which took those representations as their point of departure without ever criticizing them. He wished to present them no longer as more or less harmonious relations, but as relations of oppression and exploitation, not as relations founded *solely* upon ideas, whether religious or otherwise, but as also stemming from a predetermined material basis that corresponded to the predetermined degree of development of the material and intellectual forces of production. Marx thus uses the word class in *two* ways. In the one it refers to specific historical realities, the social groups born from the development of the capitalist mode of production and the dissolution of the feudal mode of production: that is the meaning of "classes" in the strict sense. When used in the other sense, the word refers to historical realities that are *analogous* to the classes of capitalist society, yet distinct from them; and in this sense the

---

Work of Karl Polanyi," *History and Theory* 8 (1969): 165–212 (=*Anthropology and the Greeks* [1978], 31–75); Y. Garlan, "L'oeuvre de Karl Polanyi: La place de l'économie dans les sociétés anciennes," *La Pensée* 171 (1973): 118–27.

10. I am not convinced by the way in which some of the very best contemporary historians reject any approach to the problem in terms of classes, although we find ourselves in agreement upon many other points. See M. I. Finley, *The Ancient Economy*, 49–51; P. Vidal-Naquet, "Les esclaves grecs étaient-ils une classe?" *Raison Présente* 6 (1968): 103–8 (reprinted in *The Black Hunter*, 159–167); Vidal-Naquet and M. Austin, *Economic and Social History of Ancient Greece* (1972; in English 1977); cf. Y. Garlan, "Problèmes théoriques des processus historiques: Le cas des économies et des sociétés en Grèce ancienne," *Nouvelle Critique* 246 (1973): 68; E. Will, for example in *REG* 91 (1978): 84–85.

word is used in a nonspecific, as-it-were metaphorical way, since it subsumes *only* the resemblances, not the differences.[11]

It is in this spirit—which, it seems to me, has much in common with that which prompts André Carandini to speak of "political classes" in this context[12]—that I would propose applying to slaves as a group sometimes the term "order" or "status," sometimes the term "class," depending on whether one wishes to stress the group's differences from or, on the contrary, its resemblances to the classes of the present day.

When we use concepts such as class "consciousness" or class "struggle," it is thus only those words "consciousness" and "struggle" that may still present a problem. We must, then, take them to mean whatever they may mean in the context of "primitive" societies,[13] with all the further nuances, or rather specific qualifications, necessary in the case of Antiquity.[14] Thus, in the case of chattel slaves—and to a lesser degree in that of serfs of the Helot type, with all their communal links—we must recognize all the limits placed on the arousal of their consciousness and their possibilities for action. These limits stemmed from their geographical dispersion, from the diversity of their social conditions and cultural levels, from the overwhelming nature of the dominant ideology and their fear of repression, from the lack of any perspective on freedom other than for the individual, and from their exclusion from political life as a matter of principle. We must also remember the complexity that resulted from the overlaps between on the one hand the "fundamental" or "determining" contradiction between masters and slaves (at least in certain localities and at certain periods) and, on the other, the "principal" or "dominant" contradictions among free men, which manifested themselves in a more continuous, more systematic, and more spectacular way, and so on. It is not difficult to show that the Greek slaves did not develop a "correct" and prematurely Leninist consciousness of their condition as an exploited group and did not

11. "Ordres, castes, classes," in *L'idéel*, 300–301. It is a point that I have myself tried to make, quite independently of Godelier, in a paper delivered to the ancient history group of CERM in 1975. See also the similar views of R. A. Padgug, "Classes and Society in Classical Greece," *Arethusa* 8 (1975): 85–117, in particular 98–99.

12. In the best interpretation of Marx's thought on Antiquity that I know of: *L'anatomia della scimmia* (1979), 48–50 and 158–63.

13. Note the fascinating studies by E. J. Hobsbawm in *Primitive Rebels* (1959) and *Bandits* (1969).

14. Very well explained by C. Parain, "Les caractères spécifiques de la lutte des classes dans l'Antiquité classique," *La Pensée* 108 (1963): 3–25, and by J.-P. Vernant, "La lutte des classes," *Eirene* 4 (1965): 5–19 (=*Myth and Society in Ancient Greece* [1980], 1–18).

take the firm action that such a consciousness would have imposed. But that is not to "refute Marxism" (at the very most a certain kind of Marxism). Non-Marxist historians (that is, for the most part, anti-Marxist ones) are certainly extremely punctilious in the matter of making social claims and are past masters at pitching their demands so high that those fortunate enough to have any chance of meeting them will be few and far between indeed.[15] Rather than dwell upon the impossibility of doing so, we are surely better off attempting to understand the more or less deprived and nightmarish conditions in which the dominated lived in their dominated state. In these conditions they produced forms of resistance dictated by the very process of alienation they were attempting to abolish. There too, we must go beyond the visible range of facts which does indeed constitute the proper object of the scientific method.

This study of slavery in ancient Greece thus ends not so much with a conclusion as with an outline of certain personal solutions to theoretical problems, which I have been obliged to find as I went along; or, to be more precise, an outline of the way I have (provisionally?) posed the problems to myself. I feel not the slightest regret at having thereby definitively alienated two categories of readers: those who can see Marxist history only as an affirmation of some "party position" (if any such readers still exist);[16] and those (who certainly do exist) who, in order to exercise it, complacently give a "primary"[17] representation of it, turning it into what Voltaire[18] might have called "a hideous bogey."

15. A subterfuge that I had already noticed when, together with C. Nières, I was writing *Les révoltes bretonnes de 1675: Papier timbré et bonnets rouges* (1975), 207.

16. Following L. Sève (*Une introduction à la philosophie marxiste* [1980], 562), I should like to remind the reader of what Lenin wrote in 1908 when he was relentlessly opposing the empirico-critical position adopted by Bogdanov: "We must argue out questions of philosophy in such a way that the *Proletarii* and the Bolsheviks, as a faction of the Party, do not suffer from it. And that is perfectly possible."

17. To balance the absurdity and fraudulence often imputed to a certain brand of Marxist dogmatism, we really ought to itemize and investigate the idiocies of a particular trend of anti-Marxism in ancient history: they include selecting only the most mediocre Marxist works for the attention of the public, more or less deliberately withholding information about them, and, more generally, incomprehension and malice when it comes to interpreting them. What, for example, should we make of one particular critic, usually so very prompt to denounce the slightest bibliographical omission, who finds it "all in all legitimate" (not "understandable" or "excusable" but "*legitimate*") to ignore the entire corpus of Soviet works relating to ancient slavery? (See *Latomus* 39 [1980]: 905.)

18. Cited by A. Grosrichard, *Structure du sérail: La fiction du despotisme asiatique de l'Occident classique* (1979), 40.

Translator's Note

I have used the translations of the Loeb Classical Library, published by Harvard University Press, Cambridge, and William Heinemann, London, for the following texts:
Aeneas Tacticus, 1962, trans. the Illinois Greek Club.
Aeschines, 1968, trans. Charles Darwin Adams.
Aristophanes, *Ecclesiazusae*, 1972;
——, *Frogs*, 1924;
——, *Plutus*, 1972;
——, *Wasps*, 1950; all trans. Benjamin Bickley Rogers.
Aristotle, *Athenian Constitution*, 1967;
——, *Politics*, 1972; both trans. H. Rackham.
Ps. Aristotle, *Nicomachean Ethics*, 1962, trans. H. Rackham.
Ps. Aristotle, *Oeconomica*, 1969, trans. G. Cyril Armstrong.
Athenaeus, *Deipnosophists*, 1967, trans. Charles Burton Gulick
Demosthenes, 1967, trans. A. T. Murray and J. H. Vince.
Diodorus Siculus, 1961, trans. C. H. Oldfather and 1969, trans. Russel M. Geer.
Herodotus, *Histories*, 1946–1950, trans. A. D. Godley.
Hesiod, *Works and Days*, 1960, trans. Bernadotte Perrin.
Hippocrates, 1948, trans. W. H. S. Jones.
Isocrates, 1968, trans. George Norlin.
Livy, 1966, trans. Frank Gardner Moore.
Lysias, 1943, trans. W. R. M. Lamb.
Minor Attic Orators, 1962, trans. J. O. Burtt.
Pausanias, 1966–1969, trans. H. A. Ormerod and W. H. S. Jones.

Plato, *Laws,* 1968, trans. R. G. Bury.
——, *Politicus,* 1952, trans. W. R. M. Lamb.
——, *Protagoras,* 1967, trans. W. R. M. Lamb.
——, *Republic,* 1964, trans. P. Shorey.
Plutarch, *Lives,* 1967, trans. Bernadotte Perrin.
——, *On the Fortune of Alexander,* 1962, trans. Frank Cole Babbit.
Polybius, 1967, trans. W. R. Paton.
Select Papyri, 1934, trans. A. S. Hunt and C. C. Edgar.
Strabo, 1967–1969, trans. Horace Leonard Jones.
Thucydides, 1965, trans. Charles Forster Smith.
Xenophon, *Agesilaus,* 1968, trans. E. C. Marchant.
——, *Cyropaedia,* 1968, trans. Walter Miller.
Xenophon, *Hiero,* 1968, trans. E. C. Marchant.
——, *Hellenica,* 1968, trans. Carleton L. Brownson.
——, *Memorabilia,* 1965;
——, *Oeconomicus,* 1965;
——, *Ways and Means,* 1968; all trans. E. C. Marchant.

I have used the translations published by University of Chicago Press, Chicago and London, for the following:
Aeschylus, *Persians,* 1956, trans. S. G. Benardete.
Euripides, *Helen,* 1969, trans. Richmond Lattimore.
——, *Ion,* 1958, trans. R. F. Willetts.

Others:
Homer, *Iliad,* 1950, and *Odyssey,* 1946, both trans. E. V. Rieu (Penguin Classics, Harmondsworth).
Ps. Aristotle, *Rhetorica ad Alexandrum,* Oxford, 1952, trans. E. S. Forster.

I have sometimes slightly modified these translations. Texts not mentioned in this list have been translated from the French renderings.

Index

Library of Congress Cataloging-in-Publication Data

Garlan, Yvon.
  Slavery in ancient Greece.

  Includes index.
  Translation of: Les esclaves en Grèce ancienne.
  1. Slavery—Greece—History. I. Title.
HT863.G3713   1988   306'.362'0938   87-47963
ISBN 0-8014-1841-0 (alk. paper)
ISBN 0-8014-9504-0 (pbk. : alk. paper)